WORLD AS WORD

Bernadette Waterman Ward

WORLD AS WORD

Philosophical Theology in GERARD MANLEY HOPKINS

The Catholic University of America Press
Washington, D.C.

The paper used in this publication meets the minimum requirements of American National Standards for Information Science—Permanence of Paper for Printed Library materials, ANSI Z39.48-1984.
∞

Library of Congress Cataloging-in-Publication Data

Ward, Bernadette Waterman, 1959–
World as word : philosophical theology in Gerard Manley Hopkins / Bernadette Waterman Ward.
p. cm.
Includes bibliographical references and index.
ISBN 0-8132-1016-X (alk. paper)
1. Hopkins, Gerard Manley, 1844–1889. 2. Poets, English—19th century—Biography. 3. Jesuits—Great Britain—Biography.
I. Title
BX4705.H75363 W37 2001
821′.8—dc21

CONTENTS

ACKNOWLEDGMENTS

For breathing life into the earliest glimmers of the ideas in *World as Word,* I must first thank the director of my long, strange 1991 dissertation on Arnold and Hopkins: David Halliburton of Stanford University, whose rapid mind took in immediately my most abstruse speculations about nineteenth-century poets and medieval philosophers. He will see the marks of his thought in many places, though scarcely a page of my dissertation work found its way into *World as Word,* except in footnotes. For introducing me to Scotus, patiently and rigorously, I must thank Ernst Behler of the University of Washington, who sat on my dissertation committee. Barbara Charlesworth Gelpi of Stanford was all encouragement and inspiration—and provided good coaching in prose style—during both my dissertation and the ten long, weary years afterward, when I taught large numbers of students at an underfunded state university and scant funding for research and travel slowed my work. During those years I gave birth three times, and the example of another mother in academia was a great source of strength.

In lesser ways, Stanford's Dagfinn Follesdall and Hester Gelber patiently taught me, about philosophy of language and about Scotist scholarship, respectively, though I took no courses with either. Correspondence with Canadian Scholar Stephen Dumont helped me get over some early misconceptions about Scotus. And for an understanding of the spirit in which literary study is undertaken by those who love it, I am indebted to Lawrence Ryan, who directed the Graduate Special Program in the Humanities at Stanford. All of this was preliminary to the project itself, though I did not then know it.

I am deeply in debt to Steve Seidenberg, a professional editor, who looked over an early draft for friendship's sake—a turning point in the book's development. He ruthlessly sorted out what did and did not belong in a single work. With the range of my work thus circumscribed, I could reenvision the project. Once I had a real understanding of my direction, two colleagues at SUNY Oswego read the first chapter. Tom Loe spurred me to greater clarity; Dave Hill's delight in the revision told me when I had reached it. Another colleague, Jean Troy Smith, who had just published a book herself, walked me through the maze of the publishing process. And at the very end of the project, my student Kristen Agonito proofread text so familiar to me that I could no longer see my typing errors. Kristen is responsible for a great many commas.

The Cushwa Foundation for the Study of American Catholicism supported my work in the summer of 1993 at the University of Notre Dame. I am grateful to the Department of Special Collections in the Hesburgh Memorial Library for generous access to the Wadding edition of Scotus. At SUNY Oswego, the librarians were most helpful, especially Mary Bennett in Interlibrary Loan, and Christopher Hebblethwaite, who secured a room for my use during the months when my office was undergoing asbestos removal. For the Faculty Development Grant I was then completing, which had reduced my teaching load to three courses for a term, I thank the Scholarly and Creative Activities Committee, and in particular Jack Narayan. I also am grateful for my 1998–1999 sabbatical from SUNY Oswego, which I spent at Stanford. There the Green Library reference staff was indefatigable, especially Barry Hinman. In late summer 1999, I drove to Gonzaga University, where the Crosby Library staff most helpfully assisted me in using their fine Hopkins collection. There I touched, for the first time, something that Gerard Manley Hopkins had written with his own hand.

Several scholars and organizations encouraged me in minor ways. The Central New York MLA Conference and the Northeast Conference on Christianity and Literature hosted many papers introducing tentative arguments that became portions of this book. Jorge Garcia Gomez, a philosopher and literary scholar at Long Island University, convinced me that I was onto something important with my investigations of Hopkins's Scholasticism. Columbia's Margaret Ellsberg, who had taught me at Harvard, encouraged me by phone. Harvard's William Alfred, of happy memory, did so more often. During the darkest and most depressing days of the project, I had some unforgettable visits with the late Norman Kretzmann at Cornell, and one in sunnier times with Allan Wolter at St. Bonaventure's. Their conversation about medieval philosophy was vastly enlightening and humane. On my sabbatical, I was intellectually challenged by the fortnightly meetings of the Colloquium on Religion and Violence, at which Rene Girard and Robert Hamerton Kelly preside. An Eastern Orthodox scholar, Tim McFadden, econcouraged me there by his interest in Scotus, and perhaps still has his copy of a ragged intermediate draft of this text.

The process of publication was helpful in quirky ways. I drew motivation, indeed a sense of urgency, from a viciously anti-Catholic reviewer for an important university press, who ranted about the current pope and the birthrate in Africa, but explicitly refused to discuss any argument I actually proposed in the manuscript. I declined an offer from a smaller press, but I will never forget its reviewer's fine, thoughtful advice about the Ruskin section—the loving work of a true scholar whose name I will never know.

But by far the best scholarly help came from The Catholic Universty of America Press. Director David McGonagle sent my book to two well-chosen reviewers: James Finn Cotter, the respected Hopkins scholar; and William Frank, a philosopher at the University of Dallas, who since has become my colleague there. Since Cotter and I disagree deeply about the relationship between art and spirituality in Hopkins, I had criticized his work severely; he reviewed mine with evenhanded generosity. His advice helped shape my argument for precision and graciousness in disagreement, and widened my base of secondary sources. Frank suggested that I read a few well-chosen books and articles in order to reconsider my discussion of Scotus in their light. I had taken my readers through Scotus's ideas by the same circuitous route that I myself had followed. Frank's insightful but restrained guidance revealed to me—much to my relief—that I would never have to describe the epistemological differences between Scotus and Henry of Ghent, and that articulating the Scotist doctrine of the Trinity is not essential for a discussion of his ideas about the nature of self and personality. Frank's quiet, firm expectation that my notes should be in all points accurate and authoritative sent me to Latin texts I had never dared attempt before. There is no point of Scotist scholarship on which he has left me unconvinced, and even his stylistic suggestions were enlightening. My debt to the exactitude of William Frank's scholarship is immeasurable.

Yet none of these scholars had to live with the daily stresses of my writing. With astounding hospitality, my husband's parents, Lori and Alan T. Waterman, let our whole family live with them for more than a year during my sabbatical. They also provided us, one way or another, with all of the computers used to write the book. My three little daughters endured various degrees of boredom on library visits and during Mommy's writing hours. My late mother, Doris Ward, never ceased to believe in my ability to accomplish the work, though she had long since abandoned any attempt to follow my studies.

However, the contributuion of anyone else is dwarfed by the dogged, demanding, devoted work of my husband, Dane Waterman: musician by profession, philosophical theologian by training, editor by inclination. He read the most important of my source materials; translated the Greek fragments in Hopkins's private notes; analyzed music whose rhythms I understood but could not describe in musical terminology; and disputed with me about Ruskin, Calvin, Scotus, sentence structure, and annotations. Dane read, with a keen grammarian's eye, every word of every draft of my book; fended off the children at key moments; and demanded of me a more rigorous level of thought and expression than I would have been able to achieve on my own. The midwifery was easier with the babies, I think; but this book seems almost as much his as our children are, and his work on it was a gift of his whole self. It can be reciprocated, after a fashion, but never repaid. The living community of his mind with mine is a neverending source of delight—"deep, deeper than divined." And with thanks for both the completion of this book, and for the man who upheld me through it all,

> I to him turn with tears
> Who to wedlock, his wonder wedlock
> Deals triumph and immortal years.[1]

1. Hopkins, "At the Wedding March," in *The Poetical Works of Gerard Manley Hopkins*, ed. Norman MacKenzie (Oxford, U.K.: Clarendon Press, 1990), 164; hereafter cited as *Poetical Works*.

WORLD AS WORD

CHAPTER 1

INTRODUCTORY
Of Literature and Love

God's utterance of Himself within Himself is God the Word, outside himself is this world. The world then is word, expression, news of God. Therefore its end, its purpose, its purport, its meaning, is God and its life or work to name and praise him.

—*Sermons and Devotional Writings*, 129

GERARD MANLEY HOPKINS created a poetics of revelation. He employs his pyrotechnics of rhythmic innovation, acrobatic syntax, and internal chiming to reveal that the world we meet with our senses abounds in "inscapes." They wait to be discovered, "but the beholder wanting." The wild, sensual beauties of his poetry might seem to spring from an untamable heart rebelling against the limitations of poetic form, but Hopkins was no rebel. His originality rises from philosophical engagement with the dogmas of Christian revelation: the Trinity and the Incarnation, creation and eschatology, church and sacrament, free will and salvation. He found the freedom for his bold literary experiments within the security of the Roman Catholic Church. In the metaphysics of that ancient community of faith, Hopkins discovered such an inexhaustible variety of understanding, such fierce delight in the multiplicity of truth, that he could scarcely channel it into the boundaries of language.

Hopkins wrote little, and his life and critical history may be sketched in a few strokes. He lived from 1844 to 1889, entirely within the reign of Queen Victoria (1838–1901), and was the firstborn of a large family with devout middle-class Anglican parents. His prizewinning juvenile poetry and excellence in Greek at Highgate School won him entry to Oxford (matriculated 1863) to study classics. There his piety drew him to the theologically conservative circles of the Oxford Movement, just then at the point of losing its sway over the university to the liberal "Broad Church" theologians. After a period of crisis, he followed John Henry Newman into the Roman Catholic Church (October 1866), and under Newman's guidance chose to become a Jesuit priest. Having resolved to turn his back on art and devote himself to religion, he burnt his poems, determined to write no more until he could assure himself that it was God's will that he should write. A chance word from a Jesuit superior in 1875 opened the way for him to write poems again, and he did write, but rarely. His strange and technically difficult productions were unpublishable; his aspirations as a theologian, a preacher, and a scholar were frustrated; he only half-jokingly declared that he found himself "ruined for life by my alleged singularities." Nevertheless, he maintained a supreme confidence in the worth of his poetic experiments. Posted to University College in Dublin in 1884, he ground away his last "five wearying wasted years" grading Greek examinations. He commended his poetry to the care of God and, in 1889, at forty-five, died of typhus, unknown as a poet to any but a few old friends. By all accounts, he died cheerfully and left his manuscripts in disarray.[1]

Hopkins's friend Robert Bridges had copies of his poems, but did not venture to publish them until 1918, when he carefully selected a slim volume to which he cautiously appended an introduction apologizing for their oddity. Hopkins's fame grew slowly; he was a poet's poet. But soon, within half a century, this little priest unknown in Victoria's England had become a major Victorian literary figure.[2] His

1. For the dates in this paragraph, I refer to the chronology established by Alison Sulloway in *Gerard Manley Hopkins and the Victorian Temper* (New York: Columbia University Press, 1972), 196–99.

2. For an account of the recent outpouring of scholarly work on Hopkins through about 1990, see Jerome Bump, "The Hopkins Centenary: The Current State of Criticism," in *Gerard Manley Hopkins and Critical Discourse,* ed. Eugene Hollahan (New York: AMS Press, 1993), 7–40.

popularity persists beyond critical circles; the *Hopkins Research Bulletin* and the *Hopkins Quarterly* share shelves with many biographies and two plays on his uneventful life. There are numerous popular paperback editions and reissues of his poems. Students of English literature are expected to be familiar with him at least as an unrivaled innovator in poetic technique.

A deeply thought-out philosophical structure informs Hopkins's poetry: "Design, pattern, or what I am in the habit of calling 'inscape' is what I above all aim at in poetry."[3] "Inscape," as I shall demonstrate in this study, refers to layers of meaning, of perceptible structure, in the individual things of the world; the literary concept developed over many years together with his "professional" interest in philosophical theology. His philosophy and its outworking in arresting poetry may be sampled in a few lines of "That Nature Is a Heraclitean Fire and of the Comfort of the Resurrection":

> Delightfully the bright wind boisterous ropes, wrestles, beats earth bare
> Of yestertempest's creases; in pool and rutpeel parches
> Squandering ooze to squeezed | dough, crúst, dust; stánches, starches
> Squadroned masks and manmarks | treadmire toil there
> Fóotfretted in it.[4]

Here Hopkins coalesces human and natural patterns, in mind and in mud, into a single reality awaiting fulfillment. Dissolved only to be resurrected, tempest and human tread share the same fate. As Hopkins lovingly details the precise way in which a muddy tire track curls away from the surface of the road, and then, drying by itself, gradually crumbles into the surrounding dust ("rutpeel parches"), the difficulty of the language gives the passage dignity. Hopkins's opacity and compression are designed to draw attention to matters to which we do not normally attend. Even the more conventionally literary footprints he notices are made strange: "masks and manmarks | treadmire toil there

3. Gerard Manley Hopkins, *The Letters of Gerard Manley Hopkins to Robert Bridges*, ed. Claude Colleer Abbott (London: Oxford University Press, 1955), 66 (15 Feb. 1879); hereafter cited as *Letters to Bridges*.

4. "That Nature Is a Heraclitean Fire and of the Comfort of the Resurrection," *Poetical Works*, 197–98.

footfretted." According to Hopkins's conception of poetry, we are to enjoy a poem's language in itself, even at first without understanding what it means, and allow it to gradually emerge into richer significance. Like the mud in the road, it must be accorded its own mysterious dignity. Hopkins means to draw his readers into love even of that which may not seem to deserve their regard—especially of unregarded beauty, to be regarded for its own sake. Not even the mire of the streets is unworthy of the poet's notice. Taking note of things by word and memory—a toilsome work in itself—is at one with the activity of wind and earth and water, and, as the poem continues, the Resurrection brings all to fullness, even the "mark on mind" which otherwise "time | beats level."

Hopkins's aim in poetry is to reveal the inscapes of language itself. He writes: "[P]oetry is speech framed for contemplation of the mind by the way of hearing or speech framed to be heard for its own sake and interest even over and above its interest of meaning."[5] In a poem, inscape can be known as a formal pattern of sound and syntax,[6] but

5. "Poetry and Verse," in *The Journals and Papers of Gerard Manley Hopkins,* ed. Humphry House and Graham Storey (London: Oxford University Press, 1959), 289; hereafter cited as *Journals and Papers.* Although Maria Lichtmann contends otherwise in *The Contemplative Poetry of Gerard Manley Hopkins* (Princeton, N.J.: Princeton University Press, 1989), neither here nor in most of Hopkins's writings is it necessary to make fine distinctions between contemplation and meditation. While in many ways insightful about the rigid structures that Hopkins imposed on his spiritual life, Lichtmann is on shaky ground when she claims that Hopkins gave up meditation as an elementary exercise because he was a "proficient" in the mystical ascent to God (147). His own spiritual notes indicate that he gave it up because he was depressed by a feeling of inadequacy about his accomplishments (especially professional accomplishments) when he practiced Ignatian exercises in middle age. As I will discuss more fully later, Hopkins was not engaged in the flight from the world central to mystical methods of prayer; he normally uses the word *contemplation* in the ordinary sense of "thinking about something." Only when he discusses the degree to which "contemplation" and "meditation" might be technical terms in the *Spiritual Exercises* of Saint Ignatius of Loyola would "contemplation" have a technical spiritual sense.

6. For a well-evidenced discussion of Hopkins's notes "Poetry and Verse," see Terence Allan Hoagwood, "Hopkins's Philosophical Poetics," in Hollahan, ed., *Gerard Manley Hopkins and Critical Discourse,* 183–97, especially the first four pages. I do not concur, however, with Hoagwood's poststructuralist resistance to the notion that meaning is important in literature.

also as a pattern of psychological and emotional associations. A poem deliberately brings to notice the patterns of thought that constitute language, and therefore invites meditation on the principal way that people reveal truths to one another.[7] As he "afters and oftens" the linguistic inscapes to be contemplated, sometimes, he ruefully noted, "the sense . . . gets the worst of it."[8] In both the technique and the subject matter of his poems, Hopkins draws the reader's attention to the richness of meaning in multiple aspects of the things he encounters in the world; he wants us to admire. To give one's attention fully and lovingly to anything involves a willed inattention to more immediate needs; it is the work of an artist to give that attention to a thing simply for the sake of doing justice to its beauty. Hopkins believes that such a habit of attending to things outside one's own needs allows an escape from the furnace of obsession, wherein tools are forged for one's own misery and the oppression of others. To liberate the will from domination by personal desire, a person must commit himself to the service of the perfection and success of other beings—not only human beings, but, as Hopkins sees it, trees and theologies, soldiers and syllables. His technical wizardry is meant to arrest, even compel, attention to the beauty of the scapes of language; this "bidding" he considered a great literary virtue: "saying everything right to or at the hearer, interesting him, holding him in the attitude of correspondent addressed or at least concerned, making it everywhere an act of intercourse."[9]

It is not surprising, then, that, seduced, as he says, by "labile pleasure,"[10] Jonathan Culler recited "The Leaden Echo and the Golden Echo" to the scholars assembled at the 1993 Presidential Forum of the Modern Language Association (MLA), where he had been invited to

7. Cary H. Plotkin, in "To Give Being Back: Hopkins's Theodic Language," in Hollahan, ed., *Gerard Manley Hopkins and Critical Discourse,* 226ff., convincingly argues that the uniquely poetic elements which Hopkins foregrounds are units of syntax. I would expand that argument, with, I believe Hoagwood's support, to include such figures of thought as metaphor.

8. Hopkins, *Letters to Bridges,* 163 (26 Nov. 1882).

9. Hopkins, *Letters to Bridges,* 160 (4 Nov. 1882).

10. Jonathan Culler, "Lace, Lance and Pair," *Profession 94* (New York: Modern Language Association of America, 1994), 8.

speak on the love of literature. His address confidently urges the MLA to "recapture the terrain of love of literature" from the menacing "Cultural Right," which finds an "opposition between love of literature and theory" (5). An eminent theorist himself, Culler manifests his love of literature by applying a set of assumptions collectively called "theory" to Hopkins's work. He fondly traces the lavish and delicate internal echoes of "That Nature Is a Heraclitean Fire and of the Comfort of the Resurrection"; he caresses the catalogues in "The Leaden Echo and the Golden Echo." Yet, despite his talk of love, Culler calls Hopkins's poems "painfully embarrassing" (8), because they represent poetry "whose social or political implications one may deplore" (5).

Squeamish, even censorious, about their content, Culler is nevertheless "possessed" by Hopkins's poems, captive to "something more blindly compelling, more involuntary and irrational than admiration" (6). Love of literature, as Culler understands it, spices desire with revulsion:

> If "love" were a pure, disinterested relationship, there would still be a question of whether this was the best relation to literature, but of course love is more likely to be just the opposite: a highly interested, obscure, desiring relation of overinvolvement. Love without aggressivity, transference, sadomasochism, identification or fetishism is scarcely love at all. (5)

Perhaps.

At any rate, Culler's love of Hopkins means that he finds Hopkins's combinations of words luscious and mysterious, worth repeating for the sheer beauty of the sound even when the meaning is obscure or uncongenial. Hopkins's poems exemplify the "value and force" of poetry in that they continually return to the mind in their odd, precise wording. In Hopkins's terms, the "bidding" succeeds; in Culler's terms, "[t]he iterability of verse" mechanically creates "a displaced site of language" in the memory (9).

Hopkins endorsed a species of this genus of reading. He wrote to Robert Bridges, who had protested that he did not want to read *The Wreck of the Deutschland* more than once,

> Granted that it needs study and is obscure, for indeed I was not over-desirous that the meaning of all should be quite clear, at least unmistakeable, you

might, without the effort that to make it all out would seem to have required, have nevertheless read it so that lines and stanzas should be left in the memory and superficial impressions deepened, and have liked some without exhausting all. I am sure I have read and enjoyed pages of poetry that way. Why, sometimes one enjoys and admires the very lines one cannot understand, as for instance, "If it were done when 'tis done" sqq. [and what follows], which is all obscure and disputed, though how fine it is everybody sees and nobody disputes.[11]

It is perhaps the rule among Hopkins's readers to love where they cannot understand. At the age of twelve, intoxicated by Hopkins's voice, I memorized "The Windhover" and declaimed it uncomprehending as I climbed trees or wandered in the unsown fields west of town. Later, I murmured it between classes in high school, or on Saturdays at sunrise. I was in college before I could have told anyone what the subjects and verbs of the sentences were. Nearly all Hopkins's poems exhilarated me by their gorgeous sequences of sound and imagery, yet, despite the tremendous impression of precision and power that the poems created in me, I could give no clear account of them, even to myself. In short, I loved but did not understand. And as they did in Culler's memory, the poems lived in mine, too, and gradually, over many years, they blossomed into meaning.

Hopkins was undaunted by the confusion he created in his audience. He flippantly commented that they should wait a generation and come to him again.[12] As he told Bridges, Hopkins thought it unnecessary to enjoy every aspect of a poem at once. The mere sound may be enough at some times, or the incantatory fascination of the images. Nevertheless, "some matter and meaning is essential" to poetry in order to "support and employ the shape wh. [which] is contemplated for its own sake." Poetry is "speech which afters and oftens its inscape"—that is, language designed to draw attention to its own formal aspects, its patterns of sound or syntax, metaphor, or semantic similarity. And

11. Hopkins, *Letters to Bridges,* 50 (13 May 1878), quoting *Macbeth* 1.7.1ff.

12. This comment, in its immediate context (*Letters to Bridges,* 214 [1 April 1885]), refers to some music he wrote; but in the company of such eminent scholars as Virginia Ridley Ellis I apply it to his artistic work generally; see Ellis, *Gerard Manley Hopkins and the Language of Mystery* (Columbia: University of Missouri Press, 1991), 5.

an inalienable element of the structure of language is that it has meaning beyond its internal patterns. Nonsense verse, Hopkins declares, is not poetry. It is only "if it has meaning and is meant to be heard for its own sake [that] it will be poetry."[13] Hopkins's poems, however compressed and elliptical they may be, do make grammatical sense; and, most importantly, they mount logical arguments at the same time as they are presenting chains of emotional associations. For me, discovering articulate meaning in Hopkins's poems has been a source of lasting aesthetic and intellectual pleasure, better, in its way, than my childhood's exhilaration at the mere sound of them. I know by experience that it is quite possible to admire and enjoy the poetry of Hopkins without understanding some of the matters fundamental to its meaning, but also that it is worth the trouble to uncover even the more recondite aspects of what he is talking about.

Hopkins's project of giving dignity to the unregarded goods of the world is a difficult one; he must slip past his readers' presumptions. And so Hopkins's language does—"the current language heightened, to any degree heightened and unlike itself."[14] It requires a certain commitment, even an act of will, to figure out his syntax and understand the patterns he foregrounds; the loveliness of the sound in his poetry invites readers to make that commitment. "Labile pleasure" is a free sample of the beauty of the other realities that we will discover if we attend.

But what Culler commends is the "force" of Hopkins's poetry, not its intellectual fruitfulness. "Force" means that a poem can reappear in the mind at uncalled-for moments, preserved in its verbal integrity. Culler marvels at a poem's capacity to replicate itself, "the repetitive, mechanical labor it can perform." He speculates that the "force" of poems depends on repeating patterns in poetic form, which lodge themselves in the memory like a computer virus that takes over a program, involuntarily triggered into replication by some unsuspected key. The content of the message so uncontrollably repeated is tangential to the

13. Hopkins, *Journals and Papers,* 289.
14. Hopkins, *Letters to Bridges,* 89 (14 Aug. 1879).

real purpose of the replicating code: the display of its creator's power. Hopkins's poems offer the beauty of chiming sounds and linked clusters of words, devices that constitute excellent techniques for imposing a text on a reader. Other literature appeals through commanding appetites less delicate than delight in rhyme: desire for the pleasures of nostalgia, for example, or sex, or the lust for political power. Whatever hunger may be aroused, it can lead to "love, a transferential crediting of the text with power and pertinence to one's own situation and the situation of others" (Culler, 9, 5). Love is appetency; to seem to find significance in a text is to find one's own desire mirrored there, and succumb to it. Culler can display his own power by recognizing and resisting the allurements of the text—caressing his obsessions without succumbing to the illusion of "transferential crediting." But Hopkins's project is quite the opposite; he revels in all that is attractive about words, but he explicitly writes not to force his readers into submitting to the allurements of art but to offer them freedom even from their own appetites. Hopkins spent a lifetime learning to break the narrowness of his will;[15] rather than impose his insights on others by the "force" of his poems, Hopkins seeks to share that knowledge for his readers' delight.[16] For Hopkins considered love the highest form of justice. Hopkins described love of any sort in his sermons as "wishing . . . good and happiness" to the beloved.[17] Hopkins seeks to yoke delight in beauty to a disinterested desire for the good, for the justice, of others. Culler, resisting the pull of Hopkins's verse, seeks to put the two asunder and find love only in "aggressivity, transference, sadomasochism, identification or fetishism" (5).

Culler is an important theorist among literary scholars today, and approaches Hopkins's work with all the defensiveness of one who sees literature as the use of pleasure for the purposes of control. Culler

15. See Margaret Ellsberg, *Created to Praise* (New York: Oxford University Press, 1987), chap. 1.

16. For a fine discussion of "bidding" in relation to the benefit of sharing "concentrated, heightened truth," see Ellis, *Language of Mystery,* 52–55.

17. Gerard Manley Hopkins, *Sermons and Devotional Writings of Gerard Manley Hopkins,* ed. Christopher Devlin (London: Oxford University Press, 1959), 51; hereafter cited as *Sermons and Devotional Writings.*

cannot allow the poet to persuade him into respect for matters that his poststructuralist position disfavors, even for the sake of argument or for understanding a poem's technical excellence. For instance, led by "theory," Culler finds "differentiation" and successive "variation" the nearest approach to infinity. Stability, or "stasis," he takes to oppose differentiation and diversity. Culler condemns belief in stability as self-delusion. He deplores the way "The Leaden Echo and the Golden Echo," whose "main interest lies in a splendid proliferation, call for stasis and declare that it will occur" (9). Though the "splendid proliferation" of the poems has given them permanence and rebirth in his memory, proliferation and stasis seem irreconcilable to Culler because he conceives of diversity only as the fruit of impermanence. The subject matter of the two poems is the Christian doctrine of the Resurrection of the Body; the linguistic theory that informs Culler's reading impels him to identify the idea of resurrection

> with language and its surprising incarnational effects, where the materiality of the signifier may convince us that the referent is preserved in all the particularity with which it can be named, when in fact the naming negates the object that it appears to preserve. (8)

Such theorizing is reminiscent of the delicious moment in *Gulliver's Travels* when Jonathan Swift has the intellectuals of Laputa converse by means of objects they carry on their backs, in order to avoid the theoretical inconveniences imposed by speech.[18] Of course, the greatest wizards of theory cannot in fact negate objects by naming them. Names may affect human relationships to things, but even those relationships are not absolutely negated or determined by language. Any object can be an inexhaustible locus for names. Culler uses his extravagant metaphor in consequence of a confusion that indiscriminately identifies materiality with existence. He judges that the knowledge of a thing (implied by its naming) is destructive because it is immaterial, separated by the patterns of thought and language from the matter

18. Jonathan Swift, "A Voyage to Laputa," chap. 5 in *Gulliver's Travels,* vol. 8 of *The Prose Works of Jonathan Swift, D.D.*, ed. G. Ravenscroft Dennis (London: George Bell & Sons, 1909; reprint, New York: AMS Reprint, 1971), 193.

that makes up the world.[19] Neither an incarnation nor a resurrection but rather a substitution, the concept replaces the thing, which cannot itself be encountered; memory, and, even more, language can only be about the absence of the thing remembered.

Such a position brings with it, of course, the embarrassment that it is impossible to actually live a sane life while resisting the idea that language refers to a real world, and the not unreasonable accusation that one is merely engaging in fashionable nonsense. Nevertheless, enormous respect is accorded in academia to the notion that the ability to know and to tell the truth is always utterly overwhelmed by cultural presuppositions. Theory, as Culler and a number of other Hopkins critics conceive it,[20] enables one to recognize that "truth" is at best a variation and replication of familiar language, at worst an arbitrary imposition of someone's will upon the minds of others. To escape the trap of another's illusion, one must only point out that the real issue in a text is the tragic disjunction between language and the world.

Culler resists "transferential crediting" in "The Leaden Echo and the Golden Echo" by evading any intellectual confrontation with the subject matter of the poem: the doctrine of the Resurrection of the Body—a matter that is readily available public knowledge, not an arcane invention of the poet's. Christian doctrine explicitly denies that

19. I mean not only such patterns of thought which literary theory finds upholding language, such as the *langue* of structuralism and Derrida's *"ecriture,"* but any other systems of thought that deny that knowledge by experience is possible because the mind interposes itself inescapably to block contact between consciousness and the world. About the hoary problem of the search for absolutely pure knowledge, which underlies these constructions, I shall have my say in Chapter 10. See my discussion of related matters in the work of John Henry Newman, in Chapter 5, below.

20. Jean Bricmont and Alan Sokal's *Fashionable Nonsense: Postmodern Intellectuals' Abuse of Science* (New York: Picador, 1998) well mocks the pretentiousness of literary theory. However, except in the final chapter, where political concerns arise, the authors limit their scrutiny to the misrepresentation of scientific ideas rather than making a philosophical inquiry into the literary theorists' more insidious posturing about truth itself being inaccessible. Influential poststructuralist Hopkins criticism includes Michael Sprinker, *A Counterpoint of Dissonance: The Aesthetics and Poetry of Gerard Manley Hopkins* (Baltimore: Johns Hopkins University Press, 1980); J. Hillis Miller, *The Linguistic Moment: From Wordsworth to Stevens* (Princeton, N.J.: Princeton University Press, 1985); and Hoagwood, "Hopkins's Philosophical Poetics," mentioned in note 6, above.

permanence is inimical to diversity; the resurrected are not absorbed into the Infinite One, but perfect and renew their distinctness from one another in imperishable multiplicity. God is changeless, but the Christian tradition has not accorded immutability to resurrected creatures.[21] Nor does Hopkins; it is not just the "not-by-morning matched face" but the girls' activity that will be resurrected. At first Hopkins mentions the motions baldly: "your ways and airs and looks . . . gallantry and gaiety and grace." Then he resurrects them, perfected by adjectives and alliteration: "Winning ways, airs innocent, maiden manners, sweet looks . . . going gallant, girlgrace." Culler suppresses Hopkins's conscious and confident vision of a permanence that is not undone by movement, a unity that is not disturbed by multiplicity. The critic instead scrambles to divorce religious dogma, by means of mockery, from Hopkins's exuberant catalogues, which serve in Culler's eyes only to make the poem maddeningly alluring despite its flawed premise.

Hopkins was not ashamed that poetry should evoke such grudging honor as Culler gives him. With Victorian faith in the attractive force of virtue, and Victorian English chauvinism exaggerated by his exile, he declared that a good English poem is

> an unfading bay tree. It will even be admired by and praised by and do good to those who hate England . . . who do not wish even to be benefited by her. . . . I apply to [art and its fame], and it is the true rule for dealing with them, what Christ our Lord said of virtue, Let your light shine before men that they may see your good works (say, of art) and glorify yr. Father in heaven.[22]

At least in these poems, Hopkins's improving example is lost on Culler, who flinches from recognizing even technical virtues, such as skill with allusion, much less the accuracy and consistency with which the poet presents his philosophical position. The Resurrection is also the time of the Last Judgment in Christian eschatology, yet Hopkins's lines about the unknown effects of moral action become, in Culler's version, the "merely sentimental belief that our true selves will live on

21. The images in the Book of Revelation are of feasts, the growth of fruit, music, and flowing water; later images, such as Dante's dancing circles of light, also suggest perfection without stasis.

22. Hopkins, *Letters to Bridges,* 231 (13 Oct. 1886).

forever," or, worse, the "dream to which the American cosmetics industry ministers"—"hypersentimentality" to be defused with a witticism about "no bad hair days" (8):

> See: not a hair is, not an eyelash, not the least lash lost; every hair
> Is, hair of the head, numbered.
> Nay, what we had lighthanded left in surly the mere mould
> Will have waked and have waxed and have walked in the wind what
> while we slept.

The poem is about the consequences of one's actions, sown in life like grain. Hopkins explained, "'Nay, what we lighthanded' etc means 'Nay more: the seed that we so carelessly and freely flung in the dull furrow, and then forgot it, will have come to ear meantime.'"[23] The speaker, "a good but lively girl,"[24] according to Hopkins, awakens from temporal to spiritual concerns over the course of the poem. Hopkins's text alludes to Jesus' warning about the coming judgment and the completeness of divine omniscience:

> For there is nothing covered, that shall not be revealed; nor hidden, that shall not be known. For whatsoever things you have spoken in darkness, shall be published in the light; and that which you have spoken in the ear in the chambers, shall be preached on the housetops. And I say to you, my friends: be not afraid of them that kill the body, and after that have no more that they can do. But I will shew you whom you shall fear; fear ye him, who after he hath killed, hath power to cast into hell. Yea, I say to you, fear ye him. Are not five sparrows sold for two farthings, and not one of them is forgotten before God? Yea, the very hairs of your head are all numbered.[25]

The resurrected "shall awake, some to everlasting life, and others unto reproach, to see it always" (Dan. 12.2). Physical beauty might wake and reveal itself at the lively girl's resurrection—Hopkins fully expects that resurrected saints will be physically perfect[26]—but only as an element

23. Hopkins, *Letters to Bridges*, 158 (21 Oct. 1882).

24. Hopkins, *Letters to Bridges*, 158 (18 Oct. 1882).

25. Luke 12.2–7, Douay-Rheims version. The whole pericope (12.1–12) warns about divine judgment and exhorts against cowardice.

26. Hopkins said in a sermon, "In his Passion all this strength was spent, his lissomeness crippled, this beauty wrecked, this majesty beaten down. But now it is more than all restored, and for myself I make no secret I look forward with eager desire to seeing the

of a complete self-revelation, a vehicle of divine judgment. The "spiritual body" (1 Cor. 15.44) of the Resurrection, of which Hopkins writes, unifies one's moral and physical existence in all the fullness of its consequences, both the expected and the unimagined. The critic cannot hear the admonition over the din of his own preconception that the poem must only, can only, refer to a vain desire for a permanently pretty face. Thus even Culler's comments about Hopkins's technical excellence go awry. It is as if he were to admire the daring and grace of climbers fixing ropes on the face of a sheer cliff, and then comment that it is extravagant to spend so much effort stringing such an inefficient clothesline. One has to know what the equipment is being used for in order to criticize how it is being used.

The self-justifying and self-destructive assumptions of what is often called "theory" are inadequate for reading Hopkins—and, I would claim, inadequate for full engagement with any literature. By investing in other assumptions about language, literature, and especially love, it is possible to read in a richer and more challenging way. Hopkins articulates a philosophical framework for a different kind of approach to meaning. Poststructuralists find only "absence" in language, working from an assumption that systems of language are prior to experience, and therefore block access to any "truth" not already known. Such disengagement evades a genuine philosophical dilemma, which Hopkins confronts with the help of the work of John Duns Scotus (1266–1308). Hopkins indeed holds that conceptualization, and language even more, is created within structures within which the thinker must live; but he believes that nevertheless it is possible to encounter a prelinguistic reality that can act as a basis for communication, despite the differences among different speakers' concepts. Because he believes that the world is good and that illusion is not, Hopkins is unshakable in his conviction that the structures of thought do not present an insuperable obstacle to an encounter with reality. His comment on translating Parmenides' use of the Greek verb of being sheds light on

---

matchless beauty of Christ's body in the heavenly light" (*Sermons and Devotional Writings,* 36).

his linguistic convictions: "ἔστι may roughly be expressed by *things are* or *there is truth*."[27]

If language has a foundation in a world outside language, the meaning of a proposition has decided limits, and "truth" is not an arbitrary category. Culler's concentration on structure divorced from content is supported by a notion that fixed meaning—a form of "stasis"—kills interest, play, and dialogue. But the joy, the "play," in Hopkins's philosophy of language does not depend upon deferred or undecidable meaning; quite the opposite. Hopkins writes to his friend Robert Bridges:

> You do not mean by mystery what a Catholic does. You mean an interesting uncertainty: the uncertainty ceasing the interest ceases also. . . . But a Catholic by mystery means an incomprehensible certainty: without certainty, without formulation there is no interest . . . [T]he clearer the formulation the greater the interest. At bottom the source of interest is the same in both cases, in your mind and in ours; it is the unknown, the reserve of truth beyond what the mind reaches. . . . Yours turns out to be a curiosity only; curiosity satisfied . . . it vanishes at once. But you know there are some solutions, to, say, chess problems so beautifully ingenious, some resolutions of suspensions so lovely in music that even the feeling of interest is keenest when they are known and over, and for some time survives the discovery. How must it then be when the very answer is the most tantalising statement of the problem and the truth you are to rest in the most pointed putting of the difficulty! . . . There are three persons, each God and each the same, the one, the only God: to some people this is a "dogma," a word they almost chew, that is an equation in theology, the dull algebra of schoolmen; to others it is news of their dearest friend or friends, leaving them all their lives balancing whether they have three heavenly friends or one—not that they have any doubt on the subject, but that their knowledge leaves their minds swinging; poised, but on the quiver. And this might be the ecstasy of interest, one would think. So too of the Incarnation.[28]

Meaning, even dogma, is for Hopkins a bounded infinity of understandings—not the death of language but the opportunity for it to act. And the action of language is always social, because meaning is always a communal creation. Convinced that the social reality of language is

27. Hopkins, *Journals and Papers,* 127.
28. Hopkins, *Letters to Bridges,* 187–88 (24 Oct. 1883).

not isolated from a world outside the bounds of human discourse, Hopkins attaches moral weight to both literature and criticism. To write is to enact ethics, making a human decision about what is to be done. In using language, we cannot escape responsibility toward the world we name. At the heart of Hopkins's moral passion for language is the idea that the "pure, disinterested" love that Culler mocks is possible: that one can, in fact, love something because it is a good thing, and without caring whether or not one is going to get any use out of it. In his poetry, Hopkins uses pleasure to foster that disinterested love. He believes it is possible to "merely meet" beauty: "the self can in every object it has see another self, personal or not, and . . . can treat any one thing how great or small soever as equal to any other thing."[29] There is pleasure in seeing how Hopkins's poems exercise his ideas about the nature of love and its connection to language; and indeed, Hopkins's philosophical writings reward study in themselves.

To say that Hopkins's language has decided meaning is not to say that Hopkins writes to make meaning utterly transparent. He wrote: "One of two kinds of clearness one shd. have—either the meaning to be felt without effort as fast as one reads or else, if dark at first reading, when once made out *to explode*."[30] Clearly the "unmitigated violence"[31] with which he handles the English language is intentional. What could be the advantage, though, of creating such singular and opaque lines, which lie like gorgeous land mines in the memory? Hopkins's approach to language has much of common sense about it, but is far from naïve. The nineteenth century had its own versions of the poststructuralist "radically separate heterocosm of signifiers" that creates a hermeneutic seal closing off the mind from the world.[32] Even John Henry Newman doubted at times that the evidence of his senses had any connection to an extramental world, and we shall see that his

29. Hopkins, *Sermons and Devotional Writings*, 152.

30. Hopkins, *Letters to Bridges*, 90 (8 Oct. 1879).

31. Hopkins, *Letters to Bridges*, 79 (22 April 1879, in some comments on "The Loss of the Eurydice").

32. Cary H. Plotkin minted this apt phrase of obloquy for this use in "Hopkins's Theodic Language," in Hollahan, ed., *Gerard Manley Hopkins and Critical Discourse*, 229.

confrontation with the problem deeply affected Hopkins's epistemology. Ultimately, Hopkins follows Scotus on this point and accepts the social and linguistic world as a reality in itself, a part of a larger field of experience that is accessible to knowledge. The naming of an object multiplies and extends its reality because human relationships to an object are among the constituents of the thing—rather extensions of it than substitutes for it. Memory is a legitimate augmentation of a thing's activity in the world, not a desperate and fallacious attempt to preserve it. Because Hopkins follows Scotus in the conviction that people do have prelinguistic access to reality, he is willing to grant that even the imprecise tool of language can dismantle linguistic and cultural preconceptions. The risk of finding oneself wrong, or of being confronted with something other than oneself, attends the three-way negotiation among a person who says something, a person who receives the message, and the world they variously encounter.[33]

This book is written to uncover and explain the philosophy that inhabits Hopkins's poems. Hopkins was trained as a grammarian, a philosopher, and a theologian. Many critics have justly and perceptively attended to the personal and psychological aspects of his religious and philosophical training.[34] A recent study by Daniel Brown closely examines the secular and scientific philosophical currents of Hopkins's youthful milieu.[35] Nevertheless, there has been no detailed study

33. My phrasing derives from nineteenth-century U.S. Scotist Charles Sanders Pierce, thanks to David Halliburton of Stanford University. John K. Sheriff describes Pierce's linguistic philosophy with (to a student of Hopkins) enviable clarity and clarifies Pierce's relevance to the concerns of structuralism and poststructuralism in his *The Fate of Meaning: Charles Pierce, Structuralism, and Literature* (Princeton, N.J.: Princeton University Press, 1989). Hopkins, of course, knew nothing of Pierce; nevertheless, in their attention to multiplicity of meaning and the social dimensions of language, they have much in common.

34. Extensive work on the psychology of Hopkins has been done by biographers from Fr. Lahey through Jerome Bump, Paddy Kitchen, Norman White, and the best of them, Robert Bernard Martin, as well as critics such as John Pick, Wendell Stacey Johnson, John Robinson, Walter Ong, Tom Zaniello, Allison Sulloway, David Anthony Downes, Alan Heuser, Howard Fulweiler, and James Finn Cotter.

35. Daniel Brown, *Hopkins's Idealism: Philosophy, Physics, Poetry* (Oxford, U.K.: Clarendon Press, 1997).

of the development of Hopkins's poetic practice in relation to the philosophical theology that most engaged his intellectual passions.[36]

Presuming that impassioned utterance must exclude rationality, many critics have approached Hopkins from the point of view taken in this 1986 assessment: "The true basis of Hopkins's aesthetic, in other words, is *emotional* rather than *intellectual*."[37] Having abandoned any attempts to follow Hopkins intellectually, such studies typically identify this purely emotional impulse either with sexuality[38] or with an ineffable religious inspiration inaccessible to the intellect.[39] Future

36. Marco Graziosi says of Hopkins's theories: "It is generally agreed that, while in some ways expressions of his poetic thought, they do not deserve study either in themselves or as historically relevant" ("Hopkins' Aesthetic Theory," *Hopkins Quarterly* 16, no. 3 [Oct. 1989]: 71). Leonard Cochran, whose detailed scholarship I respect, but with whom I disagree on the ontological status of instress, was certainly accurate in stating, after his listing of every occurence of certain philosophical terms, that "Gerard Manley Hopkins was not an amateur philosopher. . . . he had progressed though the very rigorous *ratio studiorum*. . . . Hopkins never abandoned his interest in philosophical studies" ("Instress and Its Place in the Poetics of Gerard Manley Hopkins," *Hopkins Quarterly* 6 [1979–1980]: 143–82).

37. Trevor McNeeley, "The Blissful Agony of Hopkins: Notes of a Neo-Reactionary," *Hopkins Quarterly* 12, nos. 3–4 (Oct. 1985–Jan. 1986): 102.

38. Studies of this type can be exemplified by Eleanor Ruggles's *Gerard Manley Hopkins: A Life* (New York: W. W. Norton, 1944); John Robinson's *In Extremity: A Study of Gerard Manley Hopkins* (Cambridge, U.K.: Cambridge University Press, 1978); and the endless attention given to Hopkins's brief acquaintance with Digby Dolben, usually treated as if it had strong sexual overtones, though Dolben's enthusiasm for vows of chastity argues against this. Lionel Trilling and Harold Bloom's hostility to Hopkins's presumed homosexual orientation taints their headnote to the Hopkins section of *Victorian Prose and Poetry*, vol. 5 of *The Oxford Anthology of English Literature* (Oxford, U.K.: Oxford University Press, 1973). The list continues with such articles as Michael Lynch's "Recovering Hopkins, Recovering Ourselves" (*Hopkins Quarterly* 6, no. 3 [Fall 1979]: 107–17) and numerous psychosexual articles following it.

39. James Finn Cotter's influential *Inscape: The Christology and Poetry of Gerard Manley Hopkins* (Pittsburgh, Pa.: University of Pittsburgh Press, 1972) treated inscape as an element of spiritual ascent to union with God; Alison Sulloway (in *Gerard Manley Hopkins and the Victorian Temper*) discusses Hopkins's aesthetics in similar terms. Donald Walhout, in *Send My Roots Rain* (Athens: Ohio University Press, 1981), which does not endorse that opinion, does list critics before 1981 who treat Hopkins as a mystic. Maria Lichtmann explicitly takes the position that Hopkins's religion was not only mystical but antirational, tending toward "*kenosis* [emptying] of intellect" (*The Contemplative Poetry of Gerard Manley Hopkins*, 140). The poet's conversion letters, which shall be

chapters will show that Hopkins did not think that artistic inspiration consisted of emotion or was inaccessible to the intellect, despite the strength of his own passions.

There are critics who do not insist on considering language an abyss of absences; nor on separating inspiration from thinking; nor on seeking dark, irrational roots for passionate or religious utterance; but who still ignore the philosophy in Hopkins's poetry. They simply do not see philosophy in the poems; and indeed, most of the time, Hopkins does not appear to be writing philosophy in them.[40] His poetic voice is fundamentally lyric, and seems less attuned to rigorously communicating an argument than to evoking emotion. Even his most didactic lines are constructed with a lyricist's attention to the niceties of structure, sound, and rhythm. One need not know philosophy to enjoy technical successes in their effect upon a reader's feeling. One need not even understand his philosophy to follow on one level (or several), the arguments of his poems. Unlike Pope's or even Wordsworth's poetry, Hopkins's poetry is rarely couched as an explication of a philosophical position or problem.

It is, of course, nearly impossible to ignore religion in Hopkins, and while studies of his theology have been spotty, there have been impressive studies of his spirituality in preceding generations. Most important to the assumptions on which I base this study are David Anthony Downes's *The Great Sacrifice* and Robert Boyle's *Metaphor in Hopkins.* Four recent, responsible, and detailed studies of Hopkins's spiritual concerns have followed them: Margaret Ellsberg's *Created to Praise,* Jeffrey Loomis's *Send My Roots Rain,* Virginia Ridley Ellis's *Gerard Manley Hopkins and the Language of Mystery,* and Margaret Johnson's *Gerard Manley Hopkins and Tractarian Poetry.* Yet there is still resistance to treating Hopkins as a philosophical theologian. James Collins's 1947 overview articles are perhaps still the most serious study; Donald

discussed below, argue on the basis of rationality in religion. See my discussion of Lichtmann in Chapter 7 below at note 19.

40. Nathan Cervo resists any notion of Hopkins as a philosopher, for instance, in "'The ooze of oil Crushed': Hopkins's Refurbishment of the 'Lady' of the Troubadour Poets," *Hopkins Quarterly* 16, no. 4 (Jan. 1990): 147–48.

Walhout's more focused article on Hopkins and Scotus is mainly a plea for more scholarship in the area.[41] Curiously, amidst his discussions of Hopkins's positions on topics in philosophical theology in *Send My Roots Rain*, Walhout states confidently that "Gerard Manley Hopkins was not a philosophical theologian" (152).

Clearly, I beg to differ; while Hopkins's poetry does not usually argue for a philosophical position, it does embody the habits of thought engendered by one. To look for the philosophy in Hopkins's work is less like interpreting an argument or unlocking an allegory than like growing to understand the manifestations of a culture. To read the poetry of Hopkins without knowledge of the ideas that motivate it is like learning spirituals without knowing about slavery in the United States. The art has its manifold delights, but a certain depth and richness remain undiscovered. Once having grasped the pervasive presence of Hopkins's theology, a literary scholar can hardly help wanting to understand the ideas and his work in relation to them. Just as spirituals record the experience but not the history of slavery, Hopkins reveals philosophical tenets in their human application without taking his readers through the reasoning on which they are based.

This book will examine how Hopkins's early thought develops from the aesthetic and epistemological concerns of his contemporaries, such as John Ruskin, Matthew Arnold, and John Henry Newman. Although this is not an intellectual biography of Hopkins but a study of some of the philosophical aspects of his work, I shall have to retrace the steps of many scholars who have studied Hopkins well in relation to his times.[42] I use a biographical arrangement to clarify the

41. Donald Walhout, "Scotism in the Poetry of Hopkins," in *Saving Beauty: Further Studies in Hopkins*, ed. Michael Allsop (New York: Garland, 1994), 113–32. James Collins demonstrates that Hopkins is a serious student of philosophy and identifies his "craving for philosophical precision" ("Philosophical Themes in Hopkins," *Thought* 22 [1947]: 79); Leonard Cochran takes a similar position, in "Instress and Its Place in the Poetics of Gerard Manley Hopkins," 171 and passim. Only recently has Daniel Brown, in *Hopkins's Idealism*, attended to even Hopkins's secular philosophical education.

42. Most important to my study are Tom Zaniello, *Hopkins in the Age of Darwin* (Iowa City, University of Iowa Press, 1988); Jude Nixon, *Gerard Manley Hopkins and His Contemporaries: Liddon, Newman, Darwin, and Pater* (New York: Garland, 1993); David DeLaura, *Hebrew and Hellene in Victorian England: Newman, Arnold, and Pater* (Austin:

relationship between Hopkins's early aesthetic philosophy and his mature poetry, which illuminates from within the humane richness of the philosophical theology of John Duns Scotus.

Scotus's works have long been difficult of access; only recently has a study such as this been made even possible, by Allan Wolter's pioneering texts with translations (among others, *Duns Scotus: Philosophical Writings, John Duns Scotus: A Treatise on God as First Principle, God and Creatures: The Quodlibetal Questions,* and *Duns Scotus on the Will and Morality*) and by the awakened interest in philosophical theology that those texts helped to engender in the United States. The dean of that movement, the late Norman Kretzmann, used

> the term "philosophical theology" in a sense that seems to be at least on its way to becoming standard. . . . Philosophical theology shares the methods of natural theology broadly conceived—i.e., analysis and argumentation of all the sorts accepted in philosophy and the sciences—but it lifts natural theology's restriction on premises. In particular, philosophical theology accepts as premises doctrinal propositions that are not also initially accessible to observation and reason . . . tests the coherence of doctrinal propositions, develops their implications, attempts explanations of them, discovers their connections with other doctrinal propositions, and so on.

Interest in this branch of thought is growing among scholars who are "more likely to be philosophers than theologians by profession."[43]

Hopkins engaged himself seriously with philosophy at Oxford, where he took his degree in classics during the English revival of Hegelianism. While his professors assigned essays on such topics as "The Position of Plato to the Greek World" and "The Probable Future of Metaphysics,"[44] he did not confine himself to considering earlier philosophers merely as examples of historical development. He did

University of Texas Press, 1969); Howard Fulwieler, *Letters from the Darkling Plain: Language and the Grounds of Knowledge in the Poetry of Arnold and Hopkins* (Columbia: University of Missouri Press, 1972); and Patricia Ball, *The Science of Aspects: The Changing Role of Fact in the Work of Coleridge, Ruskin, and Hopkins* (London: Athlone Press, 1971).

43. Norman Kretzmann, "Reason in Mystery," in *The Philosophy in Christianity,* Royal Institute of Philosophy Lecture Series 25, Supplement to *Philosophy* 1989, ed. Godfrey Vesey (Cambridge, U.K.: Cambridge University Press, 1989), 15–16, 17.

44. Hopkins, *Journals and Papers,* 115–17 and 118–21.

not openly resist the Hegelianism of his professors, but neither did he adopt it as his own.[45] Moreover, if Allison Sulloway is right about the "Socratic" innovations of his tutor Benjamin Jowett, which left students free to wrestle with philosophical questions proposed by Plato, he had some training in dialectic at Oxford that prepared him well for the practice of philosophical theology at the Jesuit seminary he attended after Oxford. Hopkins's seminary professors encouraged the "philosophers" and "theologians"—seminarians in particular phases of their education—to take ideas from all quarters and treat them as challenges to Catholic theology. Hopkins and his classmates were expected to ransack philosophies new and old for objections to theological propositions so that they could stump one another in weekly "circles" staged as training sessions in defending the faith. The objections were not taken as examples of historical positions but as challenges impinging upon the present belief system to which the young men (and their observing professor) were committed by vows.[46] Considering all philosophies as contemporary with his own position, Hopkins could be challenged or enlightened directly by what he considered to be their content. So he did with Scotus, whom he first read while training at the seminary.

The Jesuit practice of the "circle" trained seminarians primarily to pursue apologetics, but philosophical theology has another use as

45. I disagree with Brown's interpretation of the language of Hopkins's undergraduate essays. Brown argues in *Hopkins's Idealism* (147ff.) that the essays' idealist language implies that he adopted a monistic philosophical position. Hopkins did demonstrate his comprehension of his professors' Hegelian doctrines. But Hopkins's conversion to Catholicism argues in itself that he was not committed to the positions implied in his academic exercises. Hegelian monism is inconsistent with Roman Catholicism (indeed, with all monotheism) both in its doctrine of God and its anthropology. Were the decisive act of conversion insufficient to declare his position, Hopkins clearly states his rejection of monism—and explicitly Hegelian monism—in his commentary on the *Spiritual Exercises* of Ignatius of Loyola (see my discussion of *Hopkins's Sermons and Devotional Writings*, 125ff., in Chapter 8 below). For Brown's error in attributing to Hopkins the position of Hegelians and Averroists, in the passage wherein he most explicitly opposes them, see my discussion in Chapter 7. Hopkins also specifically rejects Hegel in *Letters to Bridges*, 31 (20 Feb. 1875).

46. Alfred Thomas, S.J., *Hopkins the Jesuit: The Years of Training* (London: Oxford University Press, 1969), 97.

well: "[F]or those who have matured in faith, it is a delight."[47] Hopkins does employ "genuine philosophical theology" for apologetic purposes, for instance, in his letters to Robert Bridges, but even when he is defending the mysteries of the faith (as in the letter on the Trinity quoted above), his heart is manifestly in the contemplation of the mystery rather than in the battle with his agnostic friend.

So in the next few chapters we will examine Hopkins's philosophy as it developed in the context of a skeptical age, one in which materialist concepts of history rubbed shoulders with idealisms that allowed the human mind no contact with a material world. Poststructuralist assaults on the authority of the author have their analogues[48] in nineteenth-century biblical criticism, which attacked the historical claims of Christianity. Hopkins mistrusted the retreat into a sentimental religion built on personal feelings and experience. Haunted by a sense that experience is incommunicably singular, and aware that no message comes but through the consciousness and culture of the messenger, Hopkins nevertheless was convinced that it was morally irresponsible, an assault on the dignity of the sensual world, to make one's imagination an equal or a godlike superior to the world outside the mind.

As Culler did in 1993, Hopkins started with the question of love. Although Hopkins found John Ruskin's idea of imagination too "mystical," Ruskin's aesthetic writings appealed to the poet's moralism. Ruskin considered praising the world's beauty accurately a religious duty; Ruskin made the artist's love for seeing and telling truth ("no: Truth," Hopkins wrote) seem to be noble, even a Christian sacrifice.

At Oxford, Hopkins associated himself with a religious circle of friends who believed that, by a divine fiat as firmly rooted as that which created the world, Christ is bodily present as a sacrificial victim in Communion. To be a Christian one must, he believed, participate in that sacrament, becoming physically one with Christ, and live a life of self-sacrifice. On the grounds that rational authority and the sacramental notion of sacrifice were better upheld in the Roman Catholic

47. Quoted from Saint Bonaventure in Kretzmann, "Reason in Mystery," 22.

48. And perhaps their ancestry—but that is subject matter for a different book.

Church, he made an anguished decision to leave the Anglican communion and become Roman Catholic.

That decision put him in contact with a man who was becoming one of the most important Roman Catholic theologians of the next century and more: John Henry Newman. Newman softened the edges of Hopkins's mistrust of personal feeling in religion. Hopkins taught at Newman's Oratory School and imbibed some of Newman's conviction that all knowledge is a matter of faith, and that the authority for religious belief is founded on the relationship among believers. Hopkins learned from Newman a new way of understanding how knowledge is a moral issue; all experience is incommunicably personal, but we can and must commit ourselves to knowledge beyond our personal ken. Knowledge is based on trust, either in one's senses or in one's society; human beings must depend on one another's partial understandings in order to live in the world at all. To share knowledge with someone else is an act of love. Under Newman's roof Hopkins coined the terms "inscape" to name the individual perceptions that the artist can share, and "instress" to name the activity of the artist in perceiving.

Hopkins then united his sacramental religious beliefs to Newman's epistemology of multiple perceptions which people can lovingly contribute to one another's stores of knowledge. Catholicism vigorously supports the notion that many perceivers can perceive different, but true, aspects of the same thing; sacramental theology posits two realities, divine and mundane, inhabiting the same thing at the same time. Hopkins assimilated this idea so deeply that the practice of perception could become a religious act, allowing one to participate in the creative Great Sacrifice of Christ. The whole corpus of his mature poetry calls out to the reader to recognize the sacramental presence of God in the things of the world.

Reading Duns Scotus deepened Hopkins's concept of multiple presence. Scotus introduced him to the idea that even in ordinary knowledge, untouched by sacramental grace, people encounter multiple realities that require perceiving minds in order to spring into full existence. Scotus's concept seems to resemble the romantic one of an idealist world called into existence by the imagination, but for him the imagination is neither sovereign over the things of the world, nor, emphatically, a divine faculty. Scotus argues for contact with an actual, extramental world. Only one thing about that world enters the mind unmediated by the conceptual categories of language in the mind: existence. But this single access to unmediated knowledge accords language a toehold in a world outside language. Newman was utterly skeptical about mental contact with the physical world, but Hopkins was less comfortable with uncertainty than Newman was. Hopkins rejoiced to find a philosophy in which some class of statements can be called true or false on the basis of their reference to the world, and which nevertheless honors the shaping power of the imagination. He therefore could trust his readers to find various and multiple levels of reality in his poems; his complex layering of meanings and technical effects reflect this confidence.

And along with a philosophy of meaning came a morality of language. Hopkins's approach to literature was finally based on a Scotist understanding of disinterested love. Scotus expresses with great subtlety the concept that the will is most free when seeking the good of others. This freedom he also defines as the theological virtue of charity—the very kind of love that led Christ to the Sacrifice of the Crucifixion. As Hopkins sees it, the poet's role is to do good: to notice the things of the universe, to regard them in their own goodness, and to tell others of them. Every person's perspective—and therefore the poet's perspective—is necessarily unique; there is no one else who will see the realities this artist sees. Others looking at the same things will see other realities. If they respect the unity of truth, people can reveal new realities to one another. In Scotist terms, respect for existence implies respect, in the linguistic realm, for the prohibition on contradiction: what is, is, and what is not, is not. We may make fictions but we must not lie; and since we can know existence from fiction, we are able to know the difference.

Hopkins loves the inscapes he perceives, and because of that love wishes to reveal them truthfully. Those revelations are to "do good" to those who read Hopkins's poems. Thus Hopkins returns to the moralism of Ruskin with greater maturity and philosophical sophistication. He eschews the objective, dictatorial tone in which Ruskin judges good and bad in art and morals: not just the inspired artist but many other voices can speak, and speak differently, and still speak truth. Hopkins's epistemology of revelation, which is also an epistemology of responsibility, underlies a poetry that allows a negotiation between himself and the reader. Hopkins's Scotist idea of multiple realities that do not displace one another allows for discussions of literature characterized by both liberty of thought and a sense of grounding in the reality at hand.

But the first step to that sense of reality, for Hopkins, was to look about him in the intellectual and religious world of Oxford in the 1860s. Let us see what he found there.

CHAPTER 2

TEXT AND AUTHORITY

HOPKINS WRESTLED in startling ways with the sonnet, the strictest form in English poetry; he reworked its proportions, juggled its meters, and contorted its grammar into unheard-of configurations—but never with the intent to "Break the pentameter," as Pound would seek to do two generations later. Hopkins's poetic structures served as a hothouse to force the beloved language and its forms into fresh flower of meaning. In his verse, curious and explosive pleasures of ear, and eye, and mind strain the conventions of Victorian poetry almost beyond recognition. Yet Hopkins's boldness gains artistic potency from the tension holding the experiments in check: the poet's pointed submission to form and liceity. As in art, so in life; Hopkins sought always to devote himself to some authority that he could respect.

It would be hard to judge from the calm, dapper exterior of his youthful photographs the intensity of his pleasures: in color and line and design; in "fascinations" with a face or a cast of light or a species of tree; in words (how many boys would address a friend as a "kaleidoscopic, parti-coloured, harlequinesque, thaumatropic Being"?[1]); in the joy of achievement; in friendships; in the intellectual savor of Moschus and Theocritus and Aeschylus. As susceptible to sound as a prey animal, he kept his intellect attuned to rhyme and likeness with an almost addictive fixity. The shock of each sense so keenly touched him that, in his youth, "crimson and pure blues seemed to me spiritual

1. Hopkins's entry in what seems to have been a sort of autograph book; transcription by Hamilton McKinnon, quoted in *Gerard Manley Hopkins*, by G. F. Lahey, S.J. (New York: Haskell House, 1969), 4.

and heavenly sights fit to draw tears."[2] His journals effervesce with newness of color, motion, texture, and form. But restraint is crucial to his achievement: this sensual intensity was matched by an ascetic alertness to all that he found too yielding or "unmanly" in himself. Impatient of his weaknesses, from childhood he learned to bridle his luxuriant desires by means of a sharp and unyielding will. He loved to fight from the moral high ground, and not many schoolboys could match him for his ability to conquer even the needs, much more inclinations, of nature. An old school friend wrote of the poet, in a letter of condolence to Hopkins's brother,

> Once roused by a sense of undeserved injustice he usually so quiet and docile was furiously keen for the fray, and only bristled the more, when as was usually the case the authorities tried force and browbeating to silence his arguments and beat him down. Then it was always an Homeric struggle to be fought inch by inch. Such a conflict was aroused by your brother's abstinence from all drink for three weeks, the pretext being a bet of 10/ to 6d, the real reason a conversation on seamen's sufferings and human powers of endurance. I was only the other day chatting it over with the Wilsons in Sussex, and one, then a big fellow, said he remembered Gerard showing him his tongue just before the end and it was black.[3]

To yield to mere desire without ideals seemed to him contemptible; power over himself he knew as real power, and reveled in it. His ultimate aim was devotion: to find the good thing and to seize it, to follow it embattled, to take joy in the pains of the fray. And the good thing could not be a mere yielding to desire; it had to be something difficult, something great, in his conception; and finally it had to satisfy his mind, especially his sense that the beauty of the world rests in order.

The Hopkins who went to Oxford carried with him an unusual vividness of sensuality, a "cock o' the walk" self-confidence,[4] a wicked

2. Gerard Manley Hopkins, *The Correspondence of Gerard Manley Hopkins and Richard Watson Dixon,* ed. Claude Colleer Abbott (London: Oxford University Press, 1955), 38 (22 Dec. 1880); hereafter cited as *Correspondence with Dixon.*

3. Henry Luxmoore, letter to Arthur Hopkins, June 13, 1890, in Gerard Manley Hopkins, *Further Letters of Gerard Manley Hopkins, Including His Correspondence with Coventry Patmore,* 2d ed., rev. and enlarged, ed. Claude Colleer Abbott (Oxford, U.K.: Oxford University Press, 1956), 395; hereafter cited as *Further Letters.*

4. Hopkins's phrase, in *Further Letters,* 1–2 (to Charles Noble Luxmoore, 7 May 1862).

wit, and a flaring intelligence that urged him to push the limits—but he was never the stereotypical teenaged rebel looking to differentiate himself from his parents. He saw their position of strength as his own; the poet's father, Manley Hopkins, published a volume of verse called *Pietas Metrica; or, Nature Suggestive of God and Godliness.* Hopkins dedicated much of his own art to the same notion. And his schoolfellows, even at an early age, found his devotion to his parents and his religion formidable, and respected his determined obedience. Hopkins was quite young—perhaps ten or eleven—when he won this victory:

> When he was moved into our bedroom he was the only boy who regularly read to himself a small portion of the New Testament, in accordance I think with a promise given to his mother. At first it provoked a little ridicule, in which your brother [Gerard Manley Hopkins] must have got the best of us, tho' we didn't then think so, and I remember that my set decided that the promise was quite a sufficient reason, and we all agreed that Skin was not to be hindered in any way. I think this shows that your brother even at that time was both popular and respected.[5]

Every manner of Victorian high-mindedness—moral, patriotic, artistic, religious—he took as his own, not sycophantically, but with real zeal, and as the manifestation of true and properly recognized authority. He took his stand not on mere self-assertion, but on the pursuit of ideals; he hungered to commit himself to something worth dedicating his life to, and he wanted it to make demands upon him.

The religious aspect of this matter no doubt seemed quite settled when he left for Oxford; all the authorities he knew agreed that the British Empire and the Protestant Christianity of England were alike superior over lesser entities on the earth. It was partly because Spain was the ancient enemy of England that the schoolboy poet could despise the Catholic monastery in the Escorial as

> the proudest home
> Of those who strove God's gospel to confound
> With barren rigour and a frigid gloom—[6]

5. Henry Luxmoore, in *Further Letters,* 394–95.
6. Hopkins, *Poetical Works,* 1.

Of course, Roman Catholicism held a special place of opprobrium in the English political consciousness. In 1535, by the Act of Succession, King Henry VIII had declared the reigning monarch the head of the English Church. Roman Catholics in England were therefore regarded in the light of traitors; they attributed to a foreign ruler—the pope—authority claimed by the Crown. The next three centuries of English folklore vilified Catholicism as the source of conspiracies to overthrow the English government and subject the island to foreign powers. A movement to grant Catholics civil rights caused enormous controversy early in the nineteenth century, but some political rights were finally granted in 1829. Catholic marriages were granted legal standing in 1836. Laws against the saying of masses, the Catholic Church owning property, and Catholic family inheritance were repealed in the year Hopkins was born. In the middle of Hopkins's boyhood Catholics were admitted, reluctantly, to the Oxford B.A. degree.[7] As a proud and chauvinistic English boy, Gerard Hopkins knew which religion was to be approved.

Writing to his father near the time of his conversion, Hopkins marshaled only one precedent of a Catholic who had been granted full privileges at Balliol. England's penal restriction of Catholic religious orders continued through the time in which Hopkins took his own Catholic vows. Hopkins hated to rebel; the secrecy with which he had to take his vows was not a thrill but a privation to him. When at the end of his life he found himself assigned to Ireland, his perception of the justice of the Irish Home Rulers' cause was a torment to him because it told against his loyalty to "England, whose honor O all my heart woos."[8] This was more than twenty years after he voluntarily relinquished his English respectability by converting. Through all his manhood, the state's disapproval of Catholicism was an open wound to him. From the close of *The Wreck of the Deutschland* to "The Loss of the Eurydice," from "Margaret Clitheroe" to the projected ode on the Catholic martyr Campion, even in the opening of "Henry Purcell,"

7. Edward Norman, *The English Catholic Church in the Nineteenth Century* (Oxford, U.K.: Clarendon Press, 1989), 66, 187–88.

8. Hopkins, *Poetical Works*, 181; cf. Hopkins, *Letters to Bridges*, 256 (30 July 1887).

Hopkins longs to unite his reverence for the religious martyr with the honor of the Englishman fallen in battle. He imagines Christ as a redcoat, and when he thinks of the good that poetry does, his mind turns to England as well as to religion. It took a rupture of seismic magnitude to dislodge his will from its customary obediences to parents and Crown; and the schoolboy entering Oxford had little notion of the power of the subterranean forces that would force him to judge between ultimate sources of authority.

In 1535, when he divided the Church of England from the Roman Catholic Church, Henry VIII had had no doctrinal quarrel with the pope. However, by 1576, when the 39 Articles of Religion of the Church of England were voted into law by Parliament, the winds of newborn Protestantism had brought heavy theological weather to England. The Anglican Church became, through its alienation from the pope, de facto Protestant. A masterful compromise document, the sporadically revised Articles, and the *Book of Common Prayer* regulated and defined the English Church, often by contrast to the Roman Catholic Church. Hopkins knew how Article VI delineated the source of the document's authority: "Holy scripture containeth all things necessary to salvation; so that whatsoever is not read therein, nor may be proved thereby, is not to be required of any man, that it should be believed." The article defines Anglican belief in sacred history and metaphysics as fundamentally Protestant, resting upon biblical evidence alone.

Dependence on Scripture alone sufficed so long as Anglicans understood Protestant Christendom to be unified in its most fundamental interpretive traditions, but that consensus had begun to crumble well before Hopkins came to Oxford, though he likely had little idea of the fact. From the late seventeenth to the mid-eighteenth century, French scholars working with the text of Genesis sought to disentangle the document's repeated stories on the basis of the way God was named in each pericope, thus "recovering" source documents from an ancient text.[9] Among these "higher critics," as they came to be called, questions about interpolations, editorial authority, and the reliability

9. Herbert Butterfield, *The Origins of History* (New York: Basic Books, 1981), 194–95.

of biblical source documents began to surface. Commonsense British realism had equipped Anglican divines to handle the attacks of philosophers like David Hume, who considered miracles impossible and on that ground doubted the honesty of the Apostles; but new doubts were now coming into play. The old arguments were not prepared against the argument that the Apostles' honestly held convictions were unreliable because their perceptions were mediated through their cultural expectations and beliefs. The resemblance between this reductionism and the postmodern frame of mind is not accidental. Michel Foucault merely extends the higher critics' search for political and economic subtexts in history to more of the written record.

Interpretations of the text of the Bible had long been a matter of tradition, and had, in the English Church, mostly remained within the bounds of the Creeds. The Eighth Article of Religion invokes the primacy of Scripture over dogmatic theology to enforce belief in these extrascriptural dogmatic definitions: "The Nicene Creed, and that which is commonly called the Apostles' Creed, ought thoroughly to be received and believed: for they may be proved by most certain warrants of Holy Scripture." The provenance of the Apostles' Creed is uncertain, but the Nicene Creed explicitly arose, and both were earliest used, to cope with a crisis of scriptural interpretation that forced reluctant bodies of fourth-century bishops to accept nonscriptural language as necessary for defining orthodox interpretation.[10] Many theological battles had been fought on biblical grounds to defend creedal definitions that had been made by early Christians precisely because they had found the Bible's language unclear. But in Hopkins's England the very battleground was shifting, torqued by unseen forces, and much that had seemed solid liquefied into quicksand: the legitimacy of the biblical text itself, and the trust that centuries of Protestantism had placed in it, had come into question.

Popular prejudice holds that evolutionary theory was responsible for the great Victorian crisis of faith in the reliability of the Scriptures,

10. J. N. D. Kelly, *Early Christian Doctrines*, 5th rev. ed. (London: Adam and Charles Black, 1977), 46; see discussion of the formation of the Nicene Creed, 239–49.

but the "disdain for antiquity" and religious authority that the young Newman found seductive[11] predated Darwin by two generations; nineteenth-century biology became a threat only in the wake of that doubt. In 1799, Friedrich Schleiermacher claimed his audience for *On Religion: Speeches to Its Cultured Despisers* by describing how he "began to sift the faith of my fathers and to cleanse thought and feeling from the rubbish of antiquity." He condemned the English, who "know nothing of religion, save that all preach devotion to ancient usages and defend its institutions, regarding them as a protection wisely cherished by the constitution against the natural enemy of the state."[12] By the time the new German criticism aroused serious attention at Oxford, Waterloo and prosperity had combined to soften any political alarm raised by high-minded attacks on English Erastianism. What was alarming about Schleiermacher was what John Henry Newman called "the anti-dogmatic principle." For instance, Christian tradition holds that God is a self-existent Being who creates all things; Schleiermacher presented a God interdependent with the world, asserting therefore that people created God as much as God created them. God becomes a sentiment, a recognition of dependency located within the believer, rather than an external reality judging and ruling the universe; belief in any particular proposition about God is unimportant.[13] Schleiermacher evacuates divine authority from the universe and replaces it with human need.

The critical methodology that upheld the anti-dogmatic movement was rooted in the historical scholarship of Barthold Georg Niebuhr, a

11. See John Henry Newman, *Apologia pro Vita Sua* (Garden City, N.Y.: Doubleday Image, 1956), 135.

12. Friedrich Schleiermacher, *On Religion: Speeches to Its Cultured Despisers*, trans. John Oman (New York: Harper Torchbooks, 1958), 9, 10. The shadow cast by this book in England is surprisingly long; even as late as 1887, Thomas Hardy alludes familiarly to it in his novel *The Woodlanders.*

13. Ernest Renan eloquently defends this point of view, calling religion "l'aspiration au monde ideal" and asks if his readers' "faculties, vibrating simultaneously, have never given forth that great unique being we call God?" *(Qui si vos facultés, vibrant simultanément, n'ont jamais rendu ce grand son unique que nos appelons Dieu . . . ?).* See "M. Feuerbach et la nouvelle école Hégélienne," *Oeuvres completes de Ernest Renan,* 10 vols., ed. Henriette Psichiari (Paris: Calmann-Lévy, 1947), 7:294–95.

professor of history at Berlin. In 1812 his work on Roman history revolutionized the field. Through systematic mistrust of tradition, Niebuhr "suggested the theory of the myth": that great figures gather a mythic narrative accretion. Having laid low the authority of ancient authors, Niebuhr promptly asserted his own: he "brought in inference to supply the place of discredited tradition and showed the possibility of writing history in the absence of original records."[14] He scrutinized the ancient histories for the most believable kernels of truth and speculatively reconstructed the past on the basis of probability, inference, and such evidence as he considered especially resistant to tampering. By 1824, Leopold von Ranke had established the scholarly respectability of refusing, on principle, to believe eyewitness accounts unless they were backed by other documentary records.[15] Such methods had serious implications for the Gospels, some of which claim to be, and all of which depend on, eyewitness accounts. The "German higher criticism" presented England with readings of biblical history as devoid of miracle, and of biblical narrative as historical myth shaped by the political circumstances of its time.

The first generation of English intellectuals in the nineteenth century shared the suspicions that had prompted Niebuhr's reinterpretation of written history; the radical doubt of René Descartes had preceded Niebuhr. As every scholar of our time imbibes some measure of the nihilism of Nietzsche and the anti-foundationalism of Heidegger, so English thinkers found themselves in some sympathy with continental skepticism. From religious seekers to Utilitarian economists, English thinkers encountered a crisis of epistemology.

When historians advocated doubt on the grounds that stories require tellers, who are human and undependable, religion suffered particularly. "High and Dry" Anglicanism, based on rationalizations about the social costs of abandoning religion, or upon some account of physical evidence, began to seem too intellectually feeble to command respect. The attempt to take refuge in an absolute objectivity attributed to science—which had not yet succumbed to the same with-

14. *Encyclopaedia Britannica*, 11th ed. (1910–1911), *s.v.* "Niebuhr, Barthold Georg."
15. Butterfield, *The Origins of History*, 195–97.

ering doubt—brought dire times upon traditional Anglican biblical exegesis. Charles Lyell's *The Principles of Geology* (1830–1833) provided "testimony of the rocks" to unseat Bishop Ussher's chronology of creation, which had become standard in England. Yet deeper disturbances rocked the faith of English intellectuals when Charles Darwin in 1859 contributed a plausible (though not airtight) atheist myth of origins, and later extended its reach even to human consciousness.

The new "scientific" criticism so challenged the English literalist tradition of scriptural interpretation that many religious people sought to reduce the scope of religion to a matter of purely private and personal experience. While the hermeneutical crisis was brewing—and long afterward—the moralistic Evangelical party within the Anglican Church simply and unquestioningly presumed traditional biblical interpretations, and concentrated on the personal experience of conversion. "Theology" became a term of opprobrium; a personal emotional experience, untouchable by any scientific objectivity, seemed a safer basis for religion. Newman satirized this point of view soon after his own conversion to Catholicism in his novel *Loss and Gain* (1847):

> Freeborn, in fact, thought theology itself a mistake, as substituting, as he considered, worthless intellectual notions for the vital truths of religion; so now he went on to observe, putting down his knife and fork, that it really was to him inconceivable, that real religion should depend on metaphysical distinctions, or outward observances; that it was quite a different thing in Scripture; that Scripture said much of faith and holiness, but hardly a word about Churches and forms. . . . a rite, or a creed, or a form of prayer, or good works, or communion with particular Churches—all were but "flattering unctions to the soul," if they were considered necessary; the only safe way of using them was to use them with the feeling that you might dispense with them; that none of them went to the root of the matter, for that faith, that is firm belief that God had forgiven you, was the one thing needful; that where that one thing was present, everything else was superfluous; that where it was wanting, nothing else availed.

After Freeborn enthuses that "an Arminian, a Calvinist, an Episcopalian, a Swedenborgian—nay, a Unitarian—he would go further . . . a Papist" would be saved if he had the proper feelings about being forgiven, Freeborn's fellow diners demolish his position, attacking its logical inconsistencies. They bridle at the opportunities for self-delusion: "a man need not fear to believe too little, so he feels a good deal," or that if a person "believes himself forgiven, he need not believe anything else."[16] Indeed, except for a declared allegiance to the divinely inspired status of the Bible, little distinguished Evangelical epistemology from Schleiermacher's. Nevertheless, the Evangelicals had tremendous successes at spreading "muscular Christianity" in the slums and in creating social reform. One Evangelical group, known as the Clapham Sect, can be credited with driving the agitation for the abolition of slavery in the British Empire. Newman nevertheless had scant patience for Evangelical "superficial" moralism and commonsense defenses against skepticism. He felt that the Evangelicals had abandoned the intellectual battlefront at a crucial time.[17]

In fact, when questions about the geological age of the earth and the theory of evolution filtered into the consciousness of the reading public, Evangelical piety did become intellectually unrespectable. The parson who was "one of those science-haters / Blind as a mole or a bat" became a stereotype because such clergymen could be found all over England.[18] James Collins judges that Hopkins excoriated the Evangelicals for "plaintive twaddle" primarily because of their "lack of intellectual strength and reserve."[19]

At first, Evangelicals concerned with social work were theologically the most conservative Anglicans, equally appalled by skepticism and Catholicism, and at midcentury young "muscular Christian" ministers like Charles Kingsley, actively working for social justice, generally commanded real respect. Lively, reform-minded Evangelical piety, im-

16. John Henry Newman, *Loss and Gain: The Story of a Convert,* ed. Alan G. Hill (New York: Oxford University Press, 1986), 30–31.

17. Newman, *Apologia pro Vita Sua,* 159.

18. Anonymous pantoum, "Monologue d'outre tombe," quoted in full in Babette Deutsch, *Poetry Handbook: A Dictionary of Terms,* 2d ed. (New York: Grosset & Dunlap, 1962), 102.

19. James Collins, "Philosophical Themes in G. M. Hopkins," 70. For Hopkins's excoriation of the Evangelical party at Oxford, see Hopkins, *Further Letters,* 18 (to E. W. Urquart, 6 Jan. 1865).

pregnable to the intellectual ferment around it, was very effective in work with the lower classes; literary culture was then, as it is now, rich people's culture. But moralistic zeal was not incompatible with, say, George Eliot's brand of high-minded atheism.[20] Social reformism could be divorced from Christian belief, and eventually the divorce became common; as the century wore on, the public-spirited could treat the Church as a social reform club or even respectably abandon Christianity for a "religion of humanity" or other substitutes. The Clapham Sect's descendants, physical and intellectual, progressively rejected Christian dogmatism, then the external practices of Christianity, and finally Christian morals, to become the artistic elite of Bloomsbury "immoralists"[21] whose entire way of life would doubtless have been an abomination to their Evangelical forbears.

John Stuart Mill, more intellectually rigorous than the Evangelicals, put all his faith in science, logic, and the evidence of the senses; assailed by a crisis of meaning in his early twenties, he had a nervous breakdown. His case was extreme, but throughout the century a materialist search for meaning persisted; its most powerful avatar, the Darwinian mythos, generated such god substitutes as George Bernard Shaw's Nietzschean "Life Force" in all its tragic variations. Marxist materialism inverted another response to the mistrust of worldly evidences: Hegel's idea of the absolute primacy of the mind. Hegel's theory enveloped early nineteenth-century Oxford, and was the atmosphere in which Newman's early thinking took place.[22] But both Newman and Mill—and, be it said, the movements they represent—found in Romantic poetry something that amounted to a revelation.

20. No longer Christian herself, George Eliot presented Christianity as a laudable ethical system in *Adam Bede* (1859). She explains her reasoning in the chapter "In Which the Story Pauses a Little," where she sets forth the function of the novelist as something very like the purely moral function of the parson.

21. Gertrude Himmelfarb, *Marriage and Morals among the Victorians* (New York: Alfred A. Knopf, 1986), 23–49.

22. Brown, in *Hopkins's Idealism,* provides detailed information on Oxford Hegelianism; Newman describes how Bishop Butler's *Analogy of Religion* revealed to him how a sacramental system might be an "ultimate resolution" to "the theory, to which I was inclined as a boy, viz., the unreality of material phenomena"; see *Apologia pro Vita Sua,* 132.

Coleridge and Wordsworth broke upon their countrymen as the bearers of a powerful insight about the relationship of human beings to a more complete reality than either Hegelian interiority or hardheaded materialist ratiocination could discover.

Hopkins tasted Wordsworth flavored with the religious sensibilities of the Tractarians, as the poet of "philosophical meditation" who served religion—Newman called it "Catholic truth"—by his dedication to nature. Like a scientist recording experimental results, Wordsworth described his concrete experiences—but he unashamedly evoked their spiritual dimensions. Coleridge found in "Imagination" the image of God; Wordsworth bore witness to the "divine" Imagination as a psychological phenomenon. He distilled the image of God from the moral knowledge awakened in personal, eyewitness "spots of time"—in fact, in history. For the generation of English thinkers born near the turn of the nineteenth century, there was a subtle but crucial distinction between Wordsworth's historicized embodiment of moral lessons learned and Samuel Johnson's dry eighteenth-century description of poetry as "enforcement or decoration of some moral or religious truth."[23] Both notions of poetry require a previous commitment to moral truth; the difference lies in their epistemologies. Johnson considers moral and religious truths as real but abstract principles that can be objectively codified, learned, and then illustrated from nature. Wordsworth considers the truths exclusively as insights, as concrete events in an individual psyche. His technique draws one away from the world of abstractions into moments of memory intensely realized and imbued with meaning, events in a personal history that cannot be reconstructed by ratiocination. In *The Prelude,* Wordsworth says he makes off with somebody else's trapped bird, and he hears "low breathings coming after me"; he climbs a cliff to despoil a raven's nest, and hears "strange utterance" as he hangs on the crag. Wordsworth's moral knowledge is personal, autobiographical; he taught the Tractarians who lionized him how to seek eternal truth in the tangible world,

23. Samuel Johnson, *Rasselas, Prince of Abyssinia: A Tale,* in *Poems and Selected Prose of Samuel Johnson,* ed. Bertrand Bronson (New York: Holt Rinehart and Winston, 1952), 527.

and to be comfortable with the vertigo of recognizing that human beings have no unmediated knowledge.

Of Coleridge, Newman wrote, "[T]he dry and superficial character of the religion of the last generation, or century," created "the need which was felt both by the hearts and intellects of the nation for a deeper philosophy. . . . [Coleridge] instilled a higher philosophy into inquiring minds, than they had hitherto been accustomed to accept."[24] Patricia Ball has pointed out that the necessity for humanizing the world through interpreting experience is an idea that permeates Coleridge's thought. Coleridge does not consider the imagination divine merely because he values it highly or finds it mysterious; he proposes the notion that consciousness is the only thing in creation in which being and knowing are one, as they are in God.[25] Thus, as we shall see Hopkins do in his commentary on the *Spiritual Exercises* (having certainly read Coleridge), Coleridge initiates his investigation into the doctrine of God with the self.[26] God's creative act comes through recognition—through what Coleridge titled the "PRODUCTIVE LOGOS," the Word, which is God's self-image, identical to God. To recognize and give intellectual utterance to the world is to enact its creation.[27] Coleridge made the mind not the passive recipient of objective impressions but in some sense creator of its own reality: "Imagination . . . I hold to be the living power and prime agent of all human perception, and as a repetition in the finite mind of the eternal act of creation in the infinite *I am.*" Without imagination, "all objects (*as* objects) are essentially fixed and dead."[28] This faculty of perception completes the divine work of creation; hence its association with the Name

24. Newman, *Apologia pro Vita Sua,* 202. I have been pleased to discover, since writing this, that G. B. Tennyson argues in more detail for many of the same points about the influence of Wordsworth and Coleridge on the Oxford Movement in *Victorian Devotional Poetry* (Cambridge, Mass.: Harvard University Press, 1979), 14–22.

25. Samuel Taylor Coleridge, *Biographia Literaria,* 2 vols., ed. James Engell and Walter Jackson Bate (Princeton, N.J.: Princeton University Press, 1983), 1:285.

26. For Hopkins on reading Coleridge, see his letter to Ernest Hartley Coleridge, in *Further Letters,* 7 (3 Sept. 1862).

27. *Biographia Literaria,* 1:136.

28. *Biographia Literaria,* 1:304.

of God from the Book of Exodus. This Romantic epistemology opens an aesthetic way into a sacramental theology and promotes an understanding of nature as symbol, important underpinnings of the Tractarian theology and poetics that Hopkins embraced when he encountered them at Oxford. Here Newman could find a way in which God's revelation depended upon human participation.

While Coleridge provided him with intellectual foundations for his understanding of God's relationship to human consciousness in the will and imagination, Newman chose for his motto a version of Wordsworth's solution to the problem of moral and religious knowledge: "*Cor ad cor loquitur,*" heart speaks to heart. Direct spiritual communication could come through the poetic imagination. Readers could recognize and interpret the poet's experiences in the light of their own. The Tractarians saw in the poets' theological insights something of their own; nevertheless, the Tractarian poets' main concern was not aesthetic but religious, and explicitly Christian. Not the poet's own insight but the Church's was to be displayed in poetry. The poet was to reveal not the mere reality of his own earthly history but something of God himself.[29]

John Keble's work *The Christian Year* certainly reached more English homes than any of the tracts or even the "ritualistic" liturgical practices that spread into parishes beyond Oxford's community of professional theologians. *Lyra Apostolica,* a cooperative Tractarian effort, was less successful but still widely read. Keble, the dean of Tractarian poets, drew heavily on Coleridge for his religious poetics. Keble wrote:

> Poetry lends religion her wealth of symbols and similes; religion restores these again to poetry, clothed with so splendid a radiance that they appear to be no longer symbols, but to partake (I might almost say) of the true nature of sacraments.[30]

29. Margaret Johnson, *Gerard Manley Hopkins and Tractarian Poetry* (Brookfield, Vt.: Ashgate, 1997), 30.

30. Quoted by G. B. Tennyson in "Sacramental Imagination," in *Nature and the Victorian Imagination* (Berkeley and Los Angeles: University of California Press, 1977), 376.

The sacramental notion at the heart of Tractarian poetry is bound up with the mysterious way in which Romantic poets identified human consciousness as an image of God. Like the later Coleridge and the Tractarian poets, Hopkins considered the Incarnation central to that Romantic identification.[31] The Incarnate Word is an analogy, the way in which God is like a human being; but perfect likeness is identity. God being like a man is in fact God being a man. And here, before his formal introduction to Roman Catholic sacramental theory, is the wellspring of the sacramentality in the poetic theory of Hopkins. Poets are to interpret a world inhabited by the Divine Reason, a world that is always both itself and a manifestation of God, echoing the concept that Jesus is both the Word of God and a man. There is more than one thing present in it at the same time; this notion of multiple presence is the foundation of the sacramental view.

If Keble held that humans did indeed complete God's creation, to him as a practitioner of the Tractarians' doctrine of Divine Reserve, which held certain dogmas to be too sacred for public exposure, it would have seemed immodest to proclaim that dignity of the human role. Keble found Coleridge too bold in proclaiming his theory of Imagination. Perhaps he retreated from his early enthusiasm for the Coleridgean interpenetration of divine and human action in the world because the human participation in creation smacked too much of Catholic theories of spiritual merit, or seemed to give more weight to art than to the actual sacraments of the Church.[32] But at any rate, Keble, while inspired by the notion of a sacramental poetry, retreated to the safer ground of analogy based upon Coleridge's "Fancy." We shall see the consequences of his retreat on Hopkins's undergraduate verse.

Yet it should be noted that the religious crisis was not solved by poetry; the questions of authority remained vexing. Even Newman, the

31. Cf. Margaret Johnson, *Hopkins and Tractarian Poetry*, 103. Indeed, it may be the Tractarians' teaching that first brought Hopkins to consider the Incarnation more significant in itself than the Crucifixion. That notion helped prepare him for his adherence to the Scotist doctrine of the Incarnation.

32. Margaret Johnson, *Hopkins and Tractarian Poetry*, 35, 47–48.

future founder of the Tractarian party, flirted with the German higher criticism in the 1820s, when he began to expect "an attack made on the books and canon of Scripture." Newman became uneasy with the arrogance of the approach just as his slower-moving theological colleagues began to base their biblical studies on the new theories about their ancestors' mythologizing impulses, the social pressures that affect historiography, and, as the next generation saw it, the virtues of challenging tradition with educated inference from evidence untainted by human memory.[33] Romantic epistemology had prepared Newman to handle the newfound alarm at human reportage of history with a mental flexibility that he justifiably considered uncharacteristic of his Anglican brethren; conversations with Blanco White enabled him to extend that flexibility to Scripture.[34] He was not devastated, as many of his conservative colleagues were, by the challenge to objective history in the Bible.

Some Englishmen, such as Thomas Arnold, the professor of history at Oxford, attempted to circumvent the theological implications of the new historiography by excepting Scripture from the materials over which historical theory had authority.[35] This subterfuge was a poor dike against the rising tide of suspicion that political schemes and power struggles were really behind the scriptural documents. Thomas Arnold eventually drifted with the tide. Newman's sarcastic query about Arnold in 1832—"But is *he* a Christian?"[36]—signaled, in retrospect, the inception of the Oxford Movement. He took action from the pulpit in 1833, and joined with John Keble and Edward Pusey to ward off the "National Apostasy" they saw looming from "the biblical and theological speculations of Germany."[37] They began to issue a series of

33. *Encyclopaedia Britannica,* 11th ed. (1910–11), *s.v.* "Niebuhr, Barthold Georg."

34. Newman, *Apologia pro Vita Sua,* 131.

35. See Sue Zemka, "The Arnolds and the Bible in the Age of the Great Reform Bill," a paper delivered at the West Coast Association for British Studies, March 1986, and incorporated into her Ph.D. dissertation, "Victorian Testaments: The Uses and Abuses of the Bible in Early Nineteenth-Century British Literature" (Stanford University, 1989), now published as *Victorian Testaments: The Bible, Christology, and Literary Authority in Nineteenth-Century British Culture* (Stanford, Calif.: Stanford University Press, 1997).

36. Newman, *Apologia pro Vita Sua,* 151.

37. Newman, *Apologia pro Vita Sua,* 154.

tracts to help establish ancient tradition as the basis for the authority of the Church of England; this earned them the name of Tractarians. Tractarians feared that the Church of England was built upon a shaky hermeneutical foundation, since the Anglicans had no authoritative interpreter of the Bible except another text, established by Parliament: the 39 Articles of Religion, which referred one back to the Bible for evidence. To demand absolute certainty from the Bible seemed to Newman, as it did to the German biblical critics, prima facie unreal, a begging of the question. Newman extended that suspicion about objectivity to the continental critics, to their "science" and "scientific history," sharply aware that no new evidence had arisen to change the way Scripture and history were interpreted; the decision to doubt was driven by a change of fashion in the moral world of scholarship. The theologically liberal "disdain for antiquity" amounted to a preference "for intellectual excellence over moral." The moral excellence he meant was respect for the community that had transmitted the Scriptures to his own generation.

By 1835, with a casual conviction previously found only among avowed anti-Christians, German critic David Strauss felt free to publish a life of Jesus that denied that Christ's miracles were historical. Strauss did not repudiate the Christian name, and he plausibly, even religiously, interpreted the texts. No less a stylist than George Eliot translated his book into English. Inspired by Newman, Tractarians throughout the 1830s countered such reinterpretations with tracts citing the evidence for the unity of the Christian interpretive community over time, and invitations to commit oneself to that community rather than the contemporary community of professional theologians.

Against the Broad Churchmen, who located the essence of religion in its psychological effects, Newman asserted that dogma was "the fundamental principle." He said that "religion, as a mere sentiment, is to me a dream and a mockery." Newman emphatically defined the Christian community as bounded by a set of dogmatic beliefs: "the Apostolic form of doctrine [is] essential and imperative"[38] for all time. The search for dogmatic consensus motivated Tractarians to translate

38. Newman, *Apologia pro Vita Sua,* 163–64, 160.

ancient ecclesiastical writings (theirs are still the only English versions of some works). The wider tradition made accessible by these documents was richer and more flexible than the *sola scriptura* approach that had been dominant in England; yet it supported the same creedal definitions and affirmed the historical accuracy of Scripture. Tractarians hoped for a way out of the hermeneutical crisis if they could persuade the Anglican Church to accept the tradition represented by the ancient writings as an intellectually defensible basis for the Christian faith, a thinking man's substitute for the conservatives' purely literal interpretation of the Bible.

Few Anglican clergymen went to work zealously in the slums; fewer yet pontificated against Darwin in the manner of Bishop Wilberforce. (For one thing, few had the credentials; Wilberforce's scientific expertise was far greater than popular recollection has allowed—and, though it is little known today, there were many clergy, evidently including Hopkins, who adopted a theistic evolutionism.)[39] In what was probably the most common response to the crisis of epistemology, Broad Churchmen, such as Thomas Arnold had become, sought to establish a form of Christianity that was principally a way of packaging moral exhortation. It did not require people to believe in miracles or prophecy, but did not openly repudiate them. The morality was considered to carry its own authority and therefore would provide a solid foundation for a religion that could no longer assert its historical validity. Newman despised "liberal" theology as the cowardly, but socially acceptable, approach among Oxford faculty—whose livings (benefices), after all, depended on the existence of the English Church. To Newman it seemed unmanly neither to deny Christianity nor to defend its historical basis, but rather to take refuge in vagueness, advocating morals and the need for religion without defining what religious tenets ought to be believed.

Newman, rather than break with interpretive tradition so radically as Arnold and the liberals, strongly espoused the idea that layers of

39. See Nixon, *Gerard Manley Hopkins and His Contemporaries*, 163; cf. Tom Zaniello, "A 'Beautiful but Broken Arc,'" in *Critical Essays on Gerard Manley Hopkins*, ed. Alison G. Sulloway (Boston: G. K. Hall, 1990), 155–68.

historical, moral, typological, and mystical meanings inhabited even those texts he took literally as history. The biblical text itself both provides historical context and makes use of typologies and prefigurings: Adam as a type of Christ, baptism as an antitype of Noah's flood, the Exodus from Egypt as a type of the return from the Babylonian Exile, the sufferings in the lives of the Prophets (such as the widowhood of Ezekiel or the marriage of Hosea) as images of the relationship between God and Israel, and so on.[40] The earliest Christian interpreters, such as Origen, Ambrose, and Augustine, had employed a typological hermeneutic principle, interpreting anomalous passages to be allegorical or symbolic in accord with the consensus of the Church in general.[41]

Since ancient Christian writings constantly interpret portions of the Old Testament as pure symbol,[42] the Tractarians' hermeneutic was less threatened by scientific theories about history than that of their conservative Anglican contemporaries. Against the historian's principle of suspicion Newman set a "mystical or sacramental principle" advocated by the ancient school of Alexandria, which

> spoke of various Economies or Dispensations of the Eternal. I understood them to mean that the exterior world, physical and historical, was but the outward manifestation of realities greater than itself. Nature was a parable: Scripture was an allegory: pagan literature, philosophy and mythology, properly understood, were but a preparation for the Gospel. . . . room was made for the anticipation of further and deeper disclosures, of truths still under the veil of the letter, and in their season to be revealed.[43]

Newman's "various Economies" do not mean that the Church can contradict itself to better appeal to the intellectual fashions of the times. Christian truth, Newman claims, does not change; multiple meanings demonstrate depth rather than create new truths.

40. Cf. Northrop Frye, *The Great Code: The Bible and Literature* (New York: Harcourt Brace Jovanovich, 1982), 79ff.

41. Johannes Quasten, *Patrology*, 4 vols. (Westminster, Md.: Christian Classics, 1986), 4:425. The tradition is at least as old as Origen. Cf. Quasten, *Patrology*, 2:93.

42. Cf. Quasten, *Patrology*, 1:300–308, 2:92–93, 3:91, 119, 217, 266, 404, 433, 449, 498, 540, etc.

43. Newman, *Apologia pro Vita Sua*, 145–46.

Correct dogma cannot be simply deduced from the Bible, though the Bible provides support for right doctrine,[44] and scientific evidence must be considered as an aid to interpretation. Newman feels free to interpret the story of Adam, for instance, as either symbolic or historical; if science were to prove conclusively that the human race was not descended from Adam, and that Adam was nonetheless historical, then one must conclude that the story of Adam is emblematic rather than historical. It is reasonable and part of God's plan that the interpretation of the Bible should develop over time; how can the Christian understanding of Scripture remain fixed while history, whether by scientific discoveries or other events, reveals more and more of God's plan at work in the world? Only the Church as a whole can assure the believer that "beyond all question God spoke as I thought he did."[45] Newman is very careful not to locate authority in the text of the Bible but rather in the community that creates and interprets it; the Holy Spirit is a gift not to the book but to the people, and the Holy Spirit makes "dispensations" of grace according to need. Such dispensations may include miracles, which need not happen under our own eyes to be believed. Newman trusts the people who communicated the Christian faith to him, making "an argument from Personality, which in fact is one form of the argument from Authority."[46] The moral decision to commit himself in trust or mistrust of some person in authority, rather than any "objective" standard of evidence, is ultimately the basis of his faith.

The symbolic or sacramental view of the events of history and of scriptural texts, which had opened Newman to his "Alexandrian" interpretations of the ancient books, could also be applied to the world as seen by writers operating under a lesser inspiration. Poets have intercourse not necessarily with the miraculous but certainly with the natural world, imbued with divine meaning, which they encounter personally and share with their readers. The place of Romantic episte-

44. Newman, *Apologia pro Vita Sua,* 131–32.

45. John Henry Newman, *An Essay in Aid of a Grammar of Assent* (Notre Dame, Ind.: Notre Dame University Press, 1979), 206–7; hereafter cited as *Grammar of Assent.*

46. Newman, *Apologia pro Vita Sua,* 142–43, 140.

mology in Tractarian belief is to make all knowledge personal, a matter of will as much as evidence. A believer's trust in the Christian tradition would be a personal commitment to the human, visible, unbroken community of predecessors in the faith. Tractarians preached a visible and sacramentally communicated apostolic succession of ecclesiastical authority, which seemed dangerously close to Rome. Therefore, the Tractarians carefully pointed out that their claim to the antiquity of the English Church led them only to advocate it as a theological "middle way" between the "church insane" which was Roman Catholicism and the Protestant church, whose obsession with freedom of personal scriptural interpretation had loosened its roots. During the first decade and more of the Tractarian movement, undergraduates flocked to Newman's sermons at St. Mary's in Oxford and Newman, though still an Anglican, developed a perilous reputation for losing young Englishmen to Rome.

Controversy over Newman's *Tract 90* pushed him out of the Anglican communion; his avowed purpose in that document was, in fact, to show that one could hold Roman Catholic beliefs and still subscribe to the 39 Articles of Religion. A deconstructive tour-de-force, *Tract 90* deliberately reinterpreted the Articles in a spirit that opposed the anti-Catholicism of their authors. Newman capitalized on contradictions and aporias: sermons mentioned as "wholesome doctrine" in the Articles, for instance, contradicted doctrines expressed in the Articles themselves; the article about communion left gaps in its doctrinal definitions that allowed space for dogmas defined in the Roman Catholics' fiercely anti-Protestant Council of Trent. At the time, Newman's conscious purpose was to show young men on the verge of defection to Rome that they did have a way to stay within the Anglican communion. The protests of the Anglican establishment indicated forcefully that official English anti-Catholicism extended to doctrines as well as to formal allegiances. Newman was pressured out of his post and, after a long period of reflection, himself became a Roman Catholic.

The Tractarian movement never quite recovered from the blow dealt it by Newman's conversion, though the party continued to hold power at Oxford, dealing out fellowships to men according to their theological orthodoxy, and punishing those who taught in the liberal vein. But the liberals gradually gained adherents; by the time Hopkins matriculated in 1863, clergy were no longer uniformly expected to believe in biblical miracles or in the virtuous motivations of biblical authors. Nevertheless, the Tractarian movement had been important, at Oxford and beyond, for all of Hopkins's life, and the Broad Church party was not yet altogether triumphant among the intellectual leadership of the English Church. Hopkins did not know that Tractarianism was in the waning days of its power even at Oxford, but he disdained what he saw as a liberal failure of faith and commitment. No doubt the knowledge of its hard times would only have spurred him to the defense of the party that had made Oxford, as far as he was concerned, "the head and fount of Catholicism in England and the heart of our Church."[47] Hopkins's first terms at the university were perhaps the happiest days of his life—not only because of the freedom and the intense friendships common to the first terms of college life, but also because of his joy at belonging to the party of the most earnest, theologically conservative young scholars of the Church of England.

Hopkins held himself aloof from the "enlightened Christianity" even of his much-respected tutor, Benjamin Jowett, the author of "On the Interpretation of Scripture" in the famous liberal collection *Essays and Reviews.* Some of the clerics who contributed to that book were censured by the Anglican Church for their abandonment of traditional theology, and the volume as a whole was condemned in 1864. But the crumbling of the Oxford Movement's power became evident when Canon Edward Pusey, Hopkins's mentor and soon-to-be confessor, tried but finally failed (1864–1865) to prevent a raise in Jowett's salary—at the time, about a tenth of the normal Oxford pay. Hopkins, so close to the battle, resolutely took no side; Jowett had indeed won his respect, though not his theological adherence. The inability of the Tractarians to isolate and punish Jowett demonstrated that they were not the heirs to ecclesiastical authority in England, and thus weakened their claim to be keepers of the ancient and true Christian tradition.

47. Hopkins, *Further Letters,* 16 (to E. H. Coleridge, 1 June 1864).

"It is scarcely now a party," wrote Newman in 1864 of "liberals" and their "deep, plausible scepticism"; "it is the educated lay world."[48] And indeed, so it came to be. Thomas Arnold's son was the poet Matthew Arnold, a school inspector and not a clergyman. But by the 1870s, even Matthew Arnold, who insisted upon Bible readings in public schools, could chide the Church of England for teaching that miracles actually happened: "The reign of religion as morality touched with emotion is indeed indestructible. But religion as men commonly conceive it—religion depending on the historicalness of certain supposed facts . . .—how much of this religion can be deemed unalterably secure? Our religion has materialised itself in the fact—the supposed fact; it has attached its emotion to the fact."[49] Matthew Arnold's 1884 "lay sermon" at St. Jude's, Whitechapel, disparaged from the pulpit the London Mission Society's acceptance of the "preternatural and miraculous aspect" of Christianity as "neither entirely solid nor verifiable." He did commend its moral success with the poor and urged his hearers to keep the Christian spirit and to pursue moral education.[50] One reviewer explained Arnold's principles of biblical interpretation: limit a text's meaning by its historical context and political purpose, "without reference to the adaptations of the fathers or Divines," and insist that "the apprehension of the original meaning is inconsistent with the reception of a typical or conventional one."[51]

Matthew Arnold's efforts reproduced on a popular level the efforts of Hopkins's liberal tutor Jowett and his party to establish a less supernaturally committing alternative to traditional Christianity. Having yielded the ground of historical reality to secular "science," the liberal theologians traded heavily upon a guarded region of subjectivity, in the style of Schleiermacher, as the reigning principle of religious epis-

48. Newman, *Apologia pro Vita Sua*, 335.

49. Matthew Arnold, "On Poetry," in *Complete Prose Works*, 11 vols., ed. R. H. Super (Ann Arbor: University of Michigan Press, 1971–1978), 9:63; hereafter cited as Arnold, *Prose Works.*

50. Matthew Arnold, "A Lay Sermon: On the Unveiling of a Mosaic in Whitechapel," in *Prose Works*, 10:251–52.

51. Quoted in Super's critical and explanatory notes, in Arnold, *Prose Works*, 6:456–57; cf. John O. Waller, "Matthew Arnold and Thomas Arnold: Soteriology," *Anglican Theological Review* 44 (Jan.1962): 57–70, esp. 58–59.

temology. Hopkins saw in this nothing but arrogance. He wrote to his friend E. H. Coleridge in 1864: "Beware of doing what I once thought I could do, *adopt an enlightened Christianity*, I may say, horrible as it is, *be a credit to religion*" (emphasis in original).[52] As the century wore on, of course, Hopkins was among a shrinking minority that resisted banishing the rational and discursive from religious language. All his life, Hopkins insisted that religious language had referents in the world outside the mind, though the referents could not be perceived objectively. He found little sympathy for this position even from his close friend Robert Bridges, whose attacks on his friend's religion survive in Hopkins's replies (Bridges destroyed his own letters to Hopkins). Later, Bridges proclaimed his belief in a "religion of poetry"[53] and praised religious music because it unites "in common devotion minds that are only separated by creeds and it comforts our hope with a brighter promise of unity than any logic offers."[54]

Hopkins could not speak so lightly of logic or creeds. From childhood, he believed that words signified realities, and that they could and did convey truth or falsehood, even about spiritual matters. Hopkins considered logic more than a mere human construction. Different creeds—even different Christian creeds—were not mere quibbles on different ways of saying the same thing. The different words referred to different realities; some creeds truthfully described God's action in the world and some did not. False beliefs might damn those who chose them, in spite of other virtues. Late in life, Hopkins wrote anxiously of his favorite composer, Henry Purcell, "I hope Purcell is not damned for being a Protestant, because I love his genius."[55] Recall Hopkins's deep desire for a reality worthy of his devotion; if it makes assertions about the most important reality, religious language demands a sharper standard than that of mere desire and utility, which Hopkins could master even as a boy. If language embodies a relation-

52. Hopkins, *Further Letters*, 16–17 (to E. H. Coleridge, 1 June 1864).

53. Robert Bridges, *Poems of Gerard Manley Hopkins, Now First Published* (London: Humphrey Milford, 1918), xviii.

54. Quoted in Jean-Georges Ritz, *Robert Bridges and Gerard Manley Hopkins: A Literary Friendship, 1863–1889* (London: Oxford University Press, 1960), 131.

55. Hopkins, *Letters to Bridges*, 170 (4 Jan. 1883).

ship of responsibility to the world, creeds have some meaning independent of the hortatory intentions of the speaker, however fine those intentions might be.

Hopkins, like Newman, flirted with the German higher criticism because, although repelled by emotion disengaged from the intellect, he could not deny the power of subjectivity in shaping history. The problem of authority, especially in a historically based religion such as Christianity, is that the whole of "salvation history," as it is termed, is based upon the memory of witnesses. Unless one takes the Bible to be written at dictation, as Muslims take the Koran, one must contend with the problem of the reliability of someone else's report. Observing the same difficulty in less momentous situations as well, Hopkins understood the biblical question as a particularly important instance of a more general problem: how to work out the relationship between external reality and the multifarious human perceptions of it. What any one person remembers is never exactly what anyone else remembers; what one sees is never exactly what anyone else sees. How much of what one remembers is reality and how much is just a wash of personal feelings beyond the realm of truthful communication? Hopkins was about nineteen when he considered the problem in this short poem:[56]

> It was a hard thing to undo this knot.
> The rainbow shines, but only in the thought
> Of him that looks. Yet not in that alone,
> For who makes rainbows by invention?
> And many standing round a waterfall
> See one bow each, yet not the same to all,
> But each a hand's breadth further than the next.
> The sun on falling waters writes the text
> Which yet is in the eye or in the thought.
> It was a hard thing to undo this knot.

A group of people are standing looking at a rainbow on a waterfall, such as anyone can see at Niagara Falls, and each one sees it in a different place. Where, then, is the rainbow? Whose perception can be trusted? This is not just a problem with rainbows. It is a problem with any

56. Hopkins, *Poetical Works,* 31.

event; and thus it is a problem with history. Hopkins admits, in this poem, that the text "yet is in the eye or in the thought," but nevertheless insists that the text of the world is not a human construction. He insists that human interpretation has an origin in a world of real events and relationships to which it refers, but does not forget that knowledge has its reality only in the knower. This epistemological realism throws light on matters more significant to him than the location of a rainbow; the most hotly disputed text of all in Hopkins's culture was the Bible, and that text was the issue in Hopkins's life as he wrote these lines.

His concern about subjectivity and religious knowledge never left him. Many years after his conversion to Catholicism, Hopkins published a triolet lampooning the methods of higher criticism, beginning with a well-known quotation from Wordsworth:

"The child is father to the man."
How can he be? The words are wild.
Suck any sense from that who can:
"The child is father to the man."
No; what the poet did write ran,
"The man is father to the child."
"The child is father to the man"!
How *can* he be? The words are wild.[57]

The point is, of course, that the text is misunderstood by those who want it to fit the ordinary categories of expression, just as biblical history is mangled by those who wish to reduce it to the more comfortable, less threatening category of politics. Uncomprehending critics mangled the text on the pretext of amending it, as biblical critics sought the hypothetical "sources" that had been corrupted in transmission to form the Gospels or the Old Testament texts. Hopkins's choice of Wordsworth for the subject matter of his barb is no accident; Tractarians did treat Wordsworth as, in Keble's words, "chief minister not only of sweetest poetry but also of high and sacred truth."[58] New-

57. Hopkins, "A Trio of Triolets," *Poetical Works*, 172.

58. Keble, quoted in Margaret Johnson, *Gerard Manley Hopkins and Tractarian Poetry* (Brookfield, Vt.: Ashgate, 1997), 19.

man and Keble had found that the Romantic poets fulfilled a deep need; Hopkins himself had felt that need.

As he began his Oxford career, Hopkins's own religion was, like eighteenth-century Anglicanism, "dry" in its search for objectivity. Truth seemed to demand emotional distance and distrust of "enthusiasm." It was perhaps the resistance of Tractarianism to treating religion as an emotional state that first attracted Hopkins to the Tractarians. One could oppose the sentimental religion of the liberals rationally with the scholarly weapons of antiquity wielded by the Oxford Movement. The theory of apostolic succession—that the knowledge of holy truth resided in a community of people continuous through history—offered Hopkins more certainty than could be brought to him by an appeal to deep feelings. Epistemologically, the Tractarians' scholarship in ancient documents offered a "middle way" between dependence upon a Scripture now cast into doubt and a dependence upon the authority of one's own mere sentiment for religious belief. The Tractarian union of scholarly exactitude with impassioned personal commitment has its echoes even in the technique of Hopkins as a poet.

Yet more vital to Hopkins's intellectual life at nineteen was the connection Tractarians drew between the physical world's symbolic, "sacramental" significance and the question of ecclesiastical authority. Sacrament requires external and visible signs; similarly, a Church must be visible and visibly unified. Basing their claims about the Church of England's authority on its connection to an objectively detectable tradition, rather than on an ineffable sentiment, required detectable signs by which that connection could be established. The idea of a visible and sacramental church was politically risky, of course, since Roman Catholicism had the most continuous visible and sacramental tradition. And the sacramental tradition, unlike the liberal religion Hopkins so scornfully rejected, conceives neither intellectual recognition nor even imitation as the salvation won by the Incarnation; salvation comes rather by physical participation.

The Incarnation is, as numerous critics have noted, absolutely the center of Hopkins's theology; it is also central to that of the Tractarians. Incarnation involves God "assuming" humanity, organically, as "man like us in all things but sin" (Heb. 4.15)—choosing to unify human weakness with God's nature, since a human being cannot choose to take into himself divine power. But that means that Incarnation involves a particular, messy, historical, fleshly life. Sacramental theologians acknowledge an intellectual aspect to salvation, because humans reason. But knowledge is not righteousness—not even the literary knowledge that was gaining ground among the Oxford and Cambridge elite as a reasonable substitute for religion. Recognition of even the analogy between God and man in Jesus is insufficient to save; "the devils also believe, and tremble" (James 2.19). There has to be something physical to participate in. Through contact with the Tractarians, Hopkins was convinced that he must connect himself to a communion with visible, physical sacraments in order to ensure a logical and clear connection to the authority of Christ. Now that the Anglican Church accepted even those who denied the supernatural origins of the Bible and the literal truth of biblical history, he could see no authority left in the *sola scriptura* tradition in English Protestantism.

Just when the question of authority became particularly acute in the religious circles of Oxford, Newman's autobiography, *Apologia Pro Vita Sua,* caused a stir throughout England. Newman's story of his conversion to Roman Catholicism and his sketches of ideas about the interpretation of Scripture made him again a force in English religion, especially among the remaining adherents of the Tractarian movement. As the Tractarians found their claim to unity with the great tradition of the English Church crumbling, Hopkins told his father, "the Tractarian ground I have seen broken to pieces under my feet." The same ground had crumbled under Newman's feet; when Hopkins decided that he, too, should enter the Roman Catholic Church, he took a train to Birmingham to be received by Newman.

Hopkins considered Tractarian aesthetics an outgrowth of Romanticism, classifying Newman and Keble with the "school" of the "Lake poets."[59] But, even perhaps at his conversion, he probably had not yet

59. Hopkins, *Correspondence with Dixon,* 98–99 (1–16 Dec. 1881).

seen a connection between Tractarian aesthetics and ecclesiology: that Tractarians sought not objectivity but personal loyalty in their study of the early Church. The vision of the Church as a community of knowers was connected deeply to the Romantic conviction that knowledge resides with the knower. Looking for an unbroken historical tradition to give boundaries to his traditional Christianity, the young poet sought tangible, sacramental signs of authority. But the idea of sacraments had implications for secular as well as sacred literature; it opened for Hopkins the possibility that the sensual world was also, like the Church, God's messenger. This was a poetics near to hand—a theological aesthetics.

Nevertheless, it was not the Romanticism in their poetry but the rational theological argumentation that first attracted Hopkins to the Tractarian camp. It is true, as we shall see, that Hopkins adopted Tractarian poetic practices, and other practices as well, but when he came to Oxford his aesthetic ideas were not Tractarian. They were Ruskinian. To that deeply Protestant thinker we must now turn.

CHAPTER 3

RUSKIN AND RESPONSIBILITY

JOHN RUSKIN'S ART CRITICISM was part of the intellectual equipment of any literate Victorian with aesthetic inclinations. When Hopkins entered Oxford, he was in the grip of Ruskinian hero worship. Ruskin demanded that the artist be responsible to his own vision, but emphasized that that vision, truly rendered, would reveal God's design and meaning in the world. Ruskin's insistence on truth emerges in Hopkins as a sort of preternatural exactitude of perception that calls readers to recognize in bird or tree or sky a sacredness solid enough to tingle on the skin. As long as Ruskin saw in all the world, even at its most hideous, the unity of God's purpose and the emblem of virtue, Hopkins followed him; when that theory fell apart for Ruskin, Hopkins looked for a more orderly art among the Tractarians. Yet Ruskin's lessons, unforgotten, eventually bloomed in a new synthesis of poetry and theology.

Hopkins's admiration for Ruskin was sincere and lifelong.[1] Discussing "the perfect critic" in an early letter, Hopkins naturally refers to Ruskin; the first name that comes to his mind is Ruskin's; although "Ruskin often goes astray," he is among those whose "excellences utterly outweigh their defects."[2] As a schoolboy and an undergraduate, Hopkins devoted hours to sketching the architectural details of English churches and producing landscapes and studies of foliage that imitate those Ruskin published in the later volumes of *Modern Painters.* "I venture to hope you will approve of some of the sketches,"

1. Fuller studies of this influence have been made by Alison Sulloway in *Hopkins and the Victorian Temper* and Patricia Ball in *The Science of Aspects.*

2. Hopkins, *Further Letters,* 204 (to A. W. M. Baillie, 6 Sept. 1863).

he writes to A. W. M. Baillie, "in a Ruskinese point of view."[3] Ruskinian attention to color and form imbues his description and sketching of Ruskinian subjects, mainly clouds and flora. Echoes of Ruskin's peculiar technical terms from *The Seven Lamps of Architecture* appear in Hopkins's notes on the architecture of English churches, and reappear throughout Hopkins's life as a general aesthetic vocabulary: the "flutes" of a waterfall, the "groins" of the braes, the "nave" of a knee, "furled" hearts. Hopkins even mentions Ruskin lightly in a letter written by dictation on his deathbed.[4]

Ruskin appealed to the desire of Hopkins to dedicate himself to something worthy. Like Ruskin, Hopkins already held as catechism that the purpose of life is to "witness" the glory of God. Ruskin applied it in new ways; a career dedicated to aesthetic appreciation had a higher good in it, according to Ruskin, than one whose actions served merely to preserve rather than to ennoble life. Ruskin's "Typical Beauty"—the word "type" is borrowed from biblical criticism—is "Useful" because it "sets the glory of God more brightly before us."[5] Ruskin looks to nature for more than mere illustration or decoration of known abstract moral truths. Natural beauty nourishes the recognition of intrinsic "types" of the attributes of the biblical God: purity, incomprehensibility, permanence, justice. Yet Ruskin clearly understands his purpose in writing as rather a justification of the "mental pleasures taken in beauty"[6] than as a search for God. Dismayed at the insensitivity to such pleasures in his brittle Evangelical coreligionists,

3. Hopkins, *Further Letters,* 202 (to A. W. M. Baillie, 10 July 1863).

4. He writes of the author of a sentimental song: "By every post he receives enquiries as to his meaning which he cannot give except that the Garden of Sleep is a poppy-grown churchyard in the corner of the Cliff. He gives a text from Ruskin to the effect that all pure natures admire bright colors, referring to the poppies. Accordingly with his genius and purity he must be a good catch." See Hopkins to his mother, 8 May 1889, in *Further Letters,* 198.

5. John Ruskin, *Modern Painters,* 3.1.1.4, in vol. 4 of *The Complete Works of John Ruskin,* containing part III, sections I and II: *Of the Imaginative and Theoretic Faculties,* ed. E. T. Cook and Alexander Wedderburn (New York: Longmans Green, 1903), 26–27. Hereafter this edition is cited as *C&W,* in this form: quotation from *Modern Painters,* 3.1.1.4, in *C&W,* 4:29.

6. Ruskin, *Modern Painters,* 3.1.1.2, in *C&W,* 26–28; quotation from "Preface to the Re-Arranged Edition of 1883," 7.

Ruskin "un-converted" from Christianity during the years from 1858 to 1875, but early volumes of *Modern Painters* (vol. 1, 1843, and vol. 2, 1846) and *The Seven Lamps of Architecture* (1848) are saturated in the piety Ruskin learned from his Evangelical mother as they analyze, with love and rigor, the truth an artist can tell about how color and form strike the eye.

Hopkins devoured Ruskin's argument that artistic objectivity would best serve the glory of God. If true artistic imagination does not merely indulge sentimentality or breed "Fancy"—a word Ruskin borrows from Coleridge—it is tied in a disciplined way to unfailing laws about natural growth and the balance of masses. Appreciation of beauty is a form of the worship of God, and ultimately an act of public virtue. Ruskin assigns a very important place to the beholder of art, demanding "imaginative participation from an audience."[7] Art's moral function gives it holiness; although it reveals types, they must be sought through individual encounters with the truths of experience. Ruskin exhorted young artists to train their eyes scrupulously to notice shape and pattern, and called for them to paint only the truth their eyes delivered to them. For Ruskin, such rigorous practice was evidence of moral seriousness and sincerity; Ruskin's "theoretic faculty" of appreciation employs for its force associations of guilt or rejoicing in duties "performed or omitted."[8] Hopkins, as we shall see, found the evidence of individuation in his moral sense, and deeply valued the individual vision, though finally he did not hold, as Ruskin did, that individual differences in the perception of beauty primarily have their origin in one's moral history.

Ruskin explains why he finds such individual visions valuable, despite their faults of peculiarity: they give evidence of faith in God, whose supreme "Imagination Associative" brings harmony to the universe by a comprehensiveness of vision like that of the artist who knows how to "induce in each of its component parts," as he puts it,

7. Elizabeth K. Helsinger, *Ruskin and the Art of the Beholder* (Cambridge, Mass.: Harvard University Press, 1982), 225.

8. Ruskin, *Modern Painters*, 3.1.4.10, in *C&W*, 4:73.

"such imperfection as that the other shall put it right."[9] Strict adherence to a personal vision brings about a fellowship of charity and mutual help, if one has faith in God's foresight and does not insist upon one's own perfection. Ruskin finds exemplars of the holy artist in the Gothic stonemasons he discusses in *The Stones of Venice* (1851–1853). Gothic imperfection and disorder show trust in God's ultimate authority; both the glory and the ruin of nature ultimately vindicate God's honor. Classical architecture is false and overly pretty because it was founded in slavery and the cowardice of pride, was terrified of human limitation, and sought an inhuman completeness of mastery. Christian artisans, he says, were free of shame and fearless, because they humbly trusted in God's salvation. With no pretended balance, no false dignity at stake, Gothic work stands, in its wild beauty, on the faith of the workmen. Christian charity frees workers to make mistakes and accords respect to the poor and lowly. With a dawning recognition of social "Usefulness" after all, the chapter aims a glancing blow at the standardized British factory system as Ruskin praises the aspiration made possible by Christian moral courage. Ruskin defends the dignity of the workers as he praises how, instead of repeating simple, faultless forms, Gothic stonemasons ventured, even beyond their ability, to attempt the unprecedented and unique.

Hopkins acquired a taste for Gothic, and also for the Pre-Raphaelites whom Ruskin defended as individualistic martyrs to artistic integrity.[10] His 1851 defense of them no doubt roused a strong response from Hopkins, embroiled in his dawning epistemological concerns:

> For it is always to be remembered that no one mind is like another, either in its powers or perceptions; and while the main principles of training must be the same for all, the result in each will be as various as the kinds of truth which each will apprehend; therefore, also, the modes of effort, even in men whose inner principles and final goals are exactly the same.[11]

9. Ruskin, *Modern Painters*, 3.2.2.6, in *C&W*, 4:233.

10. Ruskin, "Pre-Raphaelitism," in *Lectures on Architecture and Painting, etc.*, in *C&W*, 12:353–56, esp. 355.

11. Ruskin, *C&W*, 12:359.

Ruskin provided a way to view the artist as both a Christian hero and a thoroughly romantic artistic visionary.

Nearly all of the names of the artists of the Pre-Raphaelite circle appear in Hopkins's early notebooks, in connection either with painting or with poetry. No doubt Hopkins felt a kinship with the Pre-Raphaelite taste for psychological intensity; and, though he did not admit it, the contact with Ruskinian and Pre-Raphaelite medievalism began to soften his prejudices against Roman Catholic culture.[12] While he had written admiringly in 1862 of Tennyson's satire of Catholic asceticism, "St. Simeon Stylites,"[13] an undifferentiated admiration of the Middle Ages, including monastic and ascetic practice, begins to appear increasingly in his Oxford poems. Surviving examples of Hopkins's early poetic exercises, such as "The Queen's Crowning," "A Fragment of Anything You Like," and "A Voice from the World," maintain the Pre-Raphaelites' somewhat precious imagery and medieval "keepings," as Hopkins called them. His poem "The Half-Way House," for instance, closely resembles Richard Watson Dixon's Pre-Raphaelite publication "Dream" ("With camel's hair I clothed my skin"). His undergraduate poetry suggests that he is a disciple of Christina Rossetti, the most explicitly religious of the Pre-Raphaelites; it is in imitation of her work, not in the direct observation of nature, that Hopkins begins to write devotional poetry. His "A Voice from the World: A Reply to Christina Rossetti's 'The Convent Threshold'" was begun in June 1864, a month before the burst of enthusiasm that produced "Heaven-Haven," "New Readings," and a number of other religious poems.[14] Judging from these poems, it would be easy to see why Hopkins's father thought his aesthetic tastes had led him astray from the Church of England.

12. Hopkins did remain friendly to aesthetic medievalism. See Jerome Bump, "Hopkins's Imagery and Mediaevalist Poetics," *Victorian Poetry* 15 (1977): 99–119.

13. Hopkins, *Further Letters,* 8 (to E. H. Coleridge, 3 Sept. 1862). Ruskin also held that "Romanism" is too obsessed with pain; cf. *Modern Painters,* 1.14.29, in *C&W,* 4:202ff. Ruskin said in *Praeterita* that he could no more become a Roman Catholic than a "fire-worshipper," *Praeterita,* 3:19, in *Præterita and Dilecta,* in *C&W,* 35:492.

14. According to the dating supplied in Gerard Manley Hopkins, *Poems,* 4th ed., ed. W. H. Gardner and N. H. MacKenzie (New York: Oxford University Press, 1967), 297–309. Mackenzie's later independent edition concurs.

But Hopkins had already strayed from Ruskin before he strayed from the Anglican fold, because Hopkins could not follow Ruskin in his theory of the imagination. Ruskin grants tremendous, even divine, authority to the imagination on the grounds that "there is a reciprocal action between the intensity of moral feeling and the power of imagination; for on the one hand, those who have keenest sympathy are those who look closest and pierce deepest, and hold securest; and on the other, those who have so pierced and seen the melancholy deeps of things are filled with the most intense passion and gentleness of sympathy."[15] Ruskin continues: "Hence, I suppose that the powers of the imagination may always be tested by accompanying tenderness of emotion." Neither Hopkins nor Ruskin ever wavers in the conviction that perceiving the "vital beauty" of living things, and the meaning in each detail, calls forth sympathy, even charity. But Hopkins unsparingly rejected dependence upon the moral authority of emotion, which is finally, for Ruskin, the ultimate authority. Ruskin, although aware that feelings could be deceptive, created rules for the discipline of the feelings so as to develop proper artistic taste and thought that, properly chastened, feelings gave access to truths unavailable otherwise.

> For, as it is necessary to the existence of an idea of beauty, that the sensual pleasure which may be its basis should be accompanied first with joy, then with love of the object, then with the perception of kindness in a superior intelligence, finally, with thankfulness and veneration towards that intelligence itself; and as no idea can be at all considered as in any way an idea of beauty, until it be made up of these emotions . . . and as these emotions are in no way resultant from, nor obtainable by, any operation of the Intellect; it is evident that the sensation of beauty is not sensual on the one hand, nor is it intellectual on the other, but is dependent on a pure, right, and open state of the heart.[16]

With perfect Romantic sincerity, Ruskin held the Evangelical position that gave great theological weight to personal feelings. Emotions, springing from unknown sources, tell the believer when he is properly

15. Ruskin, *Modern Painters,* 3.2.3.9, in *C&W,* 4:257.
16. Ruskin, *Modern Painters,* 3.1.2.8, in *C&W,* 4:48–49.

understanding God's messages. Hopkins felt compelled to dissent from Ruskin here. Perhaps more than any of his own scrupulously recorded vices, Hopkins was dismayed by his own mercurial emotions. Referring to Manley Hopkins's poem on Hopkins family characteristics, Jerome Bump says, "Gerard was noticeably liable to be 'too soon depressed, too soon elate,'"[17] and indeed Gerard's early letters display a troublesome intensity of personal likes and dislikes. Distrusting his own feelings, Hopkins was particularly wary of religious insight resting upon emotion. All his life, Hopkins dreaded leading others astray into mere emotion or "d——d subjective rot," as he called it.[18] We shall see him attempting to banish emotion from his religious ideas in the next chapter.

Ruskin believed simply that truth was intrinsically lovable, and that real artistic imagination would stir the emotions properly: "[T]he pleasure which it has in things that it finds true and good is so great, that it cannot possibly be led aside by any tricks of fashion, or diseases of vanity. . . . It clasps all that it loves so hard, that it crushes it if it be hollow."[19] Yet, though imagination infallibly connects one to truth, the God glimpsed through art is seen only through the veil of analogy.[20] Hopkins craved a more substantial connection between the glory of this world and the glory of God, a real presence rather than a symbolic trace. While the distance and the veiling, to which Ruskin alludes, were congruent with the convictions of Hopkins's Tractarian colleagues at Oxford, it is here that the two aestheticians finally differ most deeply. The unity among nature, self, and Christ that Hopkins assumes in his mature poetry is alien to Ruskin's theology, even that of the times when Ruskin was a most enthusiastic Christian. Although we shall see Hopkins directly resisting Ruskin on the question of an aesthetics based in some secret power detected only by the emotions, the difference between Hopkins and Ruskin, as Hopkins developed his own aesthetic, was fundamentally theological.

17. Jerome Bump, "The Hopkins Centenary," 23.

18. Hopkins, *Letters to Bridges*, 84 (22 June 1879).

19. Ruskin, *Modern Painters*, 3.1.3.9, in *C&W*, 4:59.

20. Ruskin, *Modern Painters*, 3.1.15, in *C&W*, 4:208ff.; cf. *Modern Painters*, 3.1.11.1–2, in *C&W*, 4:142–43.

The ideas that the world's connection with God is seen only through symbolic messages, and that one must depend upon one's personal feelings to interpret those messages, were deeply ingrained in Ruskin by his Evangelical upbringing. When Ruskin lists the attributes of God, it is perhaps significant that the first is "Divine Incomprehensibility." He learned a Calvinistic reverence for keeping a distance between Creator and creature. Ruskin in *Modern Painters* expounds a severe concept of the absolute and arbitrary liberty of God, and attributes all corruptions in religion to humans seeking to usurp God's sovereignty over their salvation.[21] When Ruskin began to read Saint Augustine, whose *De trinitate* sought images of God in the physical world, Ruskin's mother reacted with great distress: she wanted him to depend on the Bible alone, conceiving that book as the only sure link to God.[22] John Calvin's epistemology disparaged human knowledge of God except through Scripture. Calvin considered art not an access to God but a frivolity, except as perhaps an aid to history lessons:

> I am not, however, so superstitious as to think that all visible representations of every kind are unlawful. But as sculpture and painting are gifts of God, what I insist for is, that both shall be used purely and lawfully. . . . Visible representations are of two classes—viz. historical, which give a representation of events, and pictorial, which merely exhibit bodily shapes and figures. The former are of some use for instruction or admonition. The latter, so far as I can see, are only fitted for amusement.

Calvin held religious art in especially deep suspicion, for "the folly of manhood cannot moderate itself, but forthwith falls away into superstitious worship."[23] In this inhospitable theological climate, Ruskin

21. Ruskin, *Modern Painters*, 3.1.10.5, in *C&W*, 4:138–39, and *Modern Painters*, 3.1.15.10–11, in *C&W*, 4:217. Hopkins's conception of divine liberty was ultimately radically different from Ruskin's; see my discussion below in Chapter 8. As to his Calvinism, Ruskin defended a preacher by saying, "His doctrine is simply Bunyan's, Baxter's, Calvin's and John Knox's." See Tim Hilton, *John Ruskin: The Early Years, 1819–1859* (New Haven, Conn.: Yale University Press, 1985), 260–61. George P. Landow, *The Aesthetic and Critical Theories of John Ruskin* (Princeton, N.J.: Princeton University Press, 1971), 247ff., gives strong evidence of Ruskin's loyalty to Calvinist views.

22. Landow, *Aesthetic and Critical Theories of John Ruskin*, 245–60. For his mother's distress over patristics, see 397n.

23. John Calvin, *Institutes of the Christian Religion*, 2 vols. in 1, trans. Henry Beveridge (Grand Rapids, Mich.: Eerdmans, 1989), I.i.11-12-13, 1:100–101.

contends passionately for the dignity of the artist's imagination. God is in Ruskin a moral judge; art gives one access to the infallible springs of morality, which are the truest feelings; therefore the great artist is God's prophet.[24] In volume 2 of *Modern Painters,* Ruskin asserts categorically that "no supreme power of art can be attained by impious men."[25]

In 1849, in the third part of *Modern Painters,* Ruskin seizes for his religious purpose Coleridge's contrast of "Imagination" to "Fancy." In describing the artist's privilege of Imagination, Ruskin alludes to the divine knowledge of the heart, such as guided the Prophet Samuel to raise up the great King David. Then Ruskin, always soaked in biblical allusion, boldly mixes magical imagery with it:

> [Imagination's] function and gift are the getting at the root, its nature and dignity depend on its holding things always by the heart. Take its hand off from the beating of that, and it will prophesy no longer. . . . This penetrating possession-taking faculty of Imagination . . . I insist upon as the highest intellectual power of man. There is no reasoning in it; it works not by algebra, nor by integral calculus; it is a piercing pholas-like mind's tongue, that works and tastes into the very rock heart; no matter what be the subject submitted to it, substance or spirit; all is alike divided asunder, joint and marrow, whatever utmost truth, life, principle it has, laid bare, and that which has no truth, life, nor principle, dissipated into its original smoke at a touch. The whispers at men's ears it lifts into visible angels. Vials that have lain sealed in the deep sea a thousand years it unseals, and brings out of them Genii.[26]

Ruskin is calling to mind the Epistle to the Hebrews 4.12–13:

> For the word of God is quick and powerful, and sharper than any two edged sword, piercing even to the dividing asunder of soul and spirit, and of the

24. He speaks of evil men being great artists in terms of the gift of prophecy being granted to Balaam and Saul (*Modern Painters,* 3.1.15.8, in *C&W,* 214). Cf. Landow, *Aesthetic and Critical Theories of John Ruskin,* 390. Helsinger, in *Ruskin and the Art of the Beholder,* 56, alludes to this divinization of imagination in her fine discussion of the participatory but nonverbal nature of the imagination in Ruskin. Helsinger attends more to Ruskin's interest in Wordsworth than to his theology, though the latter had more effect on Ruskin's views. Such a focus is understandable; Ruskin treats Wordsworth almost as a theologian.

25. Ruskin, *Modern Painters,* 3.1.15.5, in *C&W,* 4:211.

26. Ruskin, *Modern Painters,* 3.2.3.4, in *C&W,* 4:251.

joints and marrow, and is a discerner of the thoughts and intents of the heart. Neither is there any creature that is not manifest in his sight: but all things are naked, and opened unto the eyes of him with whom we have to do.

Thus Ruskin identifies Imagination with the Word of God, and makes the artist a magician as well as a prophet. The divine gift is vouchsafed, as he says, to give "by intuition and intensity of gaze (not by reasoning, but by its authoritative and opening power) a more essential truth than is seen at the surface of things. . . . [Imagination's] authority and being is its perpetual thirst for truth and purpose to be true. It has no food, no delight, no care, no perception, but that of truth. . . . the first condition of its existence is its incapability of being deceived."[27] Here, invoking inerrancy, he conflates the Evangelical view of the Bible and the artistic Imagination almost completely—a bold move indeed! It was perhaps extravagance like this that drew Keble to pull away from Coleridge's Imagination and prefer his Fancy. Ruskin, at every turn sincere, could live with the paradoxes of artistic divine right and artistic individualism—at least for a while.

In 1858, in a little Waldensian chapel in Turin, Ruskin rejected the notion that the "only children of God" were in that chapel and that an irreligious artist like Paul Veronese could have no "God-given power" of insight into truth.[28] Before Ruskin's brittle and narrow Evangelicalism broke in that chapel, he had justified art by making it divine prophecy; for the next decade and more, while he was a no less brittle "heathen," he strove to make art, or at any rate a morality of beauty, into a sort of substitute for divine grace. But Ruskin eventually lost his faith that art and virtue are intimately connected; he then turned to political economy for moral sustenance. His "Notes on a Painter's Profession as Ending Irreligiously" reflect Ruskin's perceived conflict of loyalties between goodness and artistic excellence:

Half, as I said, of his business in the world must consist in simply seeking his own pleasure, and that, in the main, a sensual pleasure. I don't mean a degrad-

27. Ruskin, *Modern Painters*, 3.2.3.29, in *C&W*, 4:284–85.

28. Landow, in *Aesthetic and Critical Theories of John Ruskin*, 282, quotes *Fors Clavigera*. Landow discusses the variant account in *Praeterita* too. With regard to matters here discussed, the accounts substantially agree.

ing one, but a bodily, not spiritual, pleasure. Seeing a fine red, or a beautiful line is a bodily and selfish pleasure, at least as compared with Gratitude or Love—or other feelings called into play by social action. And, moreover, this bodily pleasure must be sought for Itself and Himself. Not for anybody else's sake.

Ruskin lists numerous vices and crimes an artist must consider purely from the viewpoint of their usefulness in art: "[O]ur great painter must not shrink in a timid way from any form of vice or ugliness. He must know them to the full." The artist, as artist, cannot stop to do charitable deeds but must instead consider the physical appearance of the sufferer or the sinner and how he can best communicate it in art. His passion must all be aesthetic, and that passion can overwhelm, as Ruskin fears, the moral passions. Therefore, Ruskin concludes, the artist's vocation "takes away all common chances of his being affected by the feelings or imaginations which lead other men to religion."[29]

A boy of Hopkins's obedient religiosity and alarming strength of will could set himself to control those "bodily and selfish" passions. In an exuberant letter written in September 1862, just before Hopkins entered Oxford, he included his Miltonic exercise "Il Mystico," which begins:

> Hence sensual gross desires,
> Right offspring of your grimy mother Earth!
> My Spirit hath a birth
> Alien from yours . . .[30]

Then again, Hopkins had a lot to control. It was not a temptation to social irresponsibility that most concerned Hopkins, but merely letting his emotions run away with him. These lines, written the following December, consciously charge with sexual energy the sights and scents of spring:

> Summer of his sister Spring
> Crushes and tears the rare enjewelling,

29. Ruskin, *Modern Painters,* in *C&W,* 4:386–89. This chapter, not dated but not included in early versions of *Modern Painters,* was written after *The Stones of Venice.*

30. Hopkins, *Poetical Works,* 6.

And boasting "I have fairer things than these"
Plashes amidst the billowy apple-trees
His lusty hands, in gusts of scented wind
Swirling out bloom till all the air is blind
With rosy foam and pelting blossom and mists
Of driving vermeil-rain; and, as he lists,
The dainty onyx-coronals deflowers,
A glorious wanton; —[31]

In an 1868 letter, Hopkins fretted that art could lead him astray from God: "You know I once wanted to be a painter. But even if I could I wd. not, I think, now, for the fact is that the higher and more attractive parts of the art put a strain upon the passions which I shd. think it unsafe to encounter."[32] Hopkins could not so easily as Ruskin connect his sense of beauty to moral edicts from God. Long after Hopkins had turned his back on Ruskin's fusion of religious rhapsody and aesthetic analysis, he was haunted by Ruskin's example of the artist lapsing into egotistical moral subjectivity, into "d——d subjective rot." Yet more did Hopkins abhor the shallow substitution of moralism for Christianity to which Ruskin, like so many of his contemporaries, succumbed.

When Hopkins felt himself faced with the rivalry of art and Christ, he reversed Ruskin's choice: Hopkins burnt his poems and became a priest. But as Ruskin found his way to Christianity again, likewise the time would come when Hopkins could believe that an artist, in the act of articulating the truth, is a Christian hero. When he finally succeeded in doing so, the Ruskinian artist's sacrifice of praise became the self-giving of the Christian hero, and ultimately sacramental. The first steps in that direction were taken on the strength of Hopkins's mistrust of Ruskin's magical notion of Imagination. Hopkins submitted to Ruskin's analytic insistence on exactitude of observation and care in execution, but art was not, for Hopkins, a divine gnosis, nor even something above human rationality. The Aristotelian sympathies of the undergraduate Hopkins encouraged him to demand that both art

31. Hopkins, *Poetical Works,* 13.
32. Hopkins, *Further Letters,* 231 (to A. W. M. Baillie, 12 Feb.1868).

and religion be rational responses to realities, rather than responses to treacherous sentiment.

Ruskin's early Evangelical pastors had not counted religious experience genuine unless accompanied by an emotional experience.[33] When he converted to Catholicism, Hopkins wrote a letter to Canon H. P. Liddon reprehending the idea that one should allow oneself to be persuaded by an insight that supersedes reason in the way that Ruskin's divine Imagination does:

> You think I lay claim to a personal illumination which dispenses with the need of thought or knowledge on the points at issue. I have never been so unwise as to think of such a claim. There is a distinction to be made: in the sense that every case of taking truth instead of error is an illumination of course I have been illuminated, but I have never said anything to the effect that a wide subject involving history or theology or any turning-point question has been thrown into light for me by a supernatural or even unusual access of grace. If you will not think it an irreverent way of speaking, I can hardly believe that anyone ever became a Catholic because two and two make four more fully than I have.[34]

It is abundantly evident that Hopkins experienced and acted upon religious emotion, but he permitted himself to act only when he could at least defend the position that he was not acting out of emotional excitement. In the grips of his crisis over conversion, Hopkins puts it firmly in his journal: "Addis says my arguments are coloured and lose their value by personal feeling. This ought to be repressed."[35]

33. Landow, *Aesthetic and Critical Theories of John Ruskin,* 257. Then again, John Ruskin's father at least warned him about emotional turbulence with regard to religion. As he was in the midst of deciding whether or not to become a clergyman, his father wrote to him that "too much enthusiasm in religion ends in Selfishness or madness," and "Heavenly subjects require to be approached in the most worldly way. We must hold the anchor of Rationality." See Hilton, *John Ruskin: The Early Years,* 63.

34. Hopkins, *Further Letters,* 31 (15 Oct. 1866). The close resemblance between this passage and one in Newman's popular Oxford novel *Loss and Gain: The Story of a Convert,* leads me to believe that Hopkins read that novel as he was contemplating his own conversion. Cf. Newman, *Loss and Gain,* 251.

35. Hopkins, *Journals and Papers,* 58. William Edward Addis wrote in 1909, nine years before Bridges published the first edition of Hopkins's poems, "I knew him in his undergraduate days far better than anyone else did." Addis entered the Roman Catholic Church about two weeks before Hopkins did, but left it in 1888 and joined the Anglican clergy in 1901.

Hopkins's insistent rationalism, rejecting the primacy of personal preference, emerges as aesthetic theory in the surviving sections of his fragmentary 1864 verse drama, *Floris in Italy.* In one scene, Floris is arguing against loving the sympathetically portrayed heroine, Giulia. Urged to consider her beauty, Floris replies:

> Say beauty lies but in the meet of lines,
> In careful spacéd sequences of sound
> These rather are the arc where beauty shines,
> The temper'd soil where only her flower is found.
> Allow at least it has one term and part
> Beyond, and one within the looker's eye;
> And I must have the centre in my heart
> To turn the compass on the all-starred sky. . . .
> No, love prescriptive, love with place assigned. . . .
> It is a regimen on the imperfect wind,
> Piecing the elements out by plan and plot.
> Though self-made bands at last may true love bind,
> New love is free love, or true love 'tis not.

Another character, Henry, responds:

> Such spiders web he ties across his sight,
> And gives for tropes his judgment all away
> Gilds with some sparky fancies blinding night,
> And stumbling swears he walks by light of day.
> A learned fool indeed and well-bred churl
> That swinishly refuses such a pearl![36]

It is clear where the young moralist intends to draw his reader's sympathy. Even if other fragments did not indicate how sympathetically we are to view Giulia, the biblical allusion in the criticism of Floris indicates that we are to see more than contending tastes in the disagreement between the two characters. Henry proposes that Floris blinds himself to the real lights available to him when he insists that love should never be externally legislated. Hopkins deeply believed that all things should be governed by authority. The blank verse is regular and flowing until Floris talks of how rules limit love. Then the line "It is a

36. Hopkins, *Poetical Works,* 36–37. I have chosen the alternative readings of several lines, as printed on p. 37.

regimen on th'imperfect wind" displays imperfection of meter, and in Floris's mouth it is, by implication, mere imperfect wind. He wishes to have the center of the movement of the universe in his own heart; selfish, he does not wish to be bound even by marriage, except as he pleases. Floris is a morally suspect anti-rationalist; his own emotion is at the center of his universe. We are not to approve.

In a letter written as he was working on *Floris in Italy*, the twenty-year-old Hopkins gives an aggressively matter-of-fact account of the nature of the "first and highest" poetic inspiration which in a genius "raises him above himself." Hopkins's idea of inspiration contrasts radically to the artist's Imagination in Ruskin:

> The word inspiration need cause no difficulty. I mean by it a mood of great, abnormal in fact, mental acuteness, either energetic or receptive, according as the thoughts which arise in it seem generated by a stress and action of the brain, or to strike into it unasked. The mood arises from various causes, physical chiefly, as good health or the state of the air, or, prosaic as it is, length of time after a meal. . . . Everybody of course has like moods, but not being poets what they then produce is not poetry.

Hopkins makes a distinction between people who are really poets and those who are "poetasters." Ruskin had seen the artist as alternately the diligent scientist and the inspired prophet; Hopkins identifies artistic genius as a capacity that one might choose to exercise. "I think it is the case with genius that it is not when it is quiescent so very much above mediocrity . . . its greatness is *that it can be* so great." He does not see genius as an inspiration from God so much as a knack for putting things well, a "way of looking at things," whose expression he labels "Parnassian" style. Such a style is characteristic of the individualistic freedom of the true-hearted artist in that it is very recognizable yet inimitable: "Now it is a mark of Parnassian that one could conceive oneself writing it if one were the poet. . . . [Y]ou see yourself doing it, only with the difference that if you actually try to find [*sic*] you cannot write his Parnassian." Parnassian is the evidence of a fine ability, not inspiration. But when he judges a genius to be inspired, and the style rises to "Olympian," Hopkins does not make the artist's inspiration a matter of high spiritual import. Rather, circumstance and "further effort"[37] enable the artist to rise above his normal tricks of expression to say something richer.

Hopkins mounts a more philosophical attack on Ruskin's magical imagination in a dialogue on beauty written in May 1865. Unrelated to any of his assigned academic work, and too long for presentation to his essay club, the Hexameron,[38] the dialogue seems to have been written for his own satisfaction, out of his own drive for coherence and responsibility in aesthetic theory. It tastes of Ruskin everywhere. Hopkins's interlocutors look for their patterns of beauty in natural forms, as Ruskin urged. They use Ruskin's vocabulary from *Modern Painters*, and his argument about "composition" of interdependent masses; exploit his illustration from chestnut foliage; and, like Ruskin, eschew exact symmetry and likeness in favor of resemblance and antithesis.

Yet there are differences. Ruskin had unilaterally invoked Scripture to overpower the opponents of his opinions about beauty and its appreciation.[39] In the dialogue, Hopkins does not invoke Scripture at all to justify the love of beauty. Moreover, Hopkins does not cast his aesthetic theory as a Ruskinian manifesto but as a Platonic dialogue. He presumes the existence of an abstract absolute standard, but he has his three characters (Hanbury, Middleton the painter, and the Professor) seek it by reasoning together from particular, concrete examples they all encounter: a chestnut fan, a painting, some poems. The vagueness and magic of Ruskin's imagination fall before the solidity of the very observations that Ruskin has taught Hopkins to make. When the undergraduate character Hanbury says, "I am sure there is in the higher forms of beauty—at least I seem to feel—something mystical," Hopkins has the Professor proceed methodically to demonstrate that the essential thing about beauty is intellectual: comparison, contrast, and the recognition of unexpected analogies. The physical world, and not

37. All the quotations in the preceding paragraph are from a letter to A. W. M. Baillie, dated 10 Sept. 1864. The longer quotations are, respectively, on pp. 216 (longest quotation), 220, 217, and 216 of Hopkins, *Further Letters*.

38. The papers of the club, which prove Hopkins's membership, are in the special Hopkins Collection at Gonzaga University.

39. For an instance, see the discussion of biblical concepts in "The Lamp of Sacrifice," in John Ruskin, *The Seven Lamps of Architecture*, in *C&W*, 8:32–33.

"something mystical," must teach the philosopher what beauty is; the world has its own authority, which must not be traduced.

Recall that where Ruskin found it impossible to account for artistic achievement, he considered it beyond rationality and therefore divine. Ruskin denied that imagination was rational at all, since its method of operation could not be precisely described. Similarly, one can easily deny that the faculty by which one recognizes a face is rational (though computers now can do so), because one cannot trace quite how one does it.[40] Hopkins is not willing to credit this triumph of rhapsody over analysis. His "Professor of Aesthetics" takes the part of Socrates in the dialogue, and demonstrates (rather more often than necessary) that in the visual arts the relationship between symmetry and irregularity, or consistency and change, is what people recognize as beauty. "Beauty is a relation," he says, and works it out in mathematical language.[41] Thus he makes a rational activity of Ruskin's Imagination Associative.

As the dialogue proceeds, Hopkins advances a theory of "parallelism," a word garnered from form criticism of the Psalms;[42] "parallelism" applies to strict parallels, repetitive expansions, and antitheses. It applies even to metaphors. As the dialogue proceeds, a startlingly participatory theory of art emerges. In order for there to be beauty, "It seems then that it is not the excellence of any two things (or more) in themselves, but those two things as viewed in the light of each other, that makes beauty."[43] Beauty springs from an activity in the perceiver. No two things are alike, even in strict parallel structures, so that there

40. See the discussions of the gestalt of perception in Michael Polanyi, *Personal Knowledge: Towards a Post-Critical Philosophy* (Chicago: University of Chicago Press, 1958), 54–58, 97–98.

41. Gerard Manley Hopkins, "Platonic Dialogue on the Origin of Beauty," in *Journals and Papers*, 95.

42. Lichtmann (in *Contemplative Poetry of Gerard Manley Hopkins*) well examines the value of this concept in his poetic practice. Michael Raiger extends her valuable work with a discussion of its relevance to the Eastern Orthodox understanding of icons in "'Poised, but on the Quiver': The Paradox of Free Will and Grace in Hopkins's 'Spring' and '(Carrion Comfort),'" *Religion and the Arts* 3, no. 1 (Spring 1999): 87, n7.

43. Hopkins, *Journals and Papers*, 93.

is always some inequality to involve the mind in a relation. Neither are any things so unlike that no comparison is possible; beauty is potentially everywhere. A poet calls the reader's attention to a relation in making a metaphor. In the implied comparison "[n]ew meaning is generated," as Michael Potts puts it; or, in Paul Ricoeur's words, "metaphor is not the enigma but the solution of the enigma."[44] Recall how Hopkins said much the same thing when he tried to explain to Bridges how he felt about the doctrine of the Trinity:

> [T]here are some solutions, to, say, chess problems so beautifully ingenious, some resolutions of suspensions so lovely in music that even the feeling of interest is keenest when they are known and over, and for some time survives the discovery. How must it then be when the very answer is the most tantalising statement of the problem and the truth you are to rest in the most pointed putting of the difficulty.[45]

It is the activity of the mind in understanding the relation that makes the beauty, the mind contemplating likeness and contrast, as in the rhyming and chiming that electrify Hopkins's poems.[46]

In his dialogue, Hopkins, using Ruskin's own weapons, jousts with his master. The dialogue displays both Hopkins's debt to Ruskin and his independence from him: Hopkins lovingly employs Ruskin's vocabulary, many of his convictions, and even some of his arguments, but he is willing to give a rational analysis of Ruskin's ineffable Imagination. Also, abandoning the idea of the genius who comes to bless the world with his divine message, Hopkins here allows for the authority granted by the perception of beauty to reside as much in the artist's audience as in the artist himself. Hopkins also makes it clear that he is

44. Quoted by Michael Potts in "Hopkins and Metaphor," *American Catholic Philosophical Quarterly* 68, no. 4 (1995): 506. Potts insightfully suggests an understanding of the active nature of metaphor in Hopkins that puts him very close to Hopkins's actual use of "inscape" and "instress," although he falls into the customary mistake of identifying inscape with *haecceitas.* His reference to Paul Ricouer, "The Metaphoric Process as Cognition, Imagination and Feeling," in *Philosophical Perspectives on Metaphor,* ed. Mark Johnson, lacks both a date of publication and publisher; the book is from the University of Minnesota Press, 1981, and the passage that Potts quotes is on p. 232.

45. Hopkins, *Letters to Bridges,* 187–88 (24 Oct. 1883).

46. See similar speculations in Ricouer, "The Metaphoric Process," 234.

working out this theory in order to banish the vague sentimentality of "something mystical" from his theories about art.

Ruskin had fed Hopkins's imagination with the love of concrete, particular beauty, and the discipline of seeking form in it. Ruskin had taught him to regard this attention to the loveliness of the created world as a noble and holy action. Ruskin at first proclaimed the artist to be a divinely gifted prophet who must sacrifice all to reveal God's truth. In midcareer he rejected the Christian element in that notion. Suffering from conflict between his human love of worldly things and the God who was only accessible through revelation, the deeply moralistic Ruskin for a while felt compelled to take the side of what he thought to be the godless geniuses.

Alternately intoxicated by Ruskin's idea that intense aesthetic experience is holy, and sobered by an anti-Ruskinian theory of art as an intellectual rather than an irrational activity, Hopkins concluded that the responsibility to the goodness and dignity of the external world (felt by Ruskin too) demanded, for consistency, a more philosophically precise description of the nature of artistic imagination than Ruskin's magical theory, in order that the deceptions of emotional irrationalism should not reign in art.

Hopkins's name lives today primarily because of his religious nature poetry, but, ironically, the religious aspect of natural beauty, so central to Ruskin, has little part in the poetry of the undergraduate Hopkins. In 1866, at Oxford, the young poet who could be brought to tears by the "spiritual and heavenly sights" of "crimson and pure blues" could not trust that his experience of natural beauty could give him knowledge of God.

> We see the glories of the earth
> But not the hand that wrought them all:
> Night to a myriad worlds gives birth,
> Yet like a lighted empty hall
> Where stands no host at door or hearth
> Vacant creation's lamps appall.[47]

47. Hopkins, *Poetical Works*, 92.

Hopkins was unable to accept Ruskin's account of the immanence of holiness in physical beauty partly because, singularly sensitive, like Ruskin, to physical loveliness, he had qualms about his own emotional turbulence. Indeed, even for Ruskin, the symbolic link between earthly beauty and the moral qualities of the Creator could not really bind him to Christianity. As Ruskin more and more despaired of finding an outlet to aesthetic impulses that did not threaten sin, the Tractarian party seemed to offer Hopkins safe refuge; Tractarians offered Hopkins a possible niche for Christian art, in the stern and lawful manner of the early Ruskin's rules about observation. Tractarians rejoiced in the early Christian assimilation of the stoic Λόγος—the principle of rationality in the world—to Christ as the Creator, the Word of God and Wisdom of God. Hopkins found the theological content of Tractarian aesthetics compelling because the Tractarians found rationality central to both religion and art. The young Hopkins identified reason with abstract thought, generalized argumentation, and mathematics; in art, reason flowered forth in geometry and form. To the Tractarians, and Hopkins their disciple, the highest kind of knowledge seemed to be the least personal. In both his ecclesiology and his aesthetic theory, the young Hopkins appreciated Tractarian attempts to be relentlessly logical, scorning vague sentiment in favor of restrained emotion and reasoned expression. Hopkins moved beyond the Tractarian mode, eventually; the time would come when he conceived his own unity of religious and aesthetic vision, reminiscent of Ruskin's—but that did not come to birth for many years after Oxford. Ultimately, for Ruskin, as for Hopkins, the right response of a human being to the goodness of the world is joy; the Ruskin that Hopkins loved rejoiced in the very stones of the earth proclaiming the glory of God. But we shall see how at Oxford, for a while, Hopkins deafened his ear to them.

CHAPTER 4

THE TRACTARIAN LAMP OF SACRIFICE

At Oxford, Hopkins devoted himself more and more to poetry, the favorite art of the Tractarians. As we have seen, Tractarians revered poetry's likeness to the "nature of sacraments." But the holy art was to be practiced within the strictures of a spiritual reserve, which would not put forth to the common view things too sacred to be seen. Accounts of spiritual experiences or profound emotions, for instance, might spur a believer to seek such experiences for their own sake rather than to serve God according to his will. Tractarian poetry was to employ emotions and use natural images for the higher end of reminding readers of sacred truths and duties. The material world was to be approached as an analogy of the spiritual one, rather than for any value it had in itself. Margaret Johnson argues convincingly that since Hopkins was exposed to the ideals and practices of Tractarian poetry from childhood on, his poetry developed from his Tractarian roots rather than rejected them.[1] The Tractarian principles of analogy

1. Margaret Johnson, *Hopkins and Tractarian Poetry,* 16–19. Later (58) she departs from her argument to interpret Hopkins's comment that poetry might "interfere" with his clerical vocation by limiting it to the "sort of poetry he had written as a Tractarian." I attribute his uneasiness to his opinion of the spiritual risks of attention to the sensual world. Hopkins, like Ruskin, felt the pull of such sensual attractions for the seriously committed artist, and, like the Tractarians, saw them as at best distractions from his real spiritual duty. However cramping the Tractarian limitations, and however much he grew beyond them as an artist, his conversion hardly constituted a rejection of things Tractarian. Recall that Hopkins reported his first meeting with Newman with great relief: "It is needless to say he spoke with interest and kindness and appreciation of all that Tractarians reverence" (*Letters to Bridges,* 5 [22 Sept. 1866]).

and reserve,[2] which pressed poets to abstract nature into symbols for spiritual matters, would seem to lead Hopkins away from Ruskin, who taught that telling even the sacred truth requires one to speak out from within one's own perspective and give close and full renderings of the natural world. However, Hopkins in the end managed to unite Tractarian and Ruskinian principles through the notion of sacrifice. Once his Tractarian understanding of the importance of the Incarnation allowed Hopkins to believe that even the trivialities of his own life were united with the sacrifice of Christ, the poet synthesized a new idea of art. Hopkins's artist is neither God's stenographer nor his rival. The artist is a human being whose unique experiences in the material world, if united to Christ, serve not merely as analogy of, but as participation in, the sacred.

Obviously Hopkins retained Ruskin's reverence for peculiar, individual perspectives. Ruskin hates "the pursuit of beauty at the expense of manliness and truth."[3] Ruskin's artist must fearlessly confront evil and ugliness in the world and overcome the resistance offered to such truths by social convention and by his own psyche. Bold in difficulty, the artist must hold fast to the faith that the truth ultimately gives more joy and has more worth than anything that merely pleases the senses. The true is good, Ruskin says, but Keats is wrong to say "beauty is truth"; some truths are ugly, and art must first of all be true.[4] The mature Hopkins still embraced Ruskin's exhortation. Like a stonemason carving gargoyles, Hopkins expends his best energy on grotesques: poetry about sin's consequences in destruction and suffering, whether within one's own soul, as in the Terrible Sonnets, or in the external world, as in "Binsey Poplars" or "God's Grandeur." Hopkins's mature poems show God saving sinners from their own "selfbent." God exercises this mercy by bringing home to them, through suffering, their own limitation: by frightening them into repentance, as in *The Wreck*

2. I discuss Tractarian poetics in the light of G. B. Tennyson's *Victorian Devotional Poetry: The Tractarian Mode* (Cambridge, Mass.: Harvard University Press, 1981), and of Margaret Johnson's work.

3. Ruskin, "Pre-Raphaelitism," *C&W,* 12:354; cf. *C&W,* 4:50.

4. Ruskin, *Modern Painters,* 3.1.4.1, in *C&W,* 4:66–67.

of the Deutschland; or by horrifying them with the truth about their own innate vileness, as in the Terrible Sonnets; or by sacrificial suffering that accepts the consequences of sin, without desert, in order that others might not suffer. Hopkins wrote of Christ's death as the slaying of the most beautiful of men, martyred by his voluntary heroism in taking upon himself the suffering caused by sin.

In the chapter "The Lamp of Sacrifice" in *The Seven Lamps of Architecture,* Ruskin proclaims that the expense and difficulty of a work are legitimate components of its beauty. Here is already a hint of the ideal of beauty-in-suffering that Hopkins would someday preach as a Catholic priest. Daily martyrdoms "offered up"—small, inconsequential sufferings to be borne with patience, in union with the sacrificial sufferings of Christ—were standard tropes of Catholic devotional literature. Ruskin was no ascetic, but his love of the noble struggle to exhibit the artist's individual vision evolved into a fascination with exactitude and difficulty for their own sake.[5]

As he followed the common Victorian religious pattern of drift away from Christian belief toward unbelieving Christian moralism, Ruskin employed august biblical language about sacrifice in the service of a new deity: the virtuous society. In 1860, he published *Unto This Last,* a "pugnacious political economy," as Matthew Arnold snipped. The book delicately concealed Ruskin's own personal religious struggles under a rhetoric of Christian self-sacrifice applied to social reform. For Ruskin in this period, amelioration of injustice replaces salvation in a kind of Christianity manqué. Art, no longer a form of divine service, must be dragooned into human service by religious language.

5. Ruskin's aestheticism, among other things, gave nourishment to a later attraction to pain and decay among the adherents of the Decadent movement; many, such as Robinson and Ruggles, have seen in Hopkins's attention to violence some similar aberrance. But the Decadents' sensibility inverted Ruskinian sincerity. They loved pain as a matter of hedonistic taste—because suffering is an intense sensation; the less genuine, the better. When Ernest Dowson writes, "I have been faithful to thee, Cynara, in my fashion," the speaker means, of course, that he has been unfaithful but savors his own self-loathing (Ernest Dowson, "*Non sum qualis eram bonae sub regno Cynarae,*" in *Poetry of the Victorian Period,* 3d ed., ed. Jerome Hamilton Buckley and George Benjamin Woods [Glenview, Ill.: Scott Foresman, 1965], 841).

Though Hopkins eventually worked among the poor as a teacher and preacher, and wrote some prickly political and economic opinions in letters to friends, it was the spiritual state of England, not worldly politics and economics, that mattered most to him. His interest is rather in redeeming individuals than in reforming society. Hopkins took Ruskin's Christian language at face value, as a religious ethic that united sacrifice in battle, in everyday labor, and in art, where the artist's heroic duty to the world is to reveal God's truth in beauty.

Ruskin titled his controversial lectures from Christ's parable about "an householder, which went out early in the morning to hire labourers into his vineyard." The householder hires workers at various times during the day, and at the day's end generously pays them all a full day's wage, no matter how many hours they worked. Those who worked longer protest, and he replies: "Friend, I do thee no wrong; didst not thou agree with me for a penny? Take that thine is, and go thy way; I will give unto this last, even as unto thee" (Matt. 20.13–14, King James version). When he wrote this book, Ruskin had "un-converted" from Christianity; the "householder" is not for him an image of God but of good social behavior. The word οἰκοδεσπότης in New Testament Greek has a common root with modern English *economics;* Christian theology derives from the same root "the economy of salvation," which names the sacrificial covenant by which Christ redeemed the world from sin.[6] Ruskin preserves a vestige of the theological usage in his "political economy"; he argues for the moral and spiritual beauty of a merchant willing to sacrifice his power and pleasure for the sake of the common good. "Sacrifice" means a willingness to seek the good of others at a cost to oneself.

Verbal echoes of Ruskin's call for moral consistency in *Unto This Last* appear nearly twenty years later in "The Windhover"; the book's more immediate effect on Hopkins was probably to spur him toward self-sacrifice for the sake of intellectual, moral, and religious consistency. Ruskinian high-mindedness puts its stamp on both his momen-

6. According to the *Oxford English Dictionary,* in theology, the word *economy* bears the sense of "the method of the divine government of the world, or of a specific department or portion of that government."

tous decision to break with Anglicanism and his later, less momentous, but still costly, maintenance of Scotist positions against his Suarezian Thomist examiners in seminary.[7] In art, Hopkins took Ruskin's language at face value, and evolved a thoroughly religious aesthetic, which, like Ruskin's, exalted difficulty and renunciation in themselves as examples of moral beauty. For Ruskin, pain is glory insofar as it is sacrificial—insofar as the sufferer suffers to prevent evil, remove it, or transform it into good. Ruskin was very clear about the way in which sacrifice makes a despicable profession honorable.

> Philosophically, it does not, at first sight, appear reasonable . . . that a peaceable and rational person, whose trade is buying and selling, should be held in less honour than an unpeaceable and often irrational person whose trade is slaying. Nevertheless, the consent of mankind has always, in spite of the philosophers, given precedence to the soldier.
>
> And this is right.
>
> For the soldier's trade, verily and essentially, is not slaying but being slain. This . . . the world honours it for. . . . Reckless he may be—fond of pleasure or adventure . . . but our estimate of him is based on this ultimate fact . . . put him in a fortress breach, with all the pleasures of the world behind him, and only death and his duty in front of him, he will keep his face to the front; and he knows that his choice may be put to him at any moment—and he has beforehand taken his part—virtually takes such part continually—does, in reality, die daily.[8]

He alludes to Saint Paul's boast in 1 Corinthians 15.30–31: "And why stand we in jeopardy every hour? I protest by your rejoicing which I have in Christ Jesus our Lord, I die daily." Ruskin's soldier is a saint, in other words—and so may the merchant be, if he adopts the ethic of self-sacrifice.

Hopkins took up this ideal of soldierly heroism many years later and made use of it in his own poem "The Soldier": "Were I come o'er again' cries | Christ 'it should be this.'"[9] Hopkins identifies the soldier

7. Joseph Feeney settled dispute on this matter in "Hopkins' 'Failure' in Theology: Some New Archival Data and a Reevaluation," *Hopkins Quarterly* 13, no. 3 (Oct. 1986–Jan. 1987): 99–107.

8. John Ruskin, *"Unto This Last": Four Essays on the First Principles of Political Economy*, in *C&W*, 17:36–37.

9. Hopkins, *Poetical Works*, 184.

with Christ not because the soldier is in any sense perfect—he is in fact "vile clay"—but because the soldier is suffering, offering his life for the lives of others as a ransom. He absorbs the evils of war to prevent them from reaching the defenseless people behind him.[10] As a Jesuit, Hopkins preached a sermon wherein Ruskin's influence returns; he preaches about how Christ allowed his strength and beauty to be marred and crippled by crucifixion.[11] Hopkins reminds his congregation that Christ could have accomplished the world's salvation without so much suffering. Christ chose the more painful path. And why? For the greater glory of God. The greater the suffering, the greater the sacrifice; the more difficult the task, the greater the glory.

The imperious tone of Ruskin's manifestos accorded well with Hopkins's thirst to commit himself with passionate intensity to something noble. He already had shown a predilection to put himself in harm's way by sheer pertinacity; in fact, he recognized that his taste for being a sort of martyr-hero was one of his faults. His infamous scrupulosity in adulthood was at the bottom the same impulse that led Hopkins to boast, in an 1862 schoolboy letter, that when the schoolmaster, Dr. Dyne, had been too strict, Hopkins opposed him and "cheeked him wildly," though he risked—and received—a beating with a "riding-whip." He then received a continuing punishment that placed such obstacles in the way of his studies as, he complained, might cost him his future academic career.[12] The punishment did not prevent him from ultimately winning the exhibition that paved his way to Balliol College; but he was rather proud of having possibly sacrificed his chance.

At Oxford Hopkins paid hero worship to aesthetic and religious martyrs. Savonarola, "martyred in the Church," was, wrote Hopkins,

> the only person in history (except Origen) about whom I have a real feeling, and I feel such an enthusiasm about Savonarola that I can conceive what it must have been to have been of his followers. I feel this the more because he

10. Cf. the transferability of suffering and sacrifice in René Girard, *Violence and the Sacred* (Baltimore: Johns Hopkins University Press, 1977).

11. Hopkins, *Sermons and Devotional Writings*, 36.

12. Hopkins, *Further Letters*, 2 (to Charles Noble Luxmoore, 7 May 1862).

was followed by the painters, architects and other artists of his day, and is the prophet of Christian art, and it is easy to imagine oneself a painter of his following.[13]

Ruskin no doubt drew Hopkins to admire the Pre-Raphaelites as religious artists steadfast under detraction. Hopkins's vision of noble self-sacrifice was encouraged by his circle of friends at college. The "Brotherhood of the Holy Trinity"(BHT), an ascetic society of High Church undergraduates, included many of his closest friends. Hopkins was invited to join, though on the advice of his parents he refrained. Still, he remained, like the "BHT," in the orbit of Canon Pusey, who became his confessor in 1865. Hopkins kept confession diaries of sin and temptation, and there recorded in detail unkind conversation, wasting time, and overeating. The surviving volumes show him uneasy, to the point of alarm, about the uncontrollability of his sexual impulses when at the edge of sleep.[14] In the same notebook, Hopkins records a continual struggle with "scruples" that dogged him throughout his life. As time passed at Oxford, Hopkins's religious life among the young Tractarians came to dominate everything else, but the early Ruskin and the Tractarians had enough in common to give the impression of a common project.

Both Keble and Ruskin treated poets as prophets, Keble being particularly impressed by Wordsworth's prophetic credentials; but we have also seen in Hopkins an uneasiness with this idea which cannot be entirely attributed to a Tractarian principle of reserve. Tractarians did not try to reconcile their high view of religious authority, as passed

13. Hopkins, *Further Letters,* 17–18 (to E. W. Urquhart, 6 Jan. 1865). Origen (?185–254?), at seventeen, was prevented from rushing to martyrdom by his mother, who hid his clothes; later, troubled by sensual desires, he castrated himself, though he repented of his "rash act" and did not encourage others to emulate it. Renowned as an innovative theologian, who entertained, as speculations, many ideas since judged heretical, he died after torture during a Roman persecution.

14. Hopkins recorded no overt sexual activity; he did record, in English, as "temptations," glances at people that may have had sexual content; any signs of physical excitement he sanitized by describing the incident in Latin. See *The Early Poetic Manuscripts and Note-books of Gerard Manley Hopkins in Facsimile,* ed. Norman H. Mackenzie (New York: Garland, 1989).

on through apostolic teaching, with the possibility of religious authority in self-proclaimed literary prophets. In Ruskin's endorsement of the idea of the irreligious artist, Hopkins saw a dangerous side to the primacy of art as the highest guide to life. As we have seen, Hopkins's famous discussion of genius and Parnassian style stubbornly resists any implication that poetry is a divine wind with the poet as its mouthpiece; his theory is an analysis of the ways in which circumstances affect those who have a particularly fine way with words, without reference to religion at all.

However, Hopkins always held some form of the Tractarian and Ruskinian principle that the world was God's message and must be decoded. Ruskin sought divine analogies for the sake of the dignity of the world's beauty; the Tractarians canvassed the world's beauty in hope of finding news of God there. G. B. Tennyson, who identifies analogy as one of the two great principles of Tractarian aesthetics, describes its fundamental assumption: "The things of the world are insistently there as signs; what they signal is vastly more important than they."[15] In submission to this doctrine, which endorses allegory and Coleridgean Fancy over symbol and Coleridgean Imagination, Keble, for instance, gives his readers only the most general sorts of trees, fruits, and stars in his poems' imagery. Keble's primary engagement with the spiritual reality drains the physical world of its vividness. Nevertheless, although Hopkins loves God first, as a poet he ultimately follows Ruskin toward Coleridgean Imagination and a regard for the solid physical world. The *Deutschland,* for example, while invested with symbolic value as England in spiritual crisis, remains a particular boat on a voyage to and from certain solid ports, with a passenger list and a weather report.

The short poem "Spring and Death," written probably about the time that Hopkins left his school for Balliol—and eight years after his father bought *The Christian Year*—shows Hopkins exercising himself among the Tractarian allegorical conventions. It is a dream-allegory in

15. G. B. Tennyson, "Removing the Veil: Newman as Literary Artist," *Renascence* 43 (Fall 1990–Winter 1991): 34.

which the speaker meets Death, described in suitably skeletal terms, marking certain spring flowers and trees. The speaker watches, and those marked by Death die no sooner than the others, but "yet / Their fall was fuller of regret."[16] The argument about election and spiritual death, with a suitable warning for the young, is unobtrusive, but the events and scenes of the allegory never take on a life of their own. They are intellectual counters, not observed actualities. It is not that physical beauty has no use for the young poet, but its use is only as a sort of advertising ploy to make the real, spiritual truths accessible.

And even when he is relying upon allegory, he does not quite count on the transparent meaning of his chosen signs; he usually interprets them for the reader as well, or stiffly employs biblical symbolism in order to be sure of getting his message across. Some attempts fail miserably, as the allegorically chosen symbols become too literal in the hands of the poet. For instance, the conscientiously symbolic but rather macabre May 1864 "Pilate" features rock splinters driven crucifixion-style into Pilate's wrist. However, Hopkins quickly developed facility in Tractarian style, and published a straightforward Tractarian allegory, "Barnfloor and Winepress," written that July: "Scourged upon the threshing-floor . . . we found the heavenly Bread." July was fruitful for poems in that mode, such as "New Readings": "How soldiers platting thorns around CHRIST's Head / Grapes grew and drops of wine were sped." The best of these allegorical poems is the most personal, written almost a year later, "See how Spring opens with disabling cold.'" There the Parable of the Sower is illustrated with a fully realized description of slow growth in a bad year in England; with "hunting winds and the long-lying snow. . . . where is strength to make the leaf unfold?" Interpreted for the reader as "chilling remembrance" of "waste done in unreticent youth,"[17] the cold spring could stand on its own as a symbol, but Hopkins does not yet trust that his reader will follow him. He has no faith that the ordinary realities of the physical world will do his readers any good.

16. Hopkins, *Poetical Works,* 18.

17. In this paragraph, Hopkins, *Poetical Works,* 22, 26, 28, 77.

G. B. Tennyson delineates how the principle of reserve, like its twin, analogy, played a large part in Tractarian poetry's vitiation of the sensual world. "Reserve" Newman had applied to theology first, to explain why certain very important Christian theological concepts were not authoritatively defined, though he contends that they were believed, among early Christians. Tractarians thought that the *disciplina arcana*, the withholding of certain doctrines from public proclamation, served as a reverent protection against doctrines' misuse and misinterpretation by those who had not sufficiently pure hearts to take them in their full significance. Only as contested by heretics did these doctrines become part of the public life of the Church. Naturally, a notion of doctrine passed on by the authority of unwritten tradition, and not to be found on the face of the biblical text, was controversial in Anglican circles for being too "Romanising." Reserve itself became a sort of *disciplina arcana* amongst Tractarians. To promote reserve, Tractarians advocated restraint in communication about all religious and emotional matters. Especially in his crisis of decision, Hopkins appreciated this reticence. He was very pleased when he found out that his friends were startled by his change of communions; that meant that he had kept his emotions under strict control, and had not influenced anyone else's emotions by his own doubts until he was sure of his position.[18] The way in which this culture of reserve worked upon Hopkins's poems at this time was to restrain the exuberance of language and detail that makes his later poems expressive to the point of ecstasy. Appeals to emotion are, in the Tractarian view, appeals to something irrelevant to religion; one must seek to establish what is true whether one's sentiments accord with it or not. Powerful aesthetic effects are simply evil if they lead a person toward worldly consolations rather than toward God.

In the poems Hopkins wrote when he was a Tractarian, he contrives to distance the reader from the emotions associated with the subject matter. Hopkins's later poems are often frankly autobiographical, but not so the Pre-Raphaelite poems of his college days. Direct ad-

18. Hopkins, *Letters to Bridges*, 6 (22 Sept. 1866).

dress to the reader would violate Tractarian reserve. Therefore, even lyrics that seem personal to Hopkins are presented as dramatic monologues. He puts them in the mouths of such characters as "Pilate" or "One of the Spies in the Wilderness" or a character from someone else's poem. The loveliest of these monologues, "Heaven-Haven," is put in the mouth of "a nun." In "Heaven-Haven," the artifice hardly succeeds in imposing the distance it is meant to create, but it is in accord with the discipline of humility as encouraged by Canon Pusey among his followers: a strict restraint on the impulse to draw attention to one's personal feelings or virtues. Like most of his best early poems, this lyric, written at the same time as his published "Barnfloor and Winepress," reflects Hopkins's desire to master his own sensuality:

> I have desired to go
> Where springs not fail,
> To fields where flies no sharp and sided hail,
> And a few lilies blow.
>
> And I have asked to be
> Where no storms come,
> Where the green swell is in the havens dumb,
> And out of the swing of the sea.[19]

In his Tractarian poetry, Hopkins tries to describe or to create design in the world, in imitation of Christ as teacher and designer. Reserve and analogy are sometimes painfully evident as he attempts to appeal to the abstract reason at the expense of nearly everything concrete.[20] Short, allegorical, and didactic, his poems are carefully crafted in their general design, but, compared to his later works, often pallid in their execution. Even some of his most passionate religious poems are

19. Hopkins, *Poetical Works*, 29–30.

20. Lichtmann, in *Contemplative Poetry*, 159, treats Hopkins's interest in Tractarian poetics anachronistically, and therefore states that the ideas "could hold little appeal" for him. She also connects his resistance to feeling with his move beyond Tractarian poetics, while I connect it with his adherence thereto. For his mature opinion about poetry and feelings, particularly religious feelings, see *Letters to Bridges*, 66 (22 Feb. 1879): "Feeling, love in particular, is the great moving power and spring of verse and the only person that I am in love with seldom, especially now, stirs my heart sensibly and when he does I cannot always 'make capital' of it, it would be a sacrilege to do so."

weakened by an alienation from the precise observation of nature that runs riot in his journals. Some few observations of natural phenomena are distilled into allegorical meanings and then decanted into carefully ordered verses.

Moral beauty, rather than worldly beauty, increasingly consumed Hopkins's attention—especially Christian asceticism and self-sacrifice. A sampling of his undergraduate verse savors of a fascination with self-control and self-restraint, even in its extremes. Although its allegorical and fictional setting fulfills some of the requirements of reserve, no experienced ascetic would write "Easter Communion" as Hopkins did in March 1865:

> Pure fasted faces draw unto this feast:
> God comes all sweetness to your Lenten lips.
> You striped in secret with breath-taking whips,
> Those crookéd rough-scored chequers may be pieced
> To crosses meant for Jesu's; you whom the east
> With draught of thin and pursuant cold so nips,
> Breathe Easter now; you sergèd fellowships,
> You vigil-keepers with low flames decreased,
>
> God shall o'er-brim the measures you have spent
> With oil of gladness, for sackcloth and frieze
> And the ever-fretting shirt of punishment
> Give myrrhy-threaded golden folds of ease.
> Your scarce-sheathed bones are weary of being bent.
> Lo, God shall strengthen all the feeble knees.[21]

Outside of the more fevered Tractarian circles, such as the Brotherhood of the Holy Trinity, Anglicans generally considered asceticism rather perverse;[22] anti-Catholic rhetoric tarnished even celibacy, not to mention penitential flagellation. But here we see a Ruskinian fascination with suffering brought to an extreme, though clothed in medievalism. The Catholic or High Anglican interpretation of Commu-

21. Hopkins, *Poetical Works,* 70.

22. Even Hopkins had joined in the denigration of asceticism. See his *Further Letters,* 8 (to E. H. Coleridge, 3 Sept. 1862), praising Tennyson's poem hostile to asceticism; and Hopkins's drawing, 210.

nion justifies the images; God comes to the "Lenten lips" of the ascetics, and unites their sufferings with those of the scourged Christ, whose graveclothes, drenched with myrrh (John 19.39), were glorified by the Resurrection. The "oil of gladness" in Psalm 45 (46 Vulgate), anoints the bridegroom whom the Anglican Christmas liturgy identified with Christ: "upon thy right hand did stand the queen in gold of Ophir. Hearken, O daughter, and consider, and incline thine ear; forget also thine own people and thy father's house; so shall the king greatly desire they beauty: for he is thy Lord; and worship thou him" (AV). The poem alludes to the Parable of the Wise and Foolish Virgins ("vigil-keepers") awaiting the Bridegroom Christ. He comes to embrace his Bride, the Church or the soul of the believer—but the reader's attention is distracted from the bridal night's rejoicing by the awkward symbolism of the shape of the whipmarks on the back of the penitent. Hopkins attends more to the Lenten ascetic practice than to the celebration, although the poem is nominally about Easter. (His personal Lenten practices were less severe: eating meat no more than once a day, cutting back on drinking tea, and spending less time in his armchair.) A boyish fascination with intensity of suffering still characterizes his idea of asceticism; the poem has the air of an adolescent athlete or soldier boasting about the pain he endured in winning rather than enjoying the victory itself. Hopkins wrote this poem the year in which he met the strange young ascetic Digby Dolben and was drawn to the boldness of Dolben's monastic affectations; Hopkins too desired to excel at spiritual athletics.

The year of his conversion changed Hopkins's attitude toward asceticism, which in "Easter Communion" seems itself to be a sort of appetite he is tempted to indulge. Observe in "The Habit of Perfection" (subtitled "The Novice"), written in 1866, both sensuality and asceticism restrained for an effect that is rich and carefully architectural:

Elected silence, sing to me
And beat upon my whorlèd ear,
Pipe me to pastures still and be
The music that I care to hear.

Shape nothing, lips; be lovely-dumb
It is the shut, the curfew sent
From there where all surrenders come
Which only makes you eloquent.

Be shellèd, eyes, with double dark,
And find the uncreated light:
This ruck and reel which you remark
Coils, keeps, and teases simple sight.

Palate, the hutch of tasty lust,
Desire not to be rinsed with wine:
The can must be so sweet, the crust
So fresh that come in fasts divine!

Nostrils, your careless breath that spend
Upon the stir and keep of pride,
What relish shall the censers send
Along the sanctuary side!

O feel-of-primrose hands, O feet
That want the yield of plushy sward,
But you shall walk the golden street
And you unhouse and house the Lord.

And, Poverty, be thou the bride
And now the marriage-feast begun,
And lily-colored clothes provide
Your spouse not laboured-at nor spun.[23]

The carefully ordered poem touches upon self-denial in the senses of sight, taste, smell, and touch before finally invoking the ideal of evangelical poverty. But the medieval trappings are gone, and the emphasis is not on the suffering as such.

The first two stanzas enjoin two silences on the novice, his own muteness and the quiet of the cloister. Each silence has its use in one's spiritual progress, rather than as an end in itself. The peace is an opportunity to hear the divine song, which will bring him to the "pastures green" of the Twenty-Third Psalm. The obedient muteness of the

23. Hopkins, *Poetical Works*, 89–90.

spiritual aspirant will witness to his love for God more than any speech. The ambiguous "where all surrenders come" both asserts that the obedience will be received by God and that the grace to obey comes from God, who surrendered to the needs of sinners and died for them. Closing out the "ruck and reel" of distractions that entangle and delude the eye, the ascetic can encounter God in the darkness; even fasts bring food and drink of a different, sweeter sort (as Jesus said, "My meat is to do the will of Him that sent me"; John 4.34). Pride will be transformed into prayer, the pleasures of sensual touch into the pleasures of high service. The delicate allusion to celibacy in the final stanza points the reader away from the contemplation of physical luxury to the contemplation of God's provision for those who trust in him. This is no longer fashionable Victorian medievalism; its thrust is purely religious. Hopkins here begins to build a sense of direct communication with God, which stays in his work even through the "Terrible Sonnets" at the end of his life; those searing utterances achieve an immediacy and intimacy of address that implies a supreme confidence that the poet is actually addressing Someone.

As Ruskin recommended in his books, discipline of life implies discipline of form; chastity is communicated through spareness and restraint, rectitude through tight, formal meter. Only once does Hopkins indisputably go beyond the ordinary licenses of iambic tetrameter—ironically, in commending restraint, in the second foot of "Desire not to be rinsed with wine." But even the freedom of the rhythm is subtle and restrained. His astonishingly sensitive ear plays with the tension between the spoken length of syllables and the regularity of metric stress; "feel-of-primrose" must be spoken at a breath, breathlessly even, while monosyllables give the other three lines greater slowness and gravity.[24] Yet even as Hopkins preaches restraint, his enthusiasm for the beauties of language enriches the texture of the stanzas with alliteration and assonance.

This loving attention to the details of the sensual world reveals a

24. He recommends the device later in a letter describing how to confer weight and gravity on the "light" English sonnet; see *Correspondence with Dixon,* 85–86 (29 Oct. 1881).

new aspect of his spirituality. He had begun to see a way to unite his desire that the rational Logos should be the center of his religious commitment with his delight in the beauty of "all my eyes see." We find him writing to a friend in 1865,

I am now toiling through an essay for the Hexameron, but can you tell me what in music answers to realism in painting? The other arts seem to depend on truth (no: Truth) as well as Beauty. What then answers to, I mean what is, Truth in music?[25]

Here he is seeking the holy message of the universe in its design, because the universe was created by the Logos of God, which means both Word and Reason. The title is applied to Jesus in the first chapter of John's Gospel, pointing to the Incarnation of God in Christ as the principle of reason and order in the world. But Christ does more than give the world rational design and purpose. In 1866, Hopkins wrote to his friend E. H. Coleridge:

I think that the trivialness of life is, and personally to each one, ought to be seen to be, done away with by the Incarnation—or, I shd. say the difficulty wh. the trivialness of life presents ought to be. It is one adorable point of the incredible condescension of the Incarnation (the greatness of which no saint can have ever hoped to realise) that our Lord submitted not only to the pains of life, the fasting, scourging, crucifixion etc. or the insults, as the mocking, blindfolding, spitting etc, but also to the mean and trivial accidents of humanity. It leads one naturally to rhetorical antithesis to think for instance that after making the world He shd. consent to be taught carpentering, and being the eternal Reason, to be catechised in the theology of the Rabbins.[26]

The sacrifice of Christ is a sacrifice of accepting limitations, including limitations of time and place. Christianity, as Hopkins embraces it, is founded in accessible historical experience, particularized in an unrepeatable event, in accord with the experiential flavor imposed upon all truth by individual human limitations. Therefore, for a poet, the ordinary world gains meaning through the presence of God as a particular creature among his creatures—and that meaning imposes a responsi-

25. Hopkins, *Further Letters,* 224 (to A. W. M. Baillie, 5 Jan. 1865).
26. Hopkins, *Further Letters,* 19–20 (to E. H. Coleridge, 22 Jan. 1866).

bility on the world's beholder. One must respect the dignity of the world whose most ordinary details have been thus hallowed. The fascination with sacrifice is in itself very Ruskinian, of course; so is the insistence on the minor details of everyday life. But Hopkins goes beyond Ruskin in bringing not only God's intellectual plan, but God's personal participation, into the details of everyday life; and we shall see how he extends that divine participation in creatures to human participation in the divine action of redemption.

Hopkins wished to move beyond analogy, to join Christ's heroic effort and participate bodily in sacrificial, divine love rather than merely appreciating divine order. Tractarians felt free to hold that Communion offered the opportunity to be physically united with Christ incarnate; yet more did Roman Catholics. Hopkins describes how he is "drawn by a lasting strain" to the Catholic Church in a letter to his father:

> I shall hold as a Catholic what I have long held as an Anglican, that literal truth of our Lord's words by which I learn that the least fragment of the consecrated elements in the Blessed Sacrament of the Altar is the whole Body of Christ born of the Blessed Virgin, before which the whole host of saints and angels as it lies on the altar trembles in adoration. This belief once got is the life of the soul and when I doubted it I shd. become an atheist the next day.[27]

Hopkins is careful to explain to his father that it is the same Incarnation as the one at Bethlehem, not a new one—in other words, that the event is both a past and distant one and one immediate and present. The relationship of the two temporal events to the divine and eternal action of the Incarnation is precisely the same. Thus, in his theology, one physical thing could be present in multiple manners and in multiple places; and the Communion elements of bread and wine, which seem to have one reality, have in fact another present in them.

It requires explanation that his faith in God should depend upon his faith in the "Real Presence," and in the Communion elements becoming literally the body and blood of Christ. Writing to E. H. Coleridge about theodicy, Hopkins writes to justify God's ways to a man

27. Hopkins, *Further Letters,* 92 (to his father, 16 Oct. 1866).

who argues that suffering militates against the notion of God's existence:

> The great aid to belief and object of belief is the doctrine of the Real Presence in the Blessed Sacrament of the Altar. Religion without that is sombre, dangerous, illogical, with that it is—not to speak of its grand consistency and certainty—*loveable*.[28]

In Hopkins's view, then, it is not the presence of the Eternal Reason in the rationality of the world that makes religion "logical"; it is the Incarnate God's sacramental participation in the world. A clue to the solution of this paradox may be seen in the advice with which Hopkins closes his letter to his father: that his parents should try "casting yourselves" into the "five adorable wounds" of Christ. "Those who do not pray to Him in His Passion pray to God but scarcely to Christ."[29] The characteristic activity of Christ is "sacrifice," by which Hopkins means the setting aside of pleasure and privilege, and the acceptance of pain, for the good of others. The central impulse of his spirituality has become the moral rather than the aesthetic good of God's presence in the world. In the Eucharist, on the altar, a Christian sees and becomes physically one with God Incarnate in the most extreme point of sacrifice—the Body broken, the Paschal Lamb killed for the feast, "in *statu victimali*,"[30] as Hopkins writes to Bridges. Here the Christian is privileged to become one with a God who would condescend to make and love and suffer in a sin-scarred world, and thereby join God in loving the world and suffering for the world. To share in the sacrifice of God is also to share in the glory of God. In order to enter into that organic unity, Hopkins must be able to participate in the activity of God Incarnate in Communion.

The Church of England permitted but did not enforce belief in the Real Presence of Christ in the Communion elements. Identification with Christ through the Real Presence was an area of tension in Hopkins's relationship with the Anglican Church, and was an important

28. Hopkins, *Further Letters*, 17 (to E. H. Coleridge, 1 June 1864).
29. Hopkins, *Further Letters*, 95 (to his father, 16–17 Oct. 1866).
30. Hopkins, *Letters to Bridges*, 149 (16 June 1882).

element in his change of church allegiance, as his letter to his father on the topic testifies:

> But, as Monsignor Eyre says, [the physical presence of Christ in Communion] is a gross superstition unless guaranteed by infallibility. I cannot hold this doctrine confessedly except as a Tractarian or a Catholic: the Tractarian ground I have seen broken to pieces under my feet.[31]

A letter to Canon Liddon of about the same date explains exactly how he had seen the ground of Tractarian ecclesiological theory broken under his feet. He sought a certain and unbroken chain of teaching authority leading to Christ; this is what he means by "Catholic." The Tractarians, especially Pusey, had taught that there were several fallible churches with the authority of valid apostolic succession. The Roman Catholic Church simply considered it sin that these other communions did not acknowledge the authority of the Roman See. Hopkins writes, "If there are Catholics who are not Roman Catholics, can the Church of Rome hold such people under sentence of the loss of their souls and yet remain part of the Catholic Church? . . . [T]o say schism is not a deadly sin as Dr. Pusey does is useless, for a true church cannot command any sin." He rejected "the view that the whole infallible Church is made up of these three churches, singly fallible but as yet orthodox,"[32] and decided to accept Roman Catholic claims of infallibility.

The theology of participation that spoke so powerfully to Hopkins at the point of his conversion remained a part of his spirituality and thus of his poetry. The first lines of Hopkins's poem "In Honour of St. Alphonsus Rodriguez," written near the end of his life, show this aspect of Hopkins's theology of redemption at work: "Those fell strokes that once scarred flesh, scored shield, / Should tongue that time now, trumpet now that field . . . On Christ they do, they on the martyr may."[33] Sacrificial pain is glory, God's glory and the glory of the suffering creature. Hopkins took the passage literally in which Saint Paul said "In my flesh I complete what is lacking in Christ's afflictions for

31. Hopkins, *Further Letters,* 92–93 (to his father, 16 Oct. 1866).
32. Hopkins, *Further Letters,* 32–33 (to H. P. Liddon, 7 Nov. 1866).
33. Hopkins, *Poetical Works,* 200.

the sake of His Body, which is the Church" (Col. 1.24–25). Hopkins was keen to avoid the "fatal state of mind" involved in "a minimising"[34] or "an enlightened Christianity."[35] He seriously questioned whether "I shd. have no plea why my soul was not forfeit"[36] for delaying to act upon conscience in religion; he believed in hell and in salvation through sacrifice, and reveled in the heroic notion of putting oneself in harm's way for no earthly good.

Hopkins's love of the Eucharistic Christ comes from the same impulse as his delight in the Ruskinian idealization of sacrifice, of giving up one's own will and benefit. But the crucial element of identification with Christ himself is missing from Ruskin and is essential to Hopkins. Hopkins believed in an organic union of Christians with the Body of Christ, so that good done by Christians is good done by Christ. But, according to Ruskin's religious training, to unite a creature's sufferings with the redemptive action of Christ would be an encroachment on the sovereignty of God. As Calvin put it, "What is this but merely to leave the name of Christ, and at the same time make him a vulgar saintling, who can scarcely be distinguished in the crowd?"[37] But, for Hopkins, a share in the sufferings of Christ does not imply any lack on God's part, but rather a superabundant generosity; God again chooses to limit himself, as he does for the creation of the world, out of love for the glorification of his creatures. In allowing his creatures to share in his own work, he enhances their dignity as free agents working out their own salvation. Though God lacks no power to save, martyrs gain glory through their wounds; it is Christ's glory, but their whole existence is Christ's and no less their own for being his.

Hopkins's theological economy of participatory salvation owed, I think, some debt to Ruskin's political economy of heroism in *Unto This Last,* which Arnold found disturbing because Ruskin's reminders of blood sacrifice accorded ill with the sweet, reasonable, and gentle-

34. Hopkins, *Further Letters,* 22 (to John Henry Newman, 28 Aug. 1866).
35. Hopkins, *Further Letters,* 17 (to E. H. Coleridge, 1 June 1864).
36. Hopkins, *Further Letters,* 92 (to his father, 16 Oct. 1866).
37. John Calvin, *Institutes of the Christian Religion,* 2:574.

manly form of religion he thought proper to the civilized culture of the nineteenth century. Ruskin's religious language encouraged Hopkins to consider it a holy duty to spend oneself for a great cause; and, for Hopkins the Tractarian, the intensity with which he reveled in that heroic ambition could only have its justification if the ambition was hidden in Christ. Consider Ruskin's image of the plow in *Unto This Last.* Although, as wealth, a "plough might glitter in the sun . . . it becomes true capital only by another kind of splendor,—when it is seen '*splendescere sulco,*' to grow bright in the furrow; rather with diminution of its substance, than addition, by the noble friction."[38] This image begins the sestet of "The Windhover," written fourteen years after Hopkins went to Oxford. There Hopkins speaks of the glory of spending oneself completely in fulfilling one's mission: "sheer plod makes plough down sillion / Shine"[39]—"*splendescere sulco.*" Some scholarship on "The Windhover" has suggested that the poem is a condemnation of aspiration, seeing the falcon or even the coal as demonic manifestations of pride.[40] However, the allusion to Ruskin makes it clear that the poem celebrates the energy of aspiration—the Gothic energy, if you will, of the bird, with its military plumes and its apparent mission of death.

We have seen how the Tractarians encouraged Hopkins to treat all natural phenomena as emblems of Christian dogma; so he does in "The Windhover," and then moves beyond that level of meaning. In the line "I caught this morning morning's minion, king/dom of daylight's dauphin, dapple-dawn-drawn falcon," the falcon itself is not Christ per se. The word "falcon" is in apposition to "morning's minion" and "kingdom of daylight's dauphin." Rather than the son of the

38. Ruskin, *Unto This Last,* in *C&W,* 17:99.

39. MacKenzie (*Poetical Works of Gerard Manley Hopkins,* 384) also noted this allusion. William B. Templeman, in "Ruskin's Ploughshare and Hopkins's 'The Windhover,'" *English Studies* 43 (Netherlands, 1962): 103–6, preceded us both in its discovery.

40. Sulloway, *Gerard Manley Hopkins and the Victorian Temper,* 110; Loomis, *Dayspring in Darkness: Sacrament in Hopkins* (Lewisburg, Pa.: Bucknell University Press, 1988), 27; Lichtmann, *Contemplative Poetry,* discusses the matter sensitively, 119. I find Boyle's reading, in *Metaphor in Hopkins* (Chapel Hill: University of North Carolina Press, 1961), coherent and consistent with Hopkins's usual poetic practice.

King of Day, the bird is that which is ruled by the son, the servant of the coming light. As the bird circles, like a horse being trained to obey (as Christ "though a son learned obedience" in Heb. 5.8), it stoops to prey.[41] As the hawk closes for the kill, the image of Ruskin's sacrificial soldier surfaces; Hopkins addresses Christ and the bird at once: "o my chevalier!" It seems curious that Hopkins should choose this moment of violence as an image of Christian perfection—but a hawk, in "the achieve of, the mastery of the thing!" must kill. (In *The Wreck of the Deutschland,* a storm, in the perfection of its power, must overwhelm human travelers on the sea.) The beauty and skill of the bird coming to earth constitute "brute beauty"; brute creation, always obedient to God because incapable of rebellion.

The raptor, in its inarticulate beauty, is also a reminder of the Word of God, the Son who likewise "came down from heaven." Nature springs from the Word of God and is the image of it:

> as the rain and the snow come down from heaven and do not return to it without watering the earth and making it bud and flourish, so is my word that goes forth from my mouth: it will not return to me empty but will accomplish what I desire and achieve the purpose for which I sent it. (Isa. 55.10)

But nature as word has its meaning only when a human mind encounters it. When Hopkins addresses Christ as "my chevalier," his readers are overhearing a prayer of praise—but the prayer of praise is the same thing as the recognition of the falcon's capacity for flashing forth meaning. The "fire" of recognition breaks from "thee," Christ, to whom the poem is addressed, and, as Hopkins says in *The Wreck of the Deutschland,* "whom heaven and earth are word of, worded by." Hopkins's attention to Christ, the Word of God, is the same thing as interpreting the message in the flight of the hawk; the action of interpretation and the action of utterance are both praise, one inchoate, as the poet's "heart in hiding" stirs, and the other spoken to us. And the

41. MacKenzie's notes on the way kestrels dive (with a rather slower glide than one ordinarily associates with falcons) do not preclude this reading; it is not necessarily the case that a shallow dive shows less mastery than a swift one. See Hopkins, *Poetical Works,* 379–80.

windhover is itself dangerous, but so is the recognition of Christ in the world, because the recognition of the God who sacrifices himself is a peremptory invitation to join in the sacrifice: to imitate the divine victim and experience death to oneself.

So when Ruskin's image surfaces, the meaning is Ruskin's too: the plow must be worn away to bring forth the new grain from the earth. This is the glory of the plow. In the same way, in the poem's final image, the log must collapse and destroy itself in order to bring forth the energy it gathered from the sun. The apparent self-destruction is labor to bring forth the ultimate beauty: love, which is giving all for the good of another. The Christ to whom Hopkins dedicates this poem is not Arnold's schoolteacher but Ruskin's soldier. To imitate Christ's death, whether by slow attrition or swift self-immolation, is to take on the life-giving, light-bearing function of Christ in the world as he creates rich and varied glory: "gold-vermilion." And as an artist—Hopkins did call this "the best thing I ever wrote"—Hopkins is here doing, as a human being, what the windhover does as a hawk: fulfilling his function in all excellence, because the function of human beings is that of the Divine Word. In a synthesis whose theological implications a Protestant Anglican was bound to resist, the artist is honoring Christ and acting as Christ at the same time, just as the bird is; like the bird, he is and is not identified with the "daylight's dauphin," Jesus. The poem itself is a sacrifice, a sacrifice of praise, for Hopkins is regarding the kestrel in its own glory, not for some purpose of his own, and yet enriching the reality of the bird—its effect upon the world—by giving it birth into the larger pattern of divine and human meaning.

But while the dense symbolism and theology of that 1877 sonnet were far in his future, allegorical abstraction dominated Hopkins the Tractarian poet. He did his best to "repress" all that was purely personal and concrete about his knowledge, his ambitions, and his spirituality, for it was deeply intertwined with the private and isolated world of the senses. The highest art for a Tractarian had to be the least involved with the distractions of the purely sensual world. Thus Hopkins's undergraduate poetry is like his later poetry in that it manifests his religious concerns, his peculiarly sensitive ear, and his precise diction.

However, the Tractarian poetry lacks what anthropologists call *thickness:* attention to concrete details of description. Hopkins's mature work is crowded with vivid, various, and particular physical detail; his Tractarian poetry is, at its best, reserved and spare. It has a formal grace, as in a procession or ceremony well conducted: fitting utterance, with all violence of feeling removed, reserved, dispelled. In his later poetry, the violence of personal sensation and desire is not controlled so much as released at high pressure to expand the narrow space of the sonnet.

How did Hopkins find a philosophically consistent way to seize upon that which is "beautiful to individuation" and call our attention to "the differing shades of verdure in the forest," and even to the states of his own psyche, without traducing the bounds of objective truth? He found it in the company of another Tractarian, one less cowed by Coleridge than Keble had been. For this we must look to the development of the idea of inscape and thus to Hopkins's friendship with John Henry Newman.

CHAPTER 5

HOPKINS AND NEWMAN
Toward an Epistemology of Personal Commitment

NEWMAN'S CONVERSION STORY, *Apologia pro Vita Sua,* was published in 1864. Two years later, as he pondered his church allegiance, Hopkins copied out Newman's "Lead, Kindly Light" into his journal and soon "saw clearly the impossibility of staying in the Church of England."[1] Other converts among his friends went to the nearest available priest, but Hopkins wanted to speak with Newman personally. Hopkins first wrote to Newman in August 1866, more than a month after his decision, and said, "by God's mercy I am clear as to the sole authority of the Church of Rome."[2] In September he met the great man:

> Dr. Newman was most kind, I mean in the very best sense, for his manner is not that of solicitous kindness but genial and almost, so to speak, unserious. And if I may say so, he was so sensible. He asked questions which made it clear for me how to act; I will tell you presently what that is: he made sure I was acting deliberately and wished to hear my arguments, and when I had finished and said that I could see no way round them, he laughed and said, "Neither can I." He thought there appeared no reason, if it had not been for matters at home of course, why I shd. not be received at once, but in no way did he urge me on, rather the other way. . . . Amongst other things he said that he always answered those who thought the learned had no excuse in invincible ignorance, that on the contrary they had that excuse the most of all people. It is

1. Hopkins, *Journals and Papers,* 146 (17 July 1866).
2. Hopkins, *Further Letters,* 22 (28 Aug. 1866).

needless to say he spoke with interest and kindness and appreciation of all that Tractarians reverence.[3]

Others responded with less irenic sentiments toward those on the opposite side of the ecclesiastical divide. When Newman actually received Hopkins into the Roman Catholic Church in October, Hopkins's family wrote him wrenching letters; Oxford imposed bureaucratic obstacles; and Newman's successor as the head of the Tractarians, Reverend Pusey, who had been Hopkins's confessor, wrote a rancorous note calling Hopkins a "pervert" to Rome, who had chosen to serve "the unbelievers."[4]

The world beyond Oxford was not likely to be gentler. Newman offered kindly, practical advice:"[Y]our first duty is to make a good class. Show your friends at home that becoming a Catholic has not unsettled you in the plain duty that lies before you."[5] Hopkins made "a good class" at Oxford: a double first. Newman also gave Hopkins a job at his Oratory School from September 17, 1867, to April 15, 1868. Hopkins made momentous decisions in those seven months under Newman's roof. There he worked to form himself anew, not merely as a gentleman and a scholar, but in all things as a Catholic.

We are perhaps fortunate that Newman's effect on Hopkins was more theological and philosophical than poetic; Newman's supple prose and calm poetic voice have little likeness to Hopkins's gnarled intensity in writing. This Hopkins knew, but he eagerly seized Newman's epistemology as he began to articulate the central concept of his own poetic theory: "inscape." Newman's philosophy provided Hopkins with a way to link his sacramentality, his keen awareness of perspectivism, and his understanding of the unity and accessibility of truth. Trust is Newman's center. Hopkins came to agree with Newman that human knowledge depends on making a moral commitment to judge and to trust the information that one gathers. Not only is it absolutely necessary to have trust in the community that creates and in-

3. Hopkins, *Letters to Bridges*, 5 (22 Sept. 1866).

4. Hopkins, *Further Letters*, 400 (10 Oct. 1866).

5. Hopkins, *Further Letters*, 405 (6 Dec. 1866, misprinted as 1886).

terprets language; trust is also necessary even to believe one's own senses. The idea that knowledge is always and inevitably personal—an act of the will—set Hopkins free to admit imagination and feeling into his rigidly anti-emotional conception of truth. His later poems immerse the reader in sensual, particular experience almost to the point (as Hopkins admits) that they baffle attempts at straightforward rational apprehension at their first reading. Newman's philosophy of perception and language informs the "very highly wrought" theory that justifies Hopkins's much-admired boldness of expression.

Hopkins knew that Wordsworth and Coleridge had partly shaped Newman's thought. In an 1881 letter to A. W. M. Baillie, Hopkins classified poets into: "the Romantic school," of Scott, Keats, Leigh Hunt, Hood, and, eventually, Browning; its "Romantic" descendant, the "school of Rossetti"; the "sentimental school" of Byron and Moore; and "the Lake poets" such as Wordsworth and Landor. He disparaged the Lake poets' style, and noted that the school "expires in Keble and Faber and Cardinal Newman."[6] Hopkins hinted to Canon Dixon, in another letter, about what he himself had learned to admire in these poets as he wrote of Wordsworth's "Ode on the Intimations of Immortality":

> There have been in all history a few, a very few men, whom common repute, even when it did not trust them, has treated as having had something happen to them that does not happen to other men, as having *seen something*, whatever that really was. Plato is the most famous of these. . . . [H]uman nature in these men saw something, got a shock; wavers in opinion, looking back, whether there was anything in it or no; but is in a tremble ever since. Now . . . in Wordsworth when he wrote that ode human nature got another of those shocks, and the tremble from it is spreading. This opinion I do strongly share; I am, ever since I knew the ode, in that tremble. You know what happened to crazy Blake, himself a most poetically electrical subject both active and passive, at his first hearing: when the reader came to "The pansy at my feet" he fell into a hysterical excitement. Now commonsense forbid we should take on like these hysterical unstrung creatures: still it was a proof of the power of the shock.[7]

6. Hopkins, *Correspondence with Dixon,* 98–99 (1 Dec. 1881).
7. Hopkins, *Correspondence with Dixon,* 147–48 (23 Oct. 1886).

Hopkins disparages Romantic emotionalism, but he asserts that there is something intellectually deep about Romantic ideas. Newman thought that it reopened the possibility of truth in sense experience and the responding imagination. Wordsworth's Imagination half-creates, but it also half-perceives. The child or the poet, as a prophet of Nature, "Doth like an agent of the one great Mind / Create, creator and receiver both."[8] Such prophetic minds are free of the "dull and endless strife"[9] of what Newman called "notional" knowledge. But, as we saw in *Floris in Italy*, Hopkins did not trust the imagination as an agent of truth, though he was preoccupied with the way perception depends partly upon the perceiver: "Yet not on this alone / for who makes rainbows by invention?" Hopkins fretted about how one could distinguish, as Wordsworth put it, between the act of "coercing all things into sympathy" and "the power of truth coming in revelation."[10] Newman proposes that one must commit one's will to any perceptions in order to grant them "reality." Coleridge argued that things were brought into being by being perceived imaginatively;[11] for Newman, that same imaginative activity is a work of faith that makes action possible. Only commitment brings things perceived into the full reality that can impel action. In his mature work, Hopkins takes joy in making that commitment, which he compares, as we shall see, to marriage.

During Hopkins's first months at the Oratory, Newman completed the successful draft of a work on the epistemology of faith, *An Essay in Aid of a Grammar of Assent*. Its subject matter had been "teazing" Newman's mind for "twenty years"—and probably more, if one considers the challenges to his faith in the systematic doubt at the root of the German higher biblical criticism. Newman began the successful draft of *Grammar of Assent* in the Alps, a setting reminiscent of Wordsworth,

8. William Wordsworth, *The Prelude*, bk. 2, in *Wordsworth: Selected Poetry*, ed. Mark Van Doren (New York: Modern Library, 1950), 203.

9. William Wordsworth, "The Tables Turned: An Evening Scene upon the Same Subject," in Van Doren, ed., *Wordsworth: Selected Poetry*, 83.

10. William Wordsworth, *The Prelude*, bk. 2, in Van Doren, ed., *Wordsworth: Selected Poetry*, 206–7.

11. Coleridge, *Biographia Literaria*, 1:279ff.

and the opening chapters employ romantic tropes such as children's questions and meadows of alpine flowers.[12] Newman had long held that the Romantic poets apprehended deep truths about the spiritual and moral significance of imagination, and he had brought their ideas to the questions about perception and faith central to the Oxford Movement. Questions about the nature of faith, perception, and commitment were uppermost in Newman's mind—and no doubt in his conversation and preaching—while Hopkins lived at the Oratory. And into this atmosphere imbued with Wordsworth came Newman's young disciple, wary of enthusiasm, rigidly analytical in matters of faith, who had found his religious roots as "dry" as Newman had found eighteenth-century Anglicanism. He was ripe for a full awakening to the Romantic epistemology that informs the *Grammar of Assent.*

The chapters of *Grammar of Assent* that Newman composed during Hopkins's stay at the Oratory show how one may rightly believe matters one does not understand. Newman's book primarily treats faith in terms of sensory and historical evidence; he leaves aside supernatural revelations. "Scientific" classical history, after all, sparked Victorian skepticism about Scripture. Newman insists strenuously on the primacy of experience over theory—on "real" things, not "notions"—and therefore the primacy of actual, historical events over mere probabilities predicted by inference. Proof and inference are "notional." Faith requires "Real Apprehension," which need not involve understanding; a matter really apprehended is one that can move the will to desire or repulsion. Even hunger and terror require faith in the dependability of the senses; in order to desire a thing or to flee from it, one must believe that it is real.[13] "Real Apprehension is . . . an experience or information

12. Nicholas Lash, introduction to Newman, *Grammar of Assent,* 7.

13. That human beings can lose faith in the evidence of their senses, without detectable physical cause, is most strikingly exhibited in the literature on body image in patients with anorexia nervosa. See Paul Garfinkel et al., "Body Awareness in Anorexia Nervosa: Disturbances in 'Body Image' and 'Satiety,'" *Psychosomatic Medicine* 40, no. 6 (1978): 487–98, who discuss how the anorexics' body images could not be modified by "external cues." Many later studies cited in Mental Health Abstracts Online (http://dialog.carl.org:3005/cgi-bin/cw-cgi?fullrecord+31422+1+11+5) confirm the work of Garfinkel et al.

about the concrete."[14] "Notions," that is, abstractions, can be thoroughly understood—but they only move the will if they are embodied in something that comes from experience.

Newman's philosophical notebook excoriates "those who deny that all truth is ultimately from the senses." The *Grammar of Assent* has harsh words for John Locke and the philosophy that demands that everything "except such as is self-evident" be doubted and then logically proven.[15] If they cannot live with any doubt whatsoever, human beings cannot live; Newman points out that even Locke, "with noble inconsistency," permits people to assume the truth of certain unproven matters of experience. Newman argues that even sense information is not experience unless a consciousness attends to it.[16] Coleridge had discussed heaven and hell in those terms;[17] Newman's sermons on hell build on the idea; and about two decades later, Hopkins directly uses them in his own Terrible Sonnets about mental pain, and in his spiritual writings.[18] In an 1883 notebook, Hopkins uses Newman's concepts and language reminiscent of Coleridge to speak of the pains of hell that the "lost suffer":

> I suppose it to be by the imagination that the lost suffer them and that as intensely as by the senses or it may be more so. This simple explanation will never strike our scholastics, because they do not see that there is an intellectual imagination.[19]

Newman says in the *Grammar of Assent* that the mind acts so powerfully upon external impressions that we can scarcely know our own dreaming from waking. He refers readers to a pericope in the Acts of the Apostles wherein Saint Peter did not know whether an angel spoke to him in a dream or in reality (Acts 12.9–11). (He may be influenced

14. Newman, *Grammar of Assent*, 38.

15. Newman, *Grammar of Assent*, 138–39.

16. John Henry Newman, *The Philosophical Notebook*, 2 vols., ed. Edward Sillem (New York: Humanities Press, 1970), 2:79.

17. Coleridge, *Biographia Literaria*, 1:114.

18. Michael D. Moore, "Newman and the Motif of Intellectual Pain in Hopkins' Terrible Sonnets," *Mosaic* 12 (Spring 1979): 29–46, esp. 32–33.

19. Hopkins, *Sermons and Devotional Writings*, 136.

by Coleridge here.[20]) Newman's notebook states that it is a "truth conveyed by revelation that what presents itself to our senses is not a mere subjective impression of the mind, but the token of something existing." He believes that the things that strike on our senses betoken rather than reveal the unknown realities of which they are the phenomena. He continues the argument: "Two things are implied by what I have been saying: 1 that the senses convey truths or realities, 2 only partially & to a certain point."[21] So we rely on our own sight by faith in a world beyond it; and Christian revelation (Newman will admit no other sort) serves to confirm, not vitiate, reliance upon the senses. Latent in Newman's reflections is the issue of belief in a religious creed; no matter how good the evidence, assent to the evidence requires an act of the will; therefore its truth or falsehood must be really apprehended. Logic or inferential notions may assist apprehension, but assent does not mean merely judging an idea's probability through inference based on evidence. Unhesitant though not involuntary, real assent admits no argument:

> Since mere argument is not the measure of assent, no one can be called certain of a proposition, whose mind does not spontaneously and promptly reject, on their first suggestion, as idle, as impertinent, as sophistical, any objections which are directed against its truth.[22]

Newman argues that we all live by a kind of faith; we cannot know the world at all save by moral choice. People can refuse and discourage knowledge. "Science gives us the grounds or premisses from which religious truths are to be inferred; but it does not set about inferring them. . . . We have to take its facts, and to give them a meaning, and to draw our own conclusions from them."[23] We must humbly trust and embrace the goodness of creation, Newman is saying, rather than continually interrogate it for premises small enough to fit our minds:

20. Coleridge, *Biographia Literaria,* 1:262.

21. Newman, *The Philosophical Notebook,* 2:205, 210.

22. Newman, *Grammar of Assent,* 164.

23. Newman, *Grammar of Assent,* 89. Christopher Devlin, too, associates this epistemology with Hopkins, in "The Image and the Word I," *The Month,* n.s., 3 (1950): 126.

"[W]e shall never have done with beginning, if we determine to begin with proof."[24] Of course physical peculiarities, such as color blindness, warp one's perceptions, Newman says—but the consciousness that judges the imperfect information of the senses has its own distortions. To reject the senses' information militates against giving love or trust to God (as the First Principle of the universe). Indeed, nothing could escape that pervasive refusal; it is a form of damnation. Hopkins and Newman agree that the relationship between a human being and the world is fundamentally moral: voluntary and accountable to God's judgment.

Moral truths require faith no less than metaphysical truths. Wordsworth's "The Tables Turned" endorses real rather than notional assent:

One impulse from a vernal wood
Will teach you more of man,
Of moral evil and of good,
Than all the sages can.

But Wordsworth does not claim to be constructing an original morality, nor are the ethical principles of the vernal wood self-evident. Wordsworth is speaking of how experiences shaped by a moral imagination command assent. The morality that Wordsworth articulated was, as he told Matthew Arnold, "formed and fashioned by the Scottish Church having held upon him in his youth, with a power which endured his life long, 'the strong hand of her purity.'"[25] In the second book of *The Prelude,* for instance, a boy steals a boat; alarmed by a huge darkness rising up against the night sky, he returns it. "Great shapes" in the boy's imagination convict him of stealing; but he knew that his neighbors would do the same, or he would have taken his joyride in the daylight. Wordsworth was certainly enough of a mountaineer to be aware that the boy's "black and huge" pursuer, which assumes the moral character of a divinity, was a mountain emerging into view from behind a nearer hill. Likewise, Wordsworth was aware

24. Newman, *Grammar of Assent,* 90.
25. Arnold, "Address to the Wordsworth Society," *Works,* 10:131–32.

that he was investing thoroughly traditional morality with the authority of "Nature." Is it intellectual dishonesty, or sentimental self-delusion, that makes him attribute moral majesty to a bogeyman invented by a frightened child? How could the adult Hopkins, ferociously anti-sentimental as he had always been, have any respect for Wordsworthian psychological jugglery—not merely as effective rhetoric, but as producing shocks of insight on a par with Plato's?

He could because he knew that Wordsworth is not in fact urging us to learn our morality from our impulses (or other experiences) in a vernal wood. It is not possible to do so. Long before any child is old enough to corroborate his or her knowledge of moral good and evil by experiences in the wild, the human social world has passed on knowledge of such things. One need not grumble with C. S. Lewis that the wood's precepts "might not be necessarily the sort of moral philosophy Wordsworth approved. . . . We must learn our theology and philosophy elsewhere (not surprisingly, we often learn them from theologians or philosophers)."[26] Certainly, Wordsworth knew that much. He writes to transform into real assent the notional assent held by those who, like Newman, like Hopkins, like Ruskin, already attribute the works of nature to a good, almighty God. Such readers are equipped to learn Wordsworth's lessons in Wordsworth's way.

Irretrievably social, Newman argues, we need other people even to explain our own experiences to us, and to give them a context in history. A child can apprehend its mother's truthfulness and "really assent" even to ideas beyond its grasp; in fact, a child must do so in order to survive. Newman imagines a child believing its mother's saying that "the quality of mercy is not strained" is true and good, though the child cannot understand it.[27] Hopkins writes of the same idea: a child welcomes some dignitary with a compliment memorized at the behest of its parents. The child cannot understand the poem, but believes its parents and can understand that the poem gives a welcome in the parents' name. Thus the child, by faith, really means what the poem says

26. C. S. Lewis, *The Four Loves* (New York: Collins Fontana Books, 1963), 22–23. This quotation is not representative of Lewis's approach to Wordsworth, of course; Lewis loved and understood that poet very well.

27. Newman, *Grammar of Assent*, 34.

without understanding it.[28] Both Newman and Hopkins argue that if religious salvation depends on assent, the capacity to judge truth must be open to all, even the ignorant. Hopkins wrote in October 1867: "God must have made his Church such as to attract and convince the poor and unlearned as well as the learned."[29] Since all belief is an act of the will, not an inevitable intellectual conclusion, Newman says that people judge new ideas, in fact, by indwelling them in a heuristic way, to see if they conflict with things that already command real assent. Contradictions cannot be assented to; and this law is not a mere notion, either. "No man is certain of a truth, who can endure the thought of the fact of its contradictory existing."[30]

And, though ratiocination or the evidence of experience may bring one infinitely close to Newman's "certitude," the approach is asymptotic; the act of will that is assent must always cross a gap, however slender. Just as no amount of evidence can ever impose certitude on a person, so too no one can impose any perception or any certitude on another; knowledge cannot compel, but only call. Since faith is necessary, Newman counsels trust rather than suspicion in the face of history. Bridling at "scientific" historiography, he asserts that the descriptive "laws" of probability and inference are not strictly applicable to unique occurrences, such as historical events. Even those inferences most consistent with past experience have no sovereignty over real events; "laws" can only be measured approximately. Such sayings as "Every man has his price" are not always true;[31] even tomorrow's sunrise is merely probable. Newman disdained the ideological stance that the truths promulgated by the scientific community, or by historians, are more absolute and compelling than the truths perceived by other communities. Both Hopkins and Newman refused to establish a double standard for belief: the "true" for science and business, and some other, vaguer standard for religion and morals.[32] In a letter about

28. Hopkins, *Sermons and Devotional Writings*, 157.

29. Hopkins, *Further Letters*, 92–93 (16 Oct. 1866).

30. Newman, *Grammar of Assent*, 164.

31. Newman, *Grammar of Assent*, 223.

32. For the degree to which this doublethink characterized spokesmen on the other side of the doctrinal divide, see Matthew Arnold, *Literature and Dogma*, in *Works*, 6:173. For the degree to which it is still done, see the opening chapter of Karen Armstrong, *A*

Duns Scotus's birthplace, Hopkins apparently took umbrage at Mandell Creighton for seeming to imply that veracity was any less characteristic of past ages than of his own; Creighton, at any rate, wrote Hopkins apologetically that he did not mean that that age in particular had an "unhistoric character."[33]

But how can the concrete, unrepeatable experience of history evoke real assent, or even Real Apprehension? How can one apprehend realities through notional words, when the objects of belief by their very nature cannot be within the experience of the hearer? In the *Grammar of Assent,* Newman theorizes that the memory stores impressions that can be separated, classified, and recombined to create an impression sufficient to move the hearer's will. A word does not and cannot refer to the same memories in the apprehension of different people; every individual image in the mind has some peculiarities. Hopkins says that language names "relations" of things; one of the relations a thing can have is likeness. A common noun names a similarity among the things that "fall under" it, and only that similarity that can be recognized despite individual variation. Therefore, each hearer can apprehend something true and real in connection with the word, and human beings can talk to one another despite their incommunicably individual experiences.

> Nor need such an image be in any sense an abstraction; though I may have eaten a hundred peaches in times past, the impression, which remains on my memory of the flavour, may be any of them, of the ten, twenty, thirty units, as the case may be, not a general notion, distinct from every one of them, and formed from all of them by a fabrication of my mind.[34]

The importance and immediacy of memory in Hopkins's linguistic theory are evident from his first notes on the topic, written in February 1868 at Newman's Oratory. Those notes show Hopkins well prepared to think about the "intelligible species" that Duns Scotus describes as

History of God: The 4000-Year Quest of Judaism, Islam, and Christianity (New York: Alfred A. Knopf, 1993).

33. Hopkins, *Further Letters,* 421 (13 April 1880).

34. Newman, *Grammar of Assent,* 40.

formed in the mind through the accumulation of similar experiences. Hopkins's notes discuss the way in which "words mean things or relations of things." Memory's image "accenting the nerves" is the "inchoate word" that is the foundation of linguistic communication. Secondary to that great fact is the conception of the logical idea, the word proper. Note that the distinction is between the "inchoate" sensory recollection—what we shall encounter later as the medieval "sensible species"—and "definition, abstraction, vocal expression or other utterance." In other words, "we may for convenience use word and definition with a certain freedom of interchange." The analytically abstract definition does not cover the entire mental event of uttering a word,

> For the word is the expression, uttering of the idea in the mind. That idea itself has two terms, the image (of sight or sound or scapes of the other senses) which is in fact a physical and refined energy* accenting on the nerves, a word to oneself, an inchoate word, and secondly the conception.
>
> *That is when deliberately formed or when a thought is recalled [in various ways Hopkins lists.][35]

Hopkins distinguishes between definitional reasoning, which he connects with "conception," and contemplation, which he connects to the "inchoate word." Moreover, words (uttered or inchoate) have in Hopkins's theory a power of their own, both in bringing to mind the things to which they are applied, and in "prepossession, enthusiasm which it has the power of producing but not always or in everyone." A word's "prepossession" is the sum of associations it calls up in a person. (His cheerful sonnets of the 1870s, as we shall see, also acknowledge the role of the disposition of the observer's consciousness in experience.) The likeness of Hopkins's "inchoate words" to Newman's Real Apprehension is strengthened by Hopkins's inclination to call the "prepossession" the "form" of a word. He knew that Aristotle's Form inherently alters matter; perhaps recalling the Thomistic teaching that the soul is the form of the body,[36] Hopkins cautions himself against

35. Hopkins, *Journals and Papers,* 125.

36. See Hopkins, *Further Letters,* 307 (to Coventry Patmore, 24 Sept. 1883), for one of several instances of Hopkins invoking this doctrine.

calling a word's "prepossession"—its emotional associations—its "soul": "all names but proper names are general while the soul is individual."[37]

In Newman's household, Hopkins eagerly studied the mysterious relations between words and experience, already an interest from boyhood, when he thought that the onomatopoetic theory of language had "not had a fair chance."[38] Scotus too makes experience central to knowledge, though in a much more precise way than either Hopkins or Newman—but, most importantly, all three refuse to make language completely dependent on the free play of the human mind. Hopkins thinks intently about the way a unique impression externally impressed on a person's mind can be called back and associated with a word. Newman raises the problem of people's peculiar conceptions even with regard to proper nouns. Though London raises for me an image of Picadilly Circus, and for you your aunt's house, and for C. S. Lewis some particular railway platform,[39] the news that "there is a great fire in London" can be really apprehended by all three of us. A single thing can be really and truly apprehended in various ways. This is most obvious in the case of a large and complex thing, like London, but the argument holds for any thing. The images apprehended need not seem as obviously incomplete as the image of a few buildings for a whole city. Every person attends, by choice or ability, to a limited share of the world. Newman says the letter "B" appears to "face" different ways to different people. Things look different to people who have different skills. Trick pictures look like one thing and then another by

37. Hopkins, *Journals and Papers,* 125.

38. Hopkins, *Journals and Papers,* 5.

39. The illustration about the fire is from *Miracles: A Preliminary Study* (New York: Macmillan, 1947) where C. S. Lewis appears to draw on the argument of Newman's *Grammar of Assent* (41) for his popular account of how people reach certitude—what Newman calls the "illative sense." Lewis does not introduce the technical term but argues, "When I think about London I usually see a mental picture of Euston Station. But when I think (as I do) that London has several million inhabitants, I do not mean that there are several million images of people contained in my image of Euston Station. . . . It makes sense because it is not about my own mental pictures, but about the real London, outside my imagination, of which no one can have an adequate mental picture at all" (72).

turns—though never like both at once. Such apprehensions seem exclusive and complete but are not, though all are founded in reality. Descriptions of these apprehensions still refer to realities, although the thing meant is one thing and the experiences apprehended are various. Each unified ordering of the information has a foundation in reality. Moreover, veracity forbids belief in a mere construction with no such foundation. To deliberately attach faith to something imaginary, as in superstition or idolatry, is forbidden by the First Commandment. That kind of self-delusion is evil, even damnable. To create in another person an apprehension with no foundation in reality is an equally damnable abuse of the necessity of faith: lying.

Newman's idea is uncannily simple. It means that many possible apprehensions are proper to a single entity. Since a reality is what is intelligible to any person, everything real has latent in itself an endless store of real apprehensions that people may learn to know—a "relative infinite" such as Hopkins finds in the human soul.[40] The idea also implies that, if we know something really, rather than merely having a notion of it, we cannot know it fully. We can know notions fully, and prove things conclusively about them—but notions are not real, and cannot move our wills. Of any reality, we can know only a few aspects. An encounter with the world is an encounter with mystery. Every experience has unutterable depths of reality within it.

These multiple real aspects of a single thing are, I believe, what Hopkins called the "inscapes" of a thing. The first known use of the word occurs in his February 1868 notes translating and annotating some of Parmenides' philosophical fragments. Hopkins finds the philosopher's cast of thought so like his own that he renders the fragments in his own private vocabulary.[41] He begins by citing Parmenides' dictum "Being is and Not-being is not," and then explains, cryptically enough, that it seems to mean "all things are upheld by instress and are meaningless without it."[42] This is his first recorded use

40. Hopkins, *Sermons and Devotional Writings*, 153.

41. For disentangling Hopkins's translations from his commentary and providing useful clarification, editing, and discussion of the Parmenides section, I owe gratitude to independent patristics scholar Dane Waterman.

42. Hopkins, *Journals and Papers*, 127.

of "instress," a term which Hopkins uses to refer to the active role of the moral will in perception.[43] He warns himself that the fragments have an "undetermined pantheist idealism which makes it hard to translate them in a subjective or in a wholly outward sense," yet notes that Parmenides' "feeling for instress, for the flush and foredrawn, and for inscape / is most striking and from this one can understand Plato's reverence for him as the great father of Realism."[44] Then Hopkins quotes the fragment that is translated by G. S. Kirk et al. as "The one [way of inquiry] that [it] is and that it is impossible for [it] not to be, is the path of Persuasion (for she attends upon truth)."[45] Hopkins associates this adage with dialectic and then interprets ἔστι, "is," as "*things are* or *there is truth.*"

Hopkins observes less separation of subject and object in Parmenides than in his own thought; it appears that Parmenides identifies existence itself with the way a being comes into reality through the act of a perceiver. Hopkins, being committed to Catholic doctrine, is neither a monist nor a "pantheist,"[46] so he does not go so far; but he is excited by the ideas because to apprehend "being" as Parmenides does,

43. Leonard Cochran, who in "Instress and Its Place in the Poetics of Gerard Manley Hopkins" quotes every use of the term and examines most of them, supports me in my interpretation of instress as a perceiving action (164), though his understanding of "being" and his acceptance of a single "essence" as central to Hopkins's vision of a thing result ultimately in a very different understanding from mine.

44. Hopkins, *Journals and Papers,* 127. I shall discuss instress in more detail later, but here it can be seen that it has to do with the "foredrawn"; my discussion of the moral aspects of the term is in Chapter 8.

45. G. S. Kirk, J. E. Raven, and M. Schofield, eds. and trans., *The Presocratic Philosophers,* 2d ed. (Cambridge, U.K.: Cambridge University Press, 1995), 245.

46. Ludwig Ott, *Fundamentals of Catholic Dogma* (Rockford, Ill.: Tan, 1974), 79. Ott refers readers to the documents of the First Vatican Council (1868), but the declarations of the Fourth Lateran Council (1215) and the unanimous testimony of the patristic and medieval theologians would do as well. It would be impossible to persuade a man with any philosophical training (especially in Newman's company!) that he could at the same time assent to Christianity and "pantheism," as Hopkins here names Parmenides' monism. Hopkins explicitly declares his opposition to monism, Hegelian or otherwise, in his letters and in his spiritual writings. Daniel Brown, in *Hopkins's Idealism,* misreads *Sermons and Devotional Writings,* 125ff., wherein Hopkins sets out, following Aquinas but with his eye on Hegel as the main opponent, to prove that a monotheist God is the creator and monism is contrary to the known experience of moral responsibility.

with his "feeling for . . . inscape," it is necessary for a person to interact with the object—to exercise the "living power" of Coleridge's Imagination. The phrase "flush and foredrawn" gives the clue; "flush" has in Hopkins's poetry the sense of a flooding of the consciousness with an experience. In translating more of Parmenides' words about the self-contained self-consistency of being, "flushness" is in apposition to a metaphoric "temper and equality of weight." The word "foredrawn" is Hopkins's rendering of συνέχεσθαι—Greek for being held together, or being continuous.[47] Hopkins is invoking the experience of perceiving something and mentally putting it together, making sense of it.

Under Newman's roof, Hopkins approaches the great pre-Socratic through Romantic epistemology. In Parmenides even more than in Coleridge, apparently, Being is fully itself only when apprehended and acknowledged; all Being must be intelligible.[48] Hopkins's sense of the limitation of individual perspective is very keen, as we have seen in his fragment about the rainbow. It remains so even as Hopkins continues his commentary, looking, like Wordsworth, to his own moments of psychological insight: "I have often felt when I have been in this mood and felt the depth of an instress or how fast the inscape holds a thing that nothing is so pregnant and straightforward to the truth as a simple *yes* and *is*." The "yes" of instress comes from the side of the observer; the "is" of inscape comes from the side of the thing observed; both are necessary for some perception to leap into real apprehension. And one needs a real world, full of inscapes demanding assent or rejection from the will, in order to think. Hopkins translates: "Thou couldst never either know or say / what was not, there would be no coming at it." Actively "coming at" knowledge is necessary. Without an active commitment of the will, an assent to the conviction that *what is, is, and what is not, is not,*

47. Liddell and Scott (*s.v.* συνέχω 2.a, passive) renders this occurrence (Parmenides 8.23) "to be continuous." Kirk, Raven, and Schofield, in *Presocratic Philosophers* (250), following the root meaning of the word, translate it as "holding together." For Hopkins's use of "flush," see stanza 8 of *The Wreck of the Deutschland,* in *Poetical Works,* 121.

48. I will below deal with the convertibility of the transcendental attributes of being; that theory asserts that being is convertible with truth. See Jorge J. E. Gracia, "The Transcendentals in the Middle Ages: An Introduction," *Topoi* 11 (1992): 113–20.

> [t]here would be no bridge, no stem of stress between us and things to bear us out and carry the mind over. Without stress we might not and could not say Blood is red / but only / this blood is red / or / The last blood I saw was red / nor even that, for in later language not only universals would not be true but the copula would break down even in particular judgments.[49]

If being were ever seriously mixed with "what was not"—fiction—no one could define, or compare ideas, or even tell the truth. The word "universals," an anachronism here, refers to the medieval controversy over whether universal terms in language—common nouns—name realities or fictions, or are labels for perceived commonalities. (Scotus engaged in this dispute, as we shall see.) Like Parmenides, Hopkins rejects what one might call the postmodern paradigm. The bridge of judgment, of commitment, is made by "stress" without which there would be no basis for any meaning, only fictional patterns of arbitrarily chosen activity. "Stress" is a rich word for Hopkins; he equates it elsewhere with ἐνέργεια in Greek.[50] The Liddell and Scott Lexicon displays a significant cluster of meanings around ἐνέργεια and related forms: at root, production, activity, and force; in connotation, "active force," "vigour of style," "supernatural action," and "to be efficacious." It is Aristotle's technical term, usually translated as "act" or "actuality," in opposition to δύναμις, "potency" or "potentiality."

Pursuing the notion of truth in language by means of Newman's theory that real apprehension of anything excludes its contrary, Hopkins translates and then quotes Parmenides' fragments that refer to logic. He quotes the fragment that Kirk et al. translate as 297: "Nor is it divided, since it all exists alike; nor is it more here and less there, which would prevent it from holding together, but it is all full of being."[51] "From holding together"—συνέχεσθαι again—Hopkins annotates as "from foredrawing." Considering the context of Newman's thought, Hopkins seems to be denying existence to whatever does not make sense—the unforedrawn. But in fact he points out Parmenides' conflation of the logical and the ontological—"shewing the mixture of

49. Hopkins, *Journals and Papers,* 127.
50. Hopkins, *Sermons and Devotional Writings,* 123.
51. Kirk, Raven, and Schofield, *Presocratic Philosophers,* 250.

real with logical in the thought"—because he does not concur in it. He agrees with Parmenides enough to believe that nothing unintelligible can exist, but Hopkins thinks that things can exist even when we don't think of them.

Newman denies real apprehension to anything intermediate between existence and nonexistence—to "contradictiories," or to the excluded middles of logic. Hopkins follows his translation, "To be and to know or Being and thought are the same," with a phrase that puts "being" in apposition to "stress." That grammatical assertion of identity reveals the influence of Newman's epistemology. Since "stress" is also identified with "efficacy" as ἐνέργεια, and considering that he wrote these notes in Newman's household while Newman was working on the *Grammar of Assent*, it seems likeliest that "stress" refers to efficacy, the "real" in Newman's sense of Real Apprehension, rather than the fully ontological meaning of real being, when Hopkins comments: "The truth in thought is being, stress, and each word is one way of acknowledging Being and each sentence by its copula *is* (or the equivalent) the utterance and assertion of it." In other words, true thought is thought sufficient to move the will, which cannot be ambivalent about assent. Hopkins then quotes in Greek the text he began to translate. Kirk et al. translate his quotation thus: "The same thing is there to be thought and is why there is thought. For you will not find thinking without what is."[52] Hopkins comments that Parmenides places the reality of a thing in "the mind's grasp—νοεῖν [knowing],[53] the foredrawing act."

In other words, for Parmenides, things come to reality in human judgment, whose fundamental criterion is the law of noncontradiction: that nothing can both be and not-be. This makes him the "father of realism": there is not one kind of Being that is logically apprehensible and another kind that is contradictory to it. Hopkins had encountered arguments made to set up a different standard for the judgment of sci-

52. Kirk, Raven, and Schofield, *Presocratic Philosophers*, 252. The word "is," ἔστι, appears alone in the text. Adding "there" to "is" unfortunately diminishes the clarity of the translation.

53. Technically, νοεῖν is an infinitive, but it is being used the way we use gerunds in English.

ence and of morality (he was a reader of Matthew Arnold), but, like Newman, disdained them.[54] Like Parmenides in being a realist, though not a monist, Hopkins cannot be shaken from the conviction that the multiple realities in any single thing cannot contradict one another.

There is a tension between Parmenides' pantheistic position, which assumes that a thing that comes into knowledge thus comes into being,[55] and the position of Hopkins, who can believe that things exist without our making sense of them. If an inscape is, as I shall argue more fully in Chapter 7, one of many possible real mental syntheses, or understandings, of a thing, then a man's inscape is either how he is seen or how he sees himself. In a pantheistic context, such as Hopkins is discussing in Parmenides' thought, such a limited judgment is something to be left behind in order to apprehend the true Unity that is everything. So as Hopkins continues his commentary, saying "The way men judge in particular is determined for each by his own inscape," he would seem to be discussing the man's self-understanding which creates the limitations under which he views the world. The more a man has of the Parmenidean "fire-principle," which Hopkins speculates is a "vital principle," the more he is likely to be able to perceive what Parmenides believes is the truth, the Unity of All. Hopkins drops into the language Newman uses—"the phenomenal world"—and points out that Parmenides' conception of things differs from his own, in that subjectivity is unimportant to the pre-Socratic. For Parmenides, the perception of the unity of being in any thing—the "foredrawing" of an inscape—is an intimation of the all-important Unity of All Things. Here Hopkins glosses Parmenides within his own square brackets, then translates (to the close parenthesis), and emerges into the commentary (wherein is another parenthesis):

> . . . [there are ten thousand men to think and ten thousand things for them to think of but they are but names given and taken, eye and lip service to the

54. See Matthew Arnold, *St. Paul and Protestantism,* in *Works,* 6:9–10, and *Literature and Dogma,* in *Works,* 6:172–73. See also my "Ernest Renan's Averroism in the Religious Thought of Matthew Arnold," *Nineteenth Century Prose* 22 (Spring 1995): 34–53.

55. Daniel Brown, in *Hopkins's Idealism,* does not make it explicit whether the Hegelians to whom Hopkins was exposed as an undergraduate advocated a similar position.

truth, husks and scapes of it: the truth itself, the burl,] the fulness is the thought') For the phenomenal world (and the distinction between men or subjects and the things without them is unimportant in Parmenides: the contrast is between the one and the many) is the brink, limbus, lapping, run-and-mingle / of two principles which meet in the scape of everything—probably Being, under its modification or siding of particular oneness or Being, and Not-Being, under its siding of the Many. . . . The inscape will be the proportion of the mixture.[56]

"The burl" is an expression used in other private notes by Hopkins with the sense of something round that can be cut to show the beholder some "cleave" or "scape." To some degree, anyone catching an inscape will see unity and also distinguish between the thing understood and other things; the unity Parmenides would see as truth, the distinction as illusion, and, as Hopkins puts it, "The inscape will be the proportion of the mixture." Presumably each man would mix unity and distinction in different proportions, according to his degree of "fire." From Hopkins's point of view, Parmenides has it almost right: a perceiver seeks to make sense of a thing and to withdraw the will's recognition from a thing's lack of unity or "Not-being." The notebook's preceding pages define particular "oneness": "the comparison the mind has to keep making between the whole and its parts, the parts and the whole. For this reference or comparison is what the sense of unity means; mere sense or value that such a thing is one and not two has no interest or value except accidentally."[57] The object itself has its own oneness and being, the "burl," perceived in multitudinous ways. It is many in its scapes, but each of these many scapes leaves out some thing—in other words, is associated with some Not-Being, a failure to recognize some aspect of the thing in seeing only "Being under its modification or siding of particular oneness or Being." Inscape rests in the tension between a unity perceived in an object and the multiplicity of its possibilities—especially the possibility of its having no unity at all. Instress comes of having given oneself over in commitment to unity perceived.

56. Hopkins, *Journals and Papers*, 130.
57. Hopkins, *Journals and Papers*, 126.

"Catching" an inscape is always an intensely personal action. When Hopkins writes of catching inscapes, he could be Wordsworth taking notes on "spots of time":

Green-white tufts of long bleached grass like heads of hair or the crowns of heads of hair, each a whorl of slender curves, one tuft taking up another—however these I might have noticed any day. I saw the inscape though freshly, as if my eye were still growing, though with a companion the eye and the ear are for the most part shut and instress cannot come.[58]

He is also saddened by the fact that not everyone sees inscapes as he does; "I thought how sadly beauty of inscape was unknown and buried away from simple people and yet how near at hand it was if they had eyes to see it and it could be called out everywhere again."[59] The world's illimitable mystery harbors worlds that not all can see. Some leave hints of their existence: the academic world, the scientific world, the political world. Spiritual realities are apprehended by those who can find them, who must choose to have faith in them or not. Newman's epistemology of course supports and springs from the concept of multiple presence in sacraments.[60] That the word "reality" applies to spiritual matters as well as physical ones was never in doubt in Newman's mind or in Hopkins's, which is why both could believe in the Real Presence of Christ in the Eucharist before coming to the Roman Catholic opinion concerning the physical presence of Christ's body there (transubstantiation).[61] We shall see in our next chapter

58. Hopkins, *Journals and Papers,* 228.

59. Hopkins, *Journals and Papers,* 221.

60. See Newman, *Grammar of Assent,* 376–78, for an account of spiritual realities and also an indication of how the notion of spiritual realities fits with Newman's sacramental theology. In the sacramentalism of the Tractarians—which was emphatic, and accepted the notion of the Real Presence, contrary to the assertion of Lichtmann, in *Contemplative Poetry,* 177, Newman found a solution to the problem of the world seeming shadowy to him, as if it were only a symbol for something else.

61. Margaret Johnson makes this fundamental error, confusing the real with the physical in her discussion of the "Anglican viewpoint as expressed in the Book of Common Prayer that Christ was present in the bread and wine in a spiritual rather than a real sense" (*Hopkins and Tractarian Poetry,* 243, n82). The opposite of "real" in the philosophical world of these men was "logical" or, as Newman liked to put it, "notional." The Roman Catholic doctrine of transubstantiation asserts that the body of Christ is corpo-

how sacraments claim a reality beyond that of a comforting symbol or persuasive fiction. Hopkins believed that water, used sacramentally, could cleanse not just the body but the soul, and that bread and wine could be either a simple meal or God's self-sacrifice. But, for Hopkins, we shall see the world become sacramental, for all things have latent in them an infinity of realities to which our senses do not ordinarily admit us. But some people have "seen something," as Hopkins put it. Those who trust such visionaries, and indeed any people in a community who love and trust one another, can uncover new and unsuspected aspects of the world.

Hopkins does emphatically acknowledge that the world is full of spiritual realities awaiting discovery. Nevertheless, the context of the first appearance of "inscape" makes it clear that inscape is for Hopkins an intellectual phenomenon, rather than an experience of the immanence of God available only to the "pure of heart."[62] The association of mystical or contemplative spirituality with Hopkins, although common,[63] is a disservice both to the severe discipline of the contemplative vocation and to the poet. Although familiar with mystical writings, he was never a mystic, and never experienced even the "dark night of the sense," the withdrawal from the world that precedes the "dark night of the soul" in John of the Cross.[64] Guided by Catholic theology, but in-

really present in the Communion elements—but even that doctrine does not require its adherents to hold that to be real is to be corporeal.

62. Cotter, *Inscape*, 24.

63. A convenient list is provided by Donald Walhout in *Send My Roots Rain* (Athens: Ohio University Press, 1981), 140–41 and nn 47 and 48; cf. also n49. Since then, several major studies have continued the trend; see Lichtmann, *Contemplative Poetry*, 13 and also 129, where she calls inscape a "religious experience." Eleanor J. McNees, in her *Eucharistic Poetry: The Search for Presence in the Writings of John Donne, Gerard Manley Hopkins, Dylan Thomas, and Geoffrey Hill* (Lewisburg, Pa.: Bucknell University Press, 1992), seems to argue that the ability to perceive inscape is due to "prior reception and acknowledgment of grace" (77), which would exclude the pagan pantheist Parmenides, according to Hopkins's understanding of paganism. (In McNees's work, the word "Transubstantiation" seems to collect meanings rather loosely connected to those specific to philosophical theology.) Even Loomis, in *Dayspring in Darkness*, 143, has Hopkins undergoing *"deificatio"* in his Terrible Sonnets.

64. John of the Cross, *Ascent of Mount Carmel*, 3d rev. ed., ed. E. Allison Peers (Garden City, N.Y.: Image Books, 1958), 103–5.

tensely practical, Jesuit spirituality directs its adherents outward toward service and accomplishment in the world. (Hopkins bemoans to the end of his life his lack of external productivity.) Though great mystics sometimes accomplish worldly wonders, the discipline of mystical spirituality, such as that of Theresa of Avila or John of the Cross, demands an indifference to one's sensual surroundings and one's roles; the mystic seeks God alone. The *Spiritual Exercises* of Saint Ignatius Loyola constantly prod Jesuits to recollect sensory experience (the taste of tears, the feeling of flame) and consider further action, rather than flee the senses and wait in contemplative passivity. Jesuits seek no "kenosis of the intellect";[65] in the Fourth Exercise of the First Week, for example, "the intellect, carefully and without digressing onto any other subject, should range over the memory of matters contemplated in the previous Exercises."[66] Hopkins's poetry flows from a religious discipline that is meant to obey, not transcend, reason.

Hopkins's concept of "inscape" had roots in Newman's Romantic epistemology, though Hopkins's encounter with Duns Scotus deepened his insight. I will discuss Scotus in Chapter 7, but it is well to note here that Scotus developed his own epistemology in the midst of the controversy over the universals which Hopkins mentioned in his notes on Parmenides. Newman also eagerly took sides on it in a later chapter of the *Grammar of Assent*, saying that an individual human being

> is more than a universal. . . . John, Richard and Robert are individual things, independent, incommunicable. We may find some sort of common measure between them, and we may give it the name of man, man as such, the typical man. . . . Not any one of them is man, as such. . . . John is not necessarily rational, because "all men are rational."[67]

But the coining of a universal term to label a perceived commonality is only a special case of the effort to make sense of things in the world.

The judgment involved in making sense of a thing can spark an inscape into act as a *reality* in Newman's sense, which resides in the

65. Contrast to Lichtmann, *Contemplative Poetry*, 140ff.

66. Ignatius Loyola, *Saint Ignatius: Personal Writings*, trans. Joseph A. Munitz and Philip Endean (New York: Penguin Books, 1996), 298.

67. *Grammar of Assent*, 223–24.

mind of the perceiver. The perceiver is morally responsible for the truth of the judgments made. It dishonors the Creator to deny the world's internal logic; God made it good and intelligible in order to lead humankind to him. An undependable world, in which something could exist and fail to exist at the same time, would be a world that was not good. If denying the world's intelligibility is to refuse to acknowledge God's goodness, to betray it by lying is malice.

Hopkins had come to Newman with a sense that abstractions provided better access to truth than did sense experiences. Once freed of that constriction, and convinced that the real apprehension of truth is within the capacity of everyone, he discards the obtrusive efforts to provide readers with guidance that cumber his Oxford poems. He enters into informal dialogue with his readers, presuming that they share access to a common, real world.[68] Though Patricia Ball unguardedly assumes that Hopkins's language is meant to reproduce rather than reveal experience, Ball's insight does not fail her when she says that Hopkins's subjectivity leads to accessibility rather than to diminishment.[69] Hopkins's elaborate, sometimes opaque, technique displays faith that there is no unintelligible aspect of being. He wrote to Bridges of one of his pieces of music:

> [S]tudy it yourself till you see my meaning (it is slow and easy to play); it is a test too: if you do not like it is because there is something you have not seen and I see. That at least is my mind, and if the whole world agreed to condemn it or see nothing in it I should only tell them to take a generation and come to me again.[70]

He boldly invited his almost sole reader and critic constantly to "say yes" even to those elements of the poems that he could not yet understand, because Hopkins was confident that if Bridges let the words reside in his memory they would "explode" into meaning.[71]

68. Loomis, in *Dayspring in Darkness,* 86, finds some of those presumptions—well, presumptuous. He is right about the opacity that that confidence gives Hopkins's work. It does not always succeed; but when it does we get "a shock," as Hopkins put it, and the shock would not come, I think, without such confidence in his readers.

69. Ball, *The Science of Aspects,* 146.

70. Hopkins, *Letters to Bridges,* 214 (1 April 1885).

71. Hopkins, *Letters to Bridges,* 90 (8 Oct. 1879).

Having gained that confidence, Hopkins left the Oratory, two weeks after Newman reported that he was "transcribing" the "First part of my essay," the *Grammar of Assent.* Among other topics there discussed, Newman commented on how the impression of the imagination is the method for best arousing the Christian to action[72]—the Jesuit technique he had seen as particularly suitable for his young friend Hopkins:

> You are quite out, in thinking that when I offered you a "home" here, I dreamed of your having a vocation for us. This I saw clearly you had *not,* from the moment you came to us. Don't call "the Jesuit discipline hard," it will bring you to Heaven. The Benedictines would not have suited you.[73]

However, Hopkins's movement from the calculated Jesuit employment of emotion for rational ends into a more complex epistemology is partly Newman's work—for Hopkins, on his own, most likely would have striven for repression and narrow logic. Indeed, his poems are strongly marked by Jesuit meditative techniques; the emotions evoked by their imagery do serve rather than control the religious content. But they are also present for their own sake, with a candor like that of the great Romantics.

For the rest of his life, Hopkins continued to be interested in the things he had learned at the Oratory. A friend of Hopkins's from the Oratory, who had gone a very different way in his life, and had not seen or written him in years, recalled Hopkins's strong interest in the foundations of language and sent him an article on it in 1881.[74] Hopkins's interest in the *Grammar of Assent* also continued; twice in 1883, thirteen years after the book was published, Hopkins wrote to Newman requesting permission to write a commentary on it. Newman had written many books; the subject matter of this one attracted Hopkins at least as much as his desire to keep up his friendship with Newman.

72. Nicholas Lash, "Introduction" to John Henry Newman, *An Essay in Aid of a Grammar of Assent,* 7–8; Newman, *Grammar of Assent,* 79. This might be called phronesis.

73. Hopkins, *Further Letters,* 408 (14 May 1868).

74. Hopkins, *Journals and Papers,* 378. Henry Challis sent Hopkins his composition "On Language as the Vehicle of Thought" in 1881.

Newman demurred: "[T]o say that a comment may be appended to my small book because one may be made on Aristotle ought to make me blush purple!"[75] Hopkins had declared while he was at the Oratory (that is, before he read Scotus) that he thought Aristotle "the be-all and end-all of philosophy"; Newman knew what admiration Hopkins was expressing for the *Grammar of Assent*.[76] Hopkins never wrote his commentary; one can wish the cardinal had been less modest.

In an 1883 Scotist-influenced commentary on Ignatius Loyola's *Spiritual Exercises*, Hopkins continued to contemplate the simple *Yes* and *is* of his notes on Parmenides. When Hopkins discusses the freedom of the will, his thoughts turn to assertion, logic, and assent:

> . . . [S]imple positiveness, that by which being differs from and is more than nothing and not-being . . . is with precision expressed by the English *do* (the simple auxiliary), which when we employ or emphasise, as "he said it, he did say it," we do not mean that the fact is any more a fact but that we the more state it. (It is also at the bottom of the copula in logic) So that this pitch [a word designating a component of the self in Hopkins's private vocabulary] might be expressed, if it were good English, the doing be, the doing choose, the doing so-and-so in that sense. Where there was no question of will it would become mere fact; where there is will it is free action, moral action.[77]

In other words, the "truth in thought is being" for a moral agent; in some way, one's very self is a matter of *doing* choice—not in the circumstances of choice that one encounters but in the degree to which one assents to truths. Otherwise, as he puts it, one's circumstances and perceptions are "mere fact" and do not spring into full reality.

We will meet these concepts in more stringently defined ways in Scotus. But the concepts Hopkins discovered in Scotus were already crudely set forth in the notebooks he kept at the Oratory. In the same place, at the same time, Newman was writing his own accounts of the role of the will in the perception of the "phenomenal world." Hopkins, Newman, and Scotus all agree that knowledge is humanly available only within a knower who gains it through the senses, and that there is

75. Hopkins, *Further Letters*, 412 (27 Feb. and 26 April 1883).
76. Hopkins, *Further Letters*, 231 (to A. W. M. Baillie, 12 Feb. 1868).
77. Hopkins, *Sermons and Devotional Writings*, 151.

one central impulse at work in language, indeed in any human encounter with the world: moral choice, the exercise of free will.

Hopkins wrote no serious poetry between his stay at the Oratory and a word dropped by his Jesuit superior in December 1875, which opened the barrier he had set against composition and spurred the composition of *The Wreck of the Deutschland.* In the seven years between the "slaughter of the innocents" (the burning of his own copies of his undergraduate poems)[78] and *The Wreck,* he became a Catholic seminarian and a serious student of Scholastic philosophy, in particular the work of Duns Scotus. It is not possible, therefore, to find poetry in which the influence of Newman comes without that of Scotus.[79] Still, it is worth attending to the particular traces of the thought of the author of the *Grammar of Assent* in a typical poem of Hopkins's first mature phase, "The Starlight Night." Its riotous richness is utterly uncharacteristic of the poetry he wrote before his conversion. The thing he seeks to awaken in his reader is a felt reality, not a distilled idea—not notions but active realities of a number of experiences. His poetry emphasizes the moral component of perception. He urges on his readers first the basic perception that the world is good and then the further faith necessary for accepting the Christian revelation. Observe how multiplicities of presence and meaning appear also in the multiple relationships established by the way the poet plays with patterns of sound. The alliteration and the complex rhythm are not just decoration; the multilayered complexity displays Hopkins's faith that all sorts of interrelationships are important because they are real "relations of things" and therefore part of our encounter with God's intended order in the world. Listen particularly to the complex rhythm—the poem, like all Hopkins's poems, is meant for reading aloud:

The Starlight Night

Look at the stars! look, look up at the skies!
  O look at all the fire-folk sitting in the air!

78. Hopkins, *Journals and Papers,* 165 and note.

79. Hopkins published one poem, "The Elopement," in the Oratory school newspaper; it is not one of his best productions. It draws on material from his earlier diaries. He also made several free translations of classical lyrics.

The bright bóroughs, the circle-citadels there!
Down in dim woods the diamond delves! the elves'-eyes!
The grey lawns cold where gold, where quickgold lies!
Wind-beat whitebeam! airy⁀abeles set on a flare!
Flake-doves sent floating forth at a farmyard scare!—
Ah well! it is all a purchase, all is a prize.

Buy then! bid then!—What?—Prayer, pátience, alms, vows.
Look, look: a May-mess, like on orchard boughs!
Look! March-bloom, like on mealed-with-yellow sallows!
These are indeed the barn; withindoors house
The shocks. This piece-bright paling shuts the spouse
Christ home, Christ and his mother and all his hallows.[80]

The poem is an invitation to join in looking at a thing, not an authoritative description. Hopkins addresses his audience as his equals before a world he sees with a most unnerving kind of variety. Witness the kind of things he sees in the stars—cities, elves—sentient beings, mysteriously populated habitations. And he invokes hidden riches: diamond delves, that is to say, diamond mines, in dim woods. This isn't just a sky; these are the heavens, populated with mysterious beings and mysterious riches. The key to it is mystery.

Hopkins noted that this sonnet was in "standard rhythm opened and counterpointed." By "counterpointed," he means that there are two rhythms, in a way, running at once, as there are two tunes running at once in a counterpointed piece of music; musicians actually call the effect that Hopkins is describing "cross-rhythm" rather than "counterpoint." In this case, the result is, first, that there remains an exquisite uncertainty about whether the whole poem is in iambic or trochaic pentameter; and second, that in some lines the standard two-syllable rhythm suddenly breaks out into anapests. By "opened" he may mean varied in speed. Some lines must be said quickly and others are temporally very long, for they must be said very slowly. The slow "Buy, then, bid then!—What? Prayer, patience, alms, vows"—precedes a rapid exclamation—"Look, look, a May-mess, like on orchard boughs!" The variation in rhythm creates, compels, a dramatic reading of the

80. Hopkins, "The Starlight Night," in *Poetical Works*, 139–40.

sober moral advice. Moment by moment, Hopkins presents an interaction between the rhythm and the meaning that one would ordinarily associate only with an instrumental musical score. Hopkins has bound together the human drama of the poem and its rhythm in a way completely unlike the steady beat of his early poems. In those, the rhythm served mostly as an additional beauty and rarely was integrated with the subject matter except to act as a restraint in poetry about restraint; here the rhythm richly reinforces the subject matter.

His philosopher's drive for the activity of instressing he had expressed in his Oratory notebook:

> Art exacts this energy of contemplation. . . . The more intellectual, less physical, the spell of contemplation the more complex must be the object, the more close and elaborate must be the comparison the mind has to keep making between the whole and its parts, the parts and the whole.[81]

Thus he adds another layer of comparison in his patterns of alliteration, assonance, and rhyme. Each sound, considered as a unit, is a thing, an experience, and since it is real it has innumerable aspects. And each group of sounds, considered as a unit, has its own innumerable aspects, all real, all showing forth something of God's infinite store of reality. We have elves and diamond delves—say it fast and you have elves of diamond. In the same way, there is more than one thing happening even in the rhythm. And there is more than one aspect to the stars. Not only are there perhaps sentient beings looking out from the stars, or at any rate stars looking like sentient beings (in the words of another poem, perhaps "immortal diamonds"). Not only that—there are other things happening here that we cannot see. There is a harvest going on here; the imagery brings us from woods to a cultivated poplar, the whitebeam, and finally to a farmyard and a barn for harvest ingathering.

For Hopkins there is only one kind of grain that is important, and that is the biblical "grain of wheat which falls into the earth and dies": the soul of the believer united to Christ. This grain is crushed to become the Body of Christ. And deep within his account of this world of

81. Hopkins, *Journals and Papers,* 126.

stars, which seems to be populated, we find that the world he is seeing is indeed populated by that grain, by the Body of Christ in the Church Triumphant: "Christ and his mother and all his hallows."

Newman did not assume any necessary continuity between what we perceive by our senses and the actual things that those perceptions indicate.[82] Scotus did, and Hopkins, who had read Scotus before he wrote this poem, is bolder still. He simply asserts that this contact with earthly beauty is a real contact with the Communion of Saints because it is a taste of the reality that they also encounter. Hopkins invites us as his readers to inhabit his very particular and peculiar ways of seeing the stars, to trust him and enjoy whatever inscapes we can catch. He invites us by wild metaphors to take a taste of the things he is seeing. And the invitation, he ultimately makes clear to us, is a moral challenge. In order to see Christ's "paling" properly, to possess, to apprehend in the most basic sense of that word, we must engage in "prayer, patience, alms, vows." We must pitch our souls properly; alms, he once suggested to his agnostic friend Bridges, are the easiest direct access to God.[83]

Much of the imagery in the poem comes from economics, by way of an allusion to "Church Porch" by George Herbert,[84] but the exchange of "patience" for the beauty of the earth is not an ordinary Christian theme; usually it is for salvation from sin that economic metaphors of debt and redemption are used. (In ancient Israel, one redeemed property by paying the debts of a relative in order to keep the land in the family.) What is happening here is more than an exchange; it is a sacrifice. One is asked to exchange all that one is for more than one could ever comprehend. The vow demands the gift of an entire self, the taking of oneself into one's own hands to be spent for a good that is beyond the possibility of one's own experience. The vow here is

82. Newman, *Grammar of Assent,* 96. He thinks the senses are "true, but not adequate."

83. Hopkins, *Letters to Bridges,* 60 (19 Jan. 1879).

84. As pointed out by Bridges, quoted in Catherine Phillips, *The Oxford Authors Gerard Manley Hopkins* (Oxford, U.K., and New York: Oxford University Press, 1986), 348 (note to l.8).

to the Spouse: Christ considered as spouse of the soul and spouse of the Church. We are being invited to a wedding, and we are the bride.

Newman's philosophy lives in this poem, but not precisely in its argument. Hopkins is not describing but inhabiting Newman's philosophical landscape. This is what you see, he is saying, when you understand the world as a place to which we must give assent, which we can contemplate. This is the sort of thing that happens when you recognize a multiplicity of real presences in the world. Newman had asserted the need for this faith in its boldest form, as against Arnoldian pessimism: "[T]o pronounce by anticipation, what it takes a long argument to prove—that good is the rule, and evil the exception."[85] There is no security; this is a bid, a purchase, a personal commitment. Yet once we trust that our experience is good, Hopkins argues, the world opens to us; once we understand what we are doing by believing, belief becomes possible, and if we learn to look and to say a simple *yes* and *is*, we can be home with Christ and his mother and all his hallows.

Having imbibed the Romantic epistemology of Newman, Hopkins was no longer hampered on his way to the ontological by the fear of the psychological. The "religious reserve" of Tractarian poetic practice no longer had a hold over his mind. He had no need to fear inflaming emotion, no pressing obligation to be impersonal or dispassionate; he no longer resisted the world of the senses per se. Confident that though its reality resides within the knower, truth is not a convenient, subjective fiction, Hopkins was prepared for a vision of poetry as an intellectual art awakening other minds to real apprehension of meaning in the world by means of words. He learned from Newman that meaning must be real and therefore personal. Having learned that, and taken it to heart, Hopkins needed no longer to hold in reserve his passion for his God, "Beauty's self and Beauty's giver."

85. Newman, *Grammar of Assent*, 106.

CHAPTER 6

SACRAMENTS AND POETRY

HOPKINS GAINED his mature understanding of philosophical theology in the Jesuit seminary. After three years there studying "philosophy," which included rhetoric, natural sciences, mathematics, and logic, he pursued theology for three more years, and then was ordained. Forearmed with Newman's epistemology, he deepened his concept of multiple realities when he studied the sacraments according to the Jesuits' official theologian, Thomas Aquinas, as elaborated by the Jesuit Francisco Suarez (1548–1617), whose approach dominated the Jesuit *Ratio Studiorum* in theology (to the exclusion of theologians whom Hopkins found more interesting).[1] From the seminary on, a specifically Roman Catholic sacramental vision permeates Hopkins's poetic themes and practices. I will trace his sacramental theology first in the argument of a poem about a sacrament, "At the Wedding March," and then in the imagery of a nature poem, "Hurrahing in Harvest"; finally, we will see in "God's Grandeur" how even the technical innovations he pursued in meter—the machine language of poetry, as it were—manifest his understanding of sacraments.

Unfortunately, by "sacramental," critics of Hopkins too often mean a vague sense of the numinous, or enthusiastic religious emotion, or sometimes references to liturgical practices.[2] Of course, a sense of the

1. Thomas, *Hopkins the Jesuit*, 95 n1, 97. Cf. Joseph J. Feeney, S.J., "Hopkins' 'Failure' in Theology"; also *Correspondence with Dixon*, 95 (1 Dec. 1881).

2. Lichtmann's definition—"identity between heaven and earth" (*Contemplative Poetry*, 177)—makes a sacrament more like a mystical union than does Catholic theology, which divides symbol *(sacramentum)* and reality *(res)*. All Catholic sacraments do spring from the Incarnation; but only one embodies it. Sulloway ("sacrament of energy," *Gerard Manley Hopkins and the Victorian Temper*, 78ff.) and Robert Lowell ("Hop-

numinous, religious emotion, and liturgy all appear in Hopkins's poetry—but to look for the intellectual core of his work is to move beyond ritual and well beyond a mere generalized feeling about something spiritually nourishing in the beauty of the world. Sacramentality is sacrificial, having to do with loss as well as joy; it perceives God's action in scenes that are not at all attractive to the senses. Moreover, sacramental theology is an intellectually self-consistent system. It asserts that the multiple meanings of sacramental actions are not mere subjective interpretations or manipulations of feeling but realities, existent whether or not they are recognized by any human mind. Sacraments opened Hopkins to the idea that physical realities could become spiritual realities with no diminution of their physical existence. Hopkins already saw the trivialities of the world as dignified by the fact that God had deigned to become human; his sacramental vision removes all sense of incongruity from that insight. Without deifying the world, Hopkins could take all creation as a manifestation of the incar-

kins's Sanctity," in *Gerard Manley Hopkins, by the Kenyon Critics,* ed. John Crowe Ransom [Norfolk, Conn.: New Directions, 1945], 91) mostly emphasize religious emotion. The phrase "doubled presence" (McNees, *Eucharistic Poetry,* 73) describes the Real Presence, but is not the same as "inscaping," though to perceive the Presence would be to encounter an inscape. McNees is perceptive, but leans toward hyperbole; the immanent mode of Logos in the world is not technically the incarnational Real Presence (97). Margaret Johnson (in *Hopkins and Tractarian Poetry,* 188–89) correctly distinguishes between "transubstantiation" and Real Presence, but overstates the degree of identification between Christ and the world, even when conceived as the sacrament of creation (182). David McChesney, *A Hopkins Commentary* (New York: State University of New York Press, 1968); Paul Mariani, *A Commentary on the Complete Poems of Gerard Manley Hopkins* (Ithaca, N.Y.: Cornell University Press, 1970); Alan Heuser, *The Shaping Vision of Gerard Manley Hopkins* (London: Oxford University Press, 1958); David Anthony Downes, *The Great Sacrifice: Studies in Hopkins* (Lanham, Md.: University Press of America, 1983), and Loomis, *Dayspring in Darkness,* accurately describe liturgical sacramentality. I expand their understanding's aesthetic implications. Ellis implies sacramental multiplicity in her fine work on "God's Grandeur" (*Language of Mystery,* 123–33) and "Hurrahing in Harvest" (139–43), but does not explicitly discuss the theology. Good work on the theological underpinnings of sacramental language in Hopkins appears in Peter Erb, "Perichoresis and the Poetry of Hopkins," *Hopkins Quarterly* 11, nos. 3–4 (Fall 1984–Winter 1985): 67–78, and James Walter, "Perspectives of Symbol and Allegory in 'The Windhover,'" *Hopkins Quarterly* 12, nos. 3–4 (Oct. 1985–Jan. 1986): 115–17. Boyle's "existential metaphor" well communicates the role of sacraments in Hopkins, I think, though he presumes an audience better educated in theology than is common now.

nate Christ. Each thing in its own particular excellence acts the part of Christ in the world, and may be celebrated and loved in itself, because to rejoice in a thing in itself is to celebrate Christ.

Roman Catholic theology describes sacraments as the "ordinary means" to salvation. Mere human effort cannot save anyone from sin and death, but God sends grace to human beings by human, social, visible means. The practical answer to the question "What must I do to be saved?" is in sacraments, each an "effective sign of God's grace." Sacraments define Roman Catholic Church membership, its organizational structure, its primary activities, and the peculiar character of its thought.[3]

A sacrament has three modes of effectiveness. The least important, purely symbolic mode, didactic in character and visible on the physical level, is called the *sacramentum.* The most spiritually important mode of operation is called the *res,* or "reality." The *res* is the supernatural grace that the recipient receives or refuses. However, anything can be a didactic device, and God may offer grace through decidedly extraecclesiastical means. What makes a sacrament different from a clever analogy or a private religious experience is the middle mode of sacramental effectiveness, the *res et sacramentum.*[4] The *res et sacramentum* establishes relationships that symbolize the action of God in relation to his people. The sacramental language of Hopkins functions in precisely this way, creating a reality that, like a *res et sacramentum,* is itself a symbol. In the case of poetry, the relationships established are aural, grammatical, and semantic rather than social. Still, they must be recognized in order to emerge into full reality.

In a sacrament, the *sacramentum,* or symbol,[5] employs things directly accessible to the senses—water, oil, bread, wine, words—to edify

3. There is even a system of canon law, complete with courts and lawyers, almost exclusively concerned with defining who can and should, under which circumstances, receive or administer sacraments, and how a sacrament can be validly administered.

4. Msgr. Joseph Pohle, *The Sacraments: A Dogmatic Treatise,* 4 vols., 4th rev. ed., ed. Arthur Preuss (St. Louis, Mo.: B. Herder Book Co., 1917), 1:81–83. This element of a sacrament may also be called the *res et simul sacramentum.*

5. The English technical term in use is "sign," but the specialized use of that word in literary study accords less closely with the meaning than does "symbol."

witnesses, including the person administering it, about the ritual. Canon law considers a sacrament valid even if neither the recipient nor the minister understands the symbols well. Conversely, understanding does not, in itself, bring access to God's grace. A good symbol is, in Newman's terms, purely notional: it may open minds to religious reflections, which provide an opportunity for the will to turn to God, but it may not. Sometimes sacramental symbols evoke little religious reflection even for people educated in their meanings. According to the capacity of the person, some doctrinal knowledge is important to salvation—that there is one God, for instance—but no cognitive sign in itself suffices for salvific grace. Likewise, poems or art may move the intellect or the feelings, but cannot extricate a person from a corrupt moral will. Sacraments take effect neither as advertising nor as magic. A sacrament has an effect even if the sentiments and understanding of everyone involved in the ritual are skewed in some direction other than that appropriate to the grace they are supposed to receive. God's saving grace, the *res*, can be accepted or rejected by the believer. Grace does not take effect in every sacrament administered, although it is always available there. Yet even if the participants reject God's offered grace in a sacrament, the Church asserts, the rite properly performed makes something happen. That event, the *res et sacramentum*, is the same as the event that happens when everyone involved does understand the symbolism and fully experience God's grace in the sacrament.

Res et sacramentum means "the thing-which-is-also-a-sign." The *res et sacramentum* establishes a relationship between the recipient and the Christian community; this relationship is also a sign, symbolizing the relationship of God to the baptized believer.[6] For instance, in mat-

6. There are seven liturgical sacraments. Baptism initiates one into the Christian community. Confirmation establishes full membership, and is required (Canon 645) for entry into a religious order or the clerical state, and encouraged, though not required, before marriage. Penance (Confession) reestablishes a broken relationship with the Church. The Anointing of the Sick (formerly known as Extreme Unction) establishes a claim for "support" under the circumstance of serious illness and cannot be administered to one who resists unity with the community; see Canon 1007: "The Anointing of the Sick is not to be conferred upon those who obstinately persist in manifest serious sin." Holy Orders ordains a priest, with associated privileges and obligations. Matrimony creates a marriage, including the couple's relationship to the community at large. The

rimony, the vows are the *sacramentum*, symbolizing the relationship the parties wish to establish. The marriage itself, an unbreakable bond of obligation and love, is the *res et sacramentum;* that bond, in turn, symbolizes the relationship between God and his people. The relationship continues to exist even if one of the persons involved misunderstands or repudiates it; this is the reasoning behind the Catholic prohibition on divorce and remarriage. Returning excommunicates or apostates are never rebaptized, because once baptized they have the spiritual rights of Christians, regardless of their subsequent actions. The status gained is legal and, in a way, impersonal, binding upon the Church even if the member utterly rejects God's grace. Faithfully upholding one's sacramental commitments is evidence presumptive of God's action in one's life, but only God knows the state of the individual soul; the relationship established by the sacrament is only an instrument and a symbol of salvation, not salvation itself. Catholic theologians agree that grace is unfailingly available in the sacraments; still, there are countless ways for humans to thwart it.

Liberal nineteenth-century theology—what Hopkins scornfully called "an enlightened Christianity"—held that knowing about Jesus and feeling an attachment to him subdues evil tendencies. Such exemplarism is cognitive, like the *sacramentum,* but it is not supernatural. The access to the supernatural offered by the sacraments is the *res,* the reality, for which they exist. The sacramental act of Hopkins's poems does seek the liberals' real apprehension of God's presence and activity, but in a way that involves the reader in a complex of relationships. It seeks to evoke not approbation of an idea but an encounter with the reality of God in the True and the Beautiful.

Hopkins honors the sacrament of matrimony in "At the Wedding March," an unusually straightforward lyric that follows the definitions from the Code of Canon Law:

Eucharist is a special case and will be discussed in more detail below, but it at least defines Christian unity; intercommunion is church unity, and excommunication excludes one from the community. Cf. Pohle, *The Sacraments: A Dogmatic Treatise,* vol. 1; Ludwig Ott, *Fundamentals of Catholic Dogma* (Rockford, Ill.: Tan, 1974); and Canon Law Society of America, *Code of Canon Law,* Latin-English edition (Washington, D.C.: Canon Law Society of America, 1983).

The matrimonial covenant, by which a man and a woman establish between themselves a partnership of the whole of life, is by its nature ordered toward the good of the spouses and the procreation and education of the offspring.

Canon Law declares that it establishes

a bond between the spouses which by its very nature is perpetual and exclusive; furthermore, in a Christian marriage, the spouses are strengthened and, as it were, consecrated for the duties and dignity of their state by a special sacrament. Each of the spouses has equal obligations and rights to those things which pertain to the partnership of conjugal life.[7]

Hopkins opens his poem by pointing out, as the canon does, that a spiritual benefit is conferred upon those who marry; then he proceeds to consider the three necessary components of Catholic marriage. Hopkins first emphasizes its openness to procreation. Second, he indicates that the strictly marital aspects of the relationship must be equal and exclusive; adultery and polygamy are forbidden. Hopkins uses one of the few surviving dual forms in English, "other"—common enough, but quite precise here. Third, he stresses that the relationship is lifelong. To see Hopkins at work on sacramental theology in this poem is to see the difference between the notional language of the law books and the language of real encounters:

At the Wedding March

Gód with honour hang your head,
Gróom, and grace you, bride, your bed
With lissome scions, swéet scíons
Out of hallowed bodies bred.

Eách be other's comfort kind:
Déep, déeper than divined,
Divíne chárity, déar chárity
Fast you ever, fást bínd.

Then let the Márch tréad our ears
I' to hím túrn with tears
Whó to wedlock, hís wónder wedlock
Déals tríumph and immortal years.[8]

7. Canons 1055, p. 387, and 1134–35, p. 411.
8. Hopkins, "At the Wedding March," in *Poetical Works*, 164.

The poem's sprung rhythm permits two emphatic syllables placed next to each other. It also permits more "slack" syllables to separate stresses than conventional, or "running," rhythm. The subtle effects of emphasis that Hopkins counts among the advantages of sprung rhythm are here used to illuminate the theology.

He also employs alliterative devices for rhetorical effect. The opening couplet of the prayer is in simple iambic tetrameter, but the alliteration makes several theological points: it connects God, the groom, and grace; it connects "hang your head" with "honour"; and it connects the bride, the bed, and, two lines later, "bodies bred." The distinction of pattern according to sex is significant. The most important biblical text for the sacramental character of marriage is Ephesians 5.20–32.

> Giving thanks always for all things, in the name of our Lord Jesus Christ, to God and the father: Being subject one to another, in the fear of Christ. Let women be subject to their husbands, as to the Lord: Because the husband is the head of the wife, as Christ is the head of the church. He is the saviour of his body. Therefore as the church is subject to Christ, so also let the wives be to their husbands in all things. Husbands, love your wives, as Christ also loved the church, and delivered himself up for it: That he might sanctify it, cleansing it by the laver of water in the word of life: That he might present it to himself a glorious church, not having spot or wrinkle, or any such thing; but that it should be holy, and without blemish. So also ought men to love their wives as their own bodies. He that loveth his wife, loveth himself. For no man ever hated his own flesh; but nourisheth and cherisheth it, as also Christ doth the church: Because we are members of his body, of his flesh, and of his bones. For this cause shall a man leave his father and mother, and shall cleave to his wife, and they shall be two in one flesh. This is a great sacrament; but I speak in Christ and in the Church.[9]

The groom is honored by his office, and honored not merely by the bride but by God; however, the honor is in his office being that of Christ, who "loved the church and delivered himself up for it." Christ's gift was to be the victim of a rigged trial, public ridicule, and death by slow torture. An executed victim, like a sacrificial animal, suffers with

9. Douay-Rheims version, the Vatican-approved translation Hopkins used. In the King James version, the last verse is rendered, "This is a great mystery; but I speak concerning Christ and the Church."

the consent of the whole community.[10] It is this honor—the honor of being like Christ in suffering for the sake of another—that is offered the groom. The phrase "hang your head" brings to mind the garlanded sacrificial animal.[11] Alliteration also associates grace—the strength to really participate in the life of God—with the groom.

But "grace" here is a verb; its object is "bride." Hopkins connects the bride immediately to physical sexuality. Sex and the woman's power of generation are blessed; bodies that breed are not therefore the lowlier, but are in fact hallowed. It is in the sexual act, in the bed, that Hopkins first places the newly married couple. Only afterward does he begin to reflect on the side of marriage much more emphasized in the literature of his day:[12] promoting virtue and providing mutual comfort. Thomas Aquinas defined marriage as a species of friendship,[13] but Hopkins's ordering strictly follows the ordering of the purposes of marriage laid forth in nineteenth-century Catholic theology: the primary good of marriage is offspring, and its secondary good mutual aid and comfort. Hopkins does not want to lose track of the physical bond in a bath of sentiment; he celebrates the physical before the companionate.

Hopkins greatly emphasizes marital sexuality with alliteration and rhythm; the repeated word "scions" first breaks the iambic tetrameter with an abrupt sprung effect, further highlighted by the word's breaking the established rhyme scheme, which resumes on the next line. The second stanza reflects on the secondary matrimonial good of fellowship, as the priest prays that the husband and wife be blessed with depths of love beyond their understanding. Again Hopkins repeats a word to create a sprung rhythmic effect: "Déep, déeper." Hopkins suggests that the relationship established by the rite is even more significant than can be guessed by the couple whose lives it transforms. One

10. See René Girard, *Violence and the Sacred.*

11. Hopkins was a classicist, of course, but Keats's "Ode on a Grecian Urn" springs to mind here.

12. Such as Coventry Patmore's immensely popular poem, *The Angel in the House.*

13. Thomas Aquinas, *Summa Contra Gentiles,* trans. Vernon Bourke (New York: Image Books, 1956), 3.2.124, pp. 150–52.

aspect of its depth is sacramental grace: "Divine charity." The extra, unemphasized syllables hint at quiet superabundance. Hopkins also emphasizes the permanence of the relationship with sprung rhythm: "fást bínd."

The march, a song of triumph, is appropriate to the sacred dignity of matrimony. According to the canons, the priest merely stands witness to this sacrament, which the bride and groom administer to one another. In the name of the community, the priest acknowledges their new relationship and asks God's favor upon them. Hopkins evidently conceived the poem while officiating at the wedding of Mr. John Fairclough and Miss Maggie Unsworth.[14] He enjoyed weddings; "I have a kind of spooniness and delight over married people, especially if they say 'my wife,' 'my husband,' or shew the wedding ring."[15] Nevertheless, Hopkins was quite aware that in the Catholic Church, marriage is valid only during earthly life, and in heaven "there is neither marrying nor giving in marriage (Matt. 22.30)."[16] How, then, can Hopkins weep with joy at the "immortal years" of this marriage? This couple will die; the human race is doomed;[17] in what way is any marriage, then, immortal? Again, Hopkins is inhabiting, not undermining, Catholic theology. This relationship is a sign of the marriage of Christ and the Church, God's gift of "immortal years." The relationship solemnized between John and Maggie is a sign of and a participation in the death-destroying marriage of Christ and his believers. The celebrant, too, is the promised bride of Christ, and in the union of these two Christians he understands something of the physical presence of Christ at his return to earth in glory. The triumph of wedlock is not a triumph over the body, but the triumph of the body over sin and death, a foretaste of the Resurrection.

14. The poem bears the date of their wedding, at which Hopkins assisted; see *Poetical Works,* 418.

15. Hopkins, *Letters to Bridges,* 198 (11 Nov. 1884).

16. Ott, *Fundamentals of Catholic Dogma,* 466.

17. Hopkins, of course, believed that the earthly sacrament of marriage would end, at least with the end of the world. The last line of "The Sea and the Skylark" seems to refer to this, and also to a nineteenth-century version of evolutionary biologists' "primordial soup."

Marriage, in which "two become one flesh," is an image of and participation in the physical connection of the incarnate Christ to the Church. God created flesh inherently good, as the vehicle for the activity of the Divine Word. Just as a builder constructs a house, God created human bodies from a certain "order of intention." The builder buys land, collects materials, hires workers, and digs trenches. However, the intention of having a completed house comes into being first, and sets the rest in motion. Hopkins wrote of the creation of human beings: "[T]he more perfect is created in its perfection, that is to say/ if perfectible and capable of greater or less perfection, it is created at its greatest. And thus it is said, '*Ipsius enim sumus factura, created in Christo Jesu in operibus bonis, quae preparavit Deus ut in illis ambulemus.*' (Eph. II. 10)."[18] The Douay-Rheims version renders this, "For we are his workmanship, created in Christ Jesus unto good works, which God hath before ordained that we should walk in them." Hopkins no doubt underlined "created in Christ Jesus" because he thought each individual human springs from the conception of the most perfect man, God incarnate. Thus, the perfection of bodies includes not only their existence but ultimately their proper ordering to the incarnate Christ: "I am all at once what Christ is,| since he was what I am and / Thís Jack, jóke, poor pótsherd, | patch, matchwood, immortal diamond, / Is immortal diamond."[19]

The nuptial vows both symbolize and establish a relationship that the words scarcely suffice to describe. Of that relationship the couple must be aware. But the relationship itself has spiritual meaning, odd though it may be to propose meanings that might be neither intended nor understood by those who speak and hear a message. Yet even when the participants neither intend nor perceive its divine significance, the marriage itself is a medium of God's activity. Their understanding does not preclude the Church's; the meaning is multiplied. The sacrament is a sort of abstract relation requiring the possibility,

18. Hopkins, *Sermons and Devotional Writings,* 196.

19. Hopkins, "That Nature Is a Heraclitean Fire and of the Comfort of the Resurrection," in *Poetical Works,* 198.

but not necessarily the participation, of a perceiving mind. Such meanings are "inscapes": multiple real relations within individual things, relations not evident unless revealed, and inexhaustible by any revelation.

Hopkins thinks sacramentally even when an ecclesiastical sacrament is not the subject matter of his poem. In "Hurrahing in Harvest" sacramental thought operates upon his choice of metaphor; he presents the beauty of nature as a sort of *res et sacramentum* for an observer with the eye to find it when he presents an ordinary harvest in terms of the Eucharist. Certainly he saw a difference between his aesthetic practice and the "effective signs" practiced by the Church in its liturgy; poems have no use if they are not understood, and offer no sure access to God; neither do they necessarily create a real relationship with anyone or anything. Nevertheless, the poet can present the world to us with sacramental eyes—in Coleridgean terms, eyes of "faith," which is identical with fidelity to the "ideas or truths of the pure reason."[20] Coleridge conceived of history and nature as the revelation of Christ, the "Divine Humanity," and perhaps prepared Hopkins to favor the incarnational theory of Duns Scotus.[21] Scotus suggested that the Incarnation of the Word of God was the final cause of creation, the first action of the Creator in his "order of intention." John's Gospel (1.3) says "all things were made" through the Divine Reason, who would dwell bodily as a man—and Scotus says they were made for the sake of that Incarnation. Reasoning and human consciousness image forth his rationality. The Word of God in creation is a Man. Man is both himself and what God speaks as Creator. Thomas Aquinas writes that "[t]he Father, by understanding Himself, the Son and the Holy Spirit, and all other things comprised in this knowledge,

20. Quoted in Owen Barfield, *What Coleridge Thought* (Middletown, Conn.: Wesleyan University Press, 1971), 151. I discovered this incisive study late in my revisions of this book, and am encouraged to see how well Barfield's understanding of Coleridge concurs with my own. The argument of his chapter "Man and God" has emboldened my expression in this paragraph.

21. Christopher Devlin, notes to *The Sermons and Devotional Writings of Gerard Manley Hopkins*, 111.

conceives the Word; so that thus the whole Trinity is spoken in the Word; and likewise also all creatures, as the intellect of man by the word he conceives in understanding a stone, speaks a stone."[22]

"Hurrahing in Harvest" unfolds a similar understanding of the world by means of a pattern of imagery suggesting the Eucharist. In that sacrament, the *res et sacramentum* is defined as the presence of the Second Person of the Trinity, the Word of God, incarnate in body and blood under the appearance of bread and wine. Recall that Hopkins says "the least fragment of the consecrated elements of the Blessed Sacrament of the Altar is the whole Body of Christ born of the Blessed Virgin."[23] Catholic theology affirms that these physical symbols—bread, wine, words—are the means by which God announces and enacts his presence among his people. The priest who pronounces them is an instrument, whose actions constitute part of an order of the universe that he may or may not accept or recognize; the consecration is valid even if he himself has lost his faith. The sacrament is the body and blood, according to the Church, whether or not anyone perceives Christ's bodily presence in the bread and wine.

In "Hurrahing in Harvest," all nature, including human constructions, has this multiple quality of meaning, this multiplicity of inscape. All these things speak sacramentally of God. Hopkins can "lift up heart, eyes, / Down all that glory in the heavens to glean our Saviour," for "the azurous hung hills are his world-wielding shoulder majestic." Such language is not mere metaphor; Hopkins claims that he is perceiving God's immanence. Immanence is not Incarnation, but it does mark God's activity as really present: "These things, these things were here and but the beholder wanting."[24] The divine inscapes present in nature exist in reality, but are brought into actuality by the human mind.

And in the reality of a world spoken, interpreted by human beings, the immanent Logos in beauty is revealed as the same being as the Eu-

22. Thomas Aquinas, *Summa theologica,* in *Basic Writings of Saint Thomas Aquinas,* tran. Anton C. Pegis (New York: Random House, 1945), 1.1.34, art. 1, p. 335.

23. Hopkins, *Further Letters,* 92 (to his father, 16 Oct. 1866).

24. Hopkins, *Poetical Works,* 148–49.

charistic Christ. Hopkins meets him in a very Wordsworthian moment; the poet knows that his mind is working upon the things presented to him to produce the experience he records—but only because these things allow him real access to the universal order that they serve.

Hurrahing in Harvest

Summer énds now; now, bárbarous in béauty, the stóoks ríse
Around; up above, what wind-walks! what lovely behaviour
Of sílk-sack clóuds! has wilder, wilful-wávier
Méal-drift moulded ever and melted acróss skíes?

I wálk, I líft up, Í lift úp heart, éyes,
Down all that glory in the heavens to glean our Saviour;
And, éyes, heárt, what looks, what lips yet gáve you á
Ráptūrous love's greeting of realer, of rounder replies?

And the azurous hung hills are his wórld-wíelding shoulder
Majestic—as a stallion stalwart, very-violet-sweet!—
These things, these things were here and but the beholder
Wánting; whích two whén they ónce méet,
The héart réars wíngs bóld and bolder
And hurls for him, O half hurls earth for him off under his feet.

The poem describes an intense experience in a particular moment: summer ends *now.* Stooks are haystacks, and the speaker, whom I will simply identify as Hopkins,[25] is walking along at harvest time, looking up: "what wind-walks!" Remember that wind is *pneuma,* "spirit" in Greek. The clouds are "meal-drift"; think of a handful of flour tossed up in the air, how white it is and how unsubstantial. It is significant that they remind him of flour, but just as significant, considering his convictions about truth in art, that clouds really can look like that—nearly form into something, and then melt away, almost as if they had decided not to. The day is windy, with great clouds.

The repetition of "I lift up" broaches the romantic epistemological issue. Hopkins presents two kinds of lifting up. One is with the eyes. The other is with the heart. One is physical, the other is spiritual. With

25. His account of the sonnet's origin, I believe, justifies this. See Hopkins, *Letters to Bridges,* 56 (16 July 1878).

his eyes he sees grainfields, with his heart "our Saviour." He gleans the Saviour; he harvests him. In this way Hopkins's approach to nature is indeed sacramental: nature here joins grace, with only a limited part of its function available to the physical senses. The clouds are an image of the flour from which the Communion bread is made. The harvest is a real wheat harvest, and at the same time a harvest of the grain that is the Body of Christ. Usually Hopkins uses the image of grain for the members of that body, such as the "grain" carried by the *Deutschland* in his famous ode, by which he means the saved souls of those granted salvation through the tall nun's prayer. Hopkins himself undergoes his threshing as grain in "Carrion Comfort." But here the grain imagery applies to the Head of the Body, Christ. Hopkins, with special zeal, sought to pronounce the words of consecration every day of his priestly life: "He took bread, gave thanks and broke it, saying, 'Take and eat; this is my body.'"[26] Communion stands behind the imagery of this poem, though the type of communion he records in this afternoon of harvest season is purely cognitive and emotional. To take in the scene is like taking the bread. The subtle eucharistic allusion is worth noticing as the image Hopkins chooses when he speaks about his encounter with God here. But all this is analysis of the way Hopkins puts his description of the facts of the matter. What he sees, in this spot of time, is a harvested field and a wind-blown cloud over a mountain shoulder.

Hopkins's eyes and heart witness that God greets him like someone with eyes and lips—as a very particular and physical person. He is Jesus, a man, not the "Spirit of Nature." The hills, hung with blue mist, are Christ's "world wielding shoulder majestic." Hopkins describes him in the language of a lover—like a stallion, like a violet, Christ tender and powerful, and beautiful in many ways at once. Again Hopkins uses repetition to emphasize a double presence in the encountered reality: "These things, these things"—again, physical things, the cloud,

26. Hopkins even missed a rare visit with Bridges in order that he might be in a location where he could celebrate daily mass. No doubt his ability to carry out his desire was interrupted by illness, such as his surgeries and his fatal bout of typhus. The words of consecration used in the Roman ritual come originally from 1 Cor. 11.24–25.

the hills; and spiritual things, God's greeting and the shoulders of Christ upholding the world. The Creator interacts with and inheres in the world he has made.

And here we come to the philosophical center of the poem. From this line on, the sonnet is not in the first person, but phrased as an analyzed and rational account of the spot of time the audience has just experienced with Hopkins. God is of all things most desirable, but it is not so much that the beholder wants God as that the scene cries out to be made alive, in Coleridge's terms; in Hopkins's, to greet the Saviour. Unlike the nature god that Wordsworth encounters, this is not an unknown spirit inferred from feelings of awe. This is a particular, historical, and personal Saviour, whose existence Hopkins happily admits is known to him through tradition. He uses the word "Saviour" because he believes that someone who sins can beg salvation from this Presence in the clouds. Jesus isn't a Saviour here because Hopkins, as he tastes the beauty of the scene, feels the need of a Saviour. Hopkins presents it more forcefully than that. He's a Saviour because that's who he is; he's present because that's where he is. He makes himself known through those who behold him.

As in the sacramental bread, some would not see the Savior in these clouds. And if they saw only clouds, they would not be wrong; the things really are clouds—which does not stop them from being other things as well, and not just in the "prepossession" of the beholder. The book of the world may be written in a language some beholder does not know; it may require a new kind of attention, like listening to a foreign language. But Hopkins has learnt the idiom of this text. Hopkins meets God in beauty here; in *The Wreck of the Deutschland* and the Terrible Sonnets he also meets him, like Wordsworth, in fear. And Hopkins strives to make Christ present to the consciousness of his readers, bringing to mind the supreme mode in which he believes that the Word of God is present through the language of men: the Eucharist. More deeply than in the sensible world, more deeply than in its conscious manifestation in poetry, Christ is present in the Eucharist with his own meaning and his own will, uncontrollably beyond and yet inhabiting the human meaning.

Poetry honors the presence that can be perceived but not fully known, glorying in the multiplicity of language. The noises of poetry, the words and their meanings, are not for Hopkins mere signs to be manipulated for human purposes. They are part of a larger reality in which the poet is privileged, by his humanity, to share. Hopkins's sacramentality is not limited to either theological exposition or Wordsworthian encounters with natural beauty. As we shall see in "God's Grandeur," language itself is, for Hopkins, a multilayered revelation. The multiplicity of layers carries through to the style in "Hurrahing in Harvest" as well. Observe how Hopkins accented the line "Wànting; whìch two whèn they ònce mèet." This is counterpoint rhythm; by reversing the second and fifth foot—indeed, by drastically altering the structure of the fifth foot—Hopkins has mounted a new trochaic rhythm on the iambic meter, which can still be heard underneath. The language through its very rhythm implies two realities coexistent in one action, as the physical, spiritual, and symbolic coexist in sacraments, for, according to Saint Thomas, "Man's condition is such that he is brought to grasp the spiritual and intelligible naturally through the senses."[27] Words are patterns of sound, and sound is a created good. We recognize rhythm and tone and the chiming of consonance and rhyme. Language also has meaning, or inscape, of another kind, mounted upon the inscape available in its pure music: grammar, syntax, reference, argument. A poem is both a single set of sound patterns and a potential explosion of human meanings. It is at the same time one thing and many things. While Hopkins is intensely conscious of the instrumental power of language over listeners, it is not, for him, a mere tool. He loves it for itself, studies it for its intrinsic interest. His poems not only speak of experiences of beauty, but provide such experiences in themselves: repeated patterns of sound and the human meanings mounted upon them. Poetry is distinguished from other forms of speech by attention to the formal aspects of speech for their own sake:

27. Thomas Aquinas, *Summa Contra Gentiles* 4.56.3, in *St. Thomas Aquinas on the Truth of the Catholic Faith, Book Four: Salvation,* trans. Charles O'Neil (Garden City, N.Y.: Doubleday Image, 1956), 247.

Poetry is speech framed for contemplation of the mind by the way of hearing or speech framed to be heard for its own sake and interest even over and above its interest of meaning. Some matter and meaning is essential to it but only as an element necessary to support and employ the shape which is contemplated for its own sake.[28]

An attentive audience can give life and actuality to a poem's creaturely and formal inscapes. Hopkins awakens his audience to a world in which each thing has its unity and integrity, and yet has multiple inscapes present in it. His language imitates the world's multiplicities by displaying its own: real relations of sound pattern overlaid by real relations of socially active meaning both in argument and syntax.[29]

Hopkins's self-consistent theory of the nature of language and the nature of meaning freed him to experiment boldly and effectively with prosody. Though Hopkins has been taken, in the twentieth century, as a master of prosody,[30] in Victorian poetic practice, Tennysonian musicality reigned supreme. Hopkins could "err on the side of oddness," he said, because he had no broad public to please.[31] His public at the time practically consisted of Robert Bridges and the editors of *The Month,* who had just rejected *The Wreck of the Deutschland.* Although select, his readership was nevertheless repelled by Hopkins's innovations. Victorian prosodic theory, whether descriptive or prescriptive, was emphatically based on established poetic practice—on what had worked in the past. Hopkins's meticulous criticism demonstrates that he understood conventional versification as well as his contemporaries, yet his prosody challenges the conservatism of the purely practical, and his jarring experiments have uncovered tools now much valued for poetic expression.

Hopkins named three types of English rhythms: running rhythm, counterpoint rhythm, and sprung rhythm. Common or running rhythm uses feet of fixed numbers of syllables, each with a stress in a

28. Hopkins, *Journals and Papers,* 289.

29. Plotkin ("Hopkins's Theodic Language") and Lichtmann *(Contemplative Poetry)* both notice this.

30. For Hopkins's poetic descendants, see Richard Giles, ed., *Hopkins among the Poets* (Hamilton, Ont.: International Hopkins Association, 1985).

31. Hopkins, *Letters to Bridges,* 66.

specified place. It permits licenses, such as reversed feet at the beginning of a line or after the caesura. In pentameter, Hopkins's favorite meter, he observed that the rhythm against which these licenses play is set by the second foot and the last foot. If either of these "characteristic and sensitive" feet is reversed, the poet has created an effect beyond that of normally acceptable variation within a steady meter.

Hopkins was especially proud of sprung rhythm, the more radical of his two innovations, "having twice the flexibility of foot, so that any two stresses may either follow one another running or be divided by one, two or three slack syllables."[32] In sprung rhythm the only constraint is that the total number of stresses per line be retained. We have already seen this at work for effect in "At the Wedding March," when Hopkins juxtaposed stresses in "Déep, déeper" and "fást bínd," and added unstressed syllables in "Divine charity." At its most compelling, speech is rhythmic and rides upon the suggestion of breath and heartbeat. Sprung rhythm allows poetry to approach prose or speech rhythm as closely as possible without abandoning the underlying pattern of stress. Hopkins enjoyed sprung rhythm's unliterary immediacy—like the world of nature, "highly wrought" in its apparent randomness.

Sprung rhythm superimposes a prose rhythm upon a verse form. Counterpoint is a more tightly controlled departure from running rhythm, "mounting" a new poetic rhythm upon an underlying running rhythm.

> If . . . the reversal [of a foot] is repeated in two feet running, especially so as to include the sensitive second foot, it must be due either to great want of ear or else is a calculated effect, the super-inducing or *mounting* of a new rhythm upon the old; and since the new or mounted rhythm is actually heard and at the same time the mind naturally supplies the natural standard foregoing rhythm, for we do not forget what rhythm it is by rights we should be hearing, two rhythms are in some manner running at once and we have something answerable to counterpoint in music, which is two or more strains of tune going on together, and this is Counterpoint Rhythm.[33]

32. Gerard Manley Hopkins, "Author's Preface," in Gardner and MacKenzie, eds., *The Poems of Gerard Manley Hopkins,* 4th (New York: Oxford University Press, 1967), 47; hereafter cited as *Poems,* 4th ed.

33. Hopkins, "Author's Preface" to his poems, in *Poems,* 4th ed., 46.

Fallen Rain

An innovation of unusual power, counterpoint most clearly illustrates Hopkins's concern with unity and multiplicity. Musical counterpoint is not a rhythmic effect; it is, literally, point against point, that is to say, note against note—the multiplicity of harmony rather than unison singing. Counterpointed music, as Hopkins remarks, succeeds in being both a single piece and many songs at once. However, a more straightforward musical analogy to the practice of Hopkins's rhythmic counterpoint is cross-rhythm. By far the most common and useful form of cross-rhythm, from the time of Henry Purcell to that of Hopkins, was the hemiola.[34] Hemiola plays on the possibility of counting, for instance, six beats as two groups of three or three groups of two. The opening measures of Hopkins's own musical setting of R. W. Dixon's poem "Fallen Rain"[35] provide a very clear example of the effect.

The first measure establishes a clear and unambiguous 6/8 time: two groups of three eighth-notes. But the second measure—the three pairs of falling notes—falls on the ear as three groups of two. Two eighth-notes make a quarter-note, so that would normally be notated

34. The article on polyrhythms in *The New Grove Dictionary of Music and Musicians*, ed. Stanley Sadie (Washington, D.C.: Macmillan, 1980), has a more concise and graceful definition of cross-rhythm than the articles on cross-rhythm and hemiola, though both of those are also helpful.

35. Reproduced in facsimile between pp. 168 and 169 of *Correspondence with Dixon*.

as 3/4 rather than 6/8. The placement of the words corroborates this implied rhythm, since "On" must be stressed. The pattern of notes and syllables alone would indicate the hemiola clearly enough to most musicians, but Hopkins leaves no room for doubt by placing accent marks over the first, third, and fifth eighth-notes.

Hopkins knows that the principal difference between poetic and musical scansion is that the stressed beat (the primary accent) is always counted as the beginning of the musical "foot."[36] Music has no anapests or iambs; unstressed notes at the beginning of a phrase are "pickup" notes. A three-beat group in music will almost always carry both a primary and a secondary accent. The unambiguous, flowing 6/8 in the first measure of "Fallen Rain" is achieved through putting the secondary accent on the third note. So its primary stress is followed by a weak note, then a stronger one. Then another primary accent begins a new phrase.

This pattern easily accommodates the trochaic rhythm of the words by giving the stressed syllables quarter-notes (counted 1-2, since we're counting in eighths) instead of eighth-notes. The quarter-note lengthens the stressed syllable to extend through the unstressed musical beat. Let font size in the numbers stand for musical stress, and Dixon's

"Sí- lent féll the" becomes
1 - 2 - 3 4 - 5 - 6,

that is, two groups of one long note (counted 1-2) followed by one short note (3). If the second "foot" in such a pattern is reversed (so that the stresses would be 1-2-3 4-5-6), a hemiola is produced: a long note (1-2), two short notes (3 and 4), and another long one (5-6). If the musician counts in groups of three, the counting and the rhythm are in tension: 1-2; 3-1; 2-3. The new rhythm of three pairs can even predominate over the old rhythm of two triplets if the fifth beat is strong enough to compete with the fourth for primary stress.

The musical "foot" 1-2-3 is the "running rhythm" in "Fallen Rain."

36. Hopkins, "Author's Preface," in *Poems*, 4th ed., 45.

The hemiola of measure 2 is a moment of rhythmic "counterpoint" created by mounting the rhythm of three pairs of notes upon the second measure of the three-measure phrase:

Sí- lent féll the | ráin ón the | éarth- ly gróund;
1 - 2 - 3 4 - 5 - 6 | 1 - 2 - 3 4 - 5 - 6 | 1 - 2 - 3 4 - 5 - 6
measure 1 *measure 2* *measure 3*

The running rhythm returns for the end of the phrase. The second phrase begins in running 6/8 rhythm, like the first, but Hopkins puts a hemiola in its second measure too. This second hemiola is considerably more complicated—a double hemiola, one might say, in which a larger hemiola is mounted upon two smaller ones. Measure 5 contains a hemiola similar to its counterpart in measure 2, except that there is less stress on the second pair (third beat). The fourth beat is empty, offering no competition whatsoever to the hemiola accent of beat 5.

| thén a- róse a | sóund tó com-| pláin—
| **1** - 2 - 3 **4** - 5 - 6 | 1 - 2 - 3 4 - **5** - 6 | **1** - 2 - **3** 4 - 5 - 6
measure 4 *measure 5* *measure 6*

The following measure has a hemiola too, but its third pair is unequivocally slack. The smoothly flowing phrase ends with the *f* that is reached on the third beat, which makes that a very strong rival to the first beat for primary stress. Hopkins writes a crescendo to the *f*, as if to emphasize that all this is intentional. We now have two hemiolas back to back, making the two big groups of three sound like three big pairs; I underline the beats that create this illusion. We shall see that at the end of "God's Grandeur," Hopkins manages a similar effect through reversals that create something resembling two anapests in a line of iambic pentameter.[37]

The effect of counterpoint rhythm in the sonnet "God's Grandeur" demonstrates the interrelations among layers of meaning—that is to say, detectable pattern—in his poetry. Rhythm; the chiming of sound

37. I have relied on Dane Waterman, a professional pianist, for the above analysis of Hopkins's music.

created by rhyme, alliteration, consonance and assonance; syntax; and imagery all have patterns of their own, and those patterns work together to further the argument of the poem. Hopkins was not seeking subconscious effects in doing this—for one thing, because the theory of the subconscious could scarcely be part of his mental equipment[38] —but seeking to, as Keats put it, "load every rift with ore." All these graces and orderings are themselves ordered to the service of the greatest, the most human one, Christ. As in the creation of the world, the less perfect depends upon the more perfect in order of intention, so does the rhythm of the poem depend upon the meaning of the argument. The argument of the poem is set up as the chief good; upon that the construction of each syntactic element depends. One only knows how to accent the word "perfect," for instance, if one knows whether it is a noun or a verb; in this poem the rhythm of "Why do men then" depends upon meaning. Upon the construction of the sentences, the rhythm of the words depends. The relationships among vowels and consonants gain significance because of the words they connect. Rhythm serves syntax; auditory rhyme serves both; a sort of mental rhyme, punning, serves imagery; all serve argument; and the whole is, as it were, one body, imaged forth in its many members.

Hopkins advised his friends that his poetry was to be performed and heard rather than read "slovenly with the eyes." "God's Grandeur" is a tour-de-force of interrelationships among sounds and imagery, rhythms and argument. (The boldface words support my comments on meter below.)

The **world** is charged **wíth** the **grán**deur of **God.**
  It will flame **out,** like **shin**ing from **shook foil;**
  It **gath**ers to a **great**ness, like the **ooze** of **oil**
Crushed. Why do **men** then **now** not **reck** his **rod?**
Gén**erá**tions have **trod,** have **trod,** have **trod;**
  And **all** is **seared** with **trade;** bleared, **smeared** with **toil;**
  And **wears** man's **smudge** and **shares** man's **smell:** the **soil**
Is **bare** now, **nor** can **foot** feel, being **shod.**

38. He does occasionally mention something he calls an "underthought," but to burden that expression with Freudian psychological theory is to strain it beyond reason.

Ánd, for all **this, náture** is **never spent;**
  There **lives** the **dear**est **fresh**ness **deep down** things;
And **though** the last **lights off** the black **West went**
  Oh, **morn**ing, at the **brown brink east**wards, **springs**—
Be**cause** the **Ho**ly **Ghost** óver the **bent**
  World broods with warm **breast** and with **ah!** bright **wings.**[39]

The first quatrain proclaims the dignity of God and the danger of disregarding it; the dignity itself is described, the warning implied. The imagery is drawn from lightning and violence. The first line implies a danger of lightning, the second of fire; the third recalls the slow buildup of electrical charge, which had not yet been quantized but was still considered a "continuous fluid."[40] Here Hopkins makes the fluid oil, associating it with the anointing of kings and prophets. The rod of rulership appears in the final line—but we are not to forget the lightning rod, any more than we are to forget the double meaning of "charge" as electrical power and mandate. As Hopkins put it in a sermon,

> Much more has God a purpose, an end, a meaning in his work. He meant the world to give him praise, reverence and service; *to give him glory.* It is like a garden, a field he sows; what should it bear him? Praise, reverence and service; it should yield him glory. . . . He has infinite glory without it and what is infinite can be made no bigger. Nevertheless he takes it: he wishes it, asks it, he commands it, he enforces it, he gets it.[41]

The growling in "grandeur" and "charged" is echoed by that in "greatness," and reminiscent of the threatening "crushed." Hopkins had noted in his undergraduate notebooks on language formation the close association between "c" and "g." "R" continues to rumble in "reck" and "rod"—associated by rhyme (as well as syntax) with this very threatening God. "Flame" leaps out at the hearer, rather a shock in its sharpness after a train of vowels dominated by a softening "r." After "flame," the second line sizzles with "shining" and "shook." The growling, the

39. Hopkins, *Poetical Works,* 139.

40. David Halliday and Robert Resnick, *Physics* (New York: John Wiley and Sons, 1978), 2:571. The electron theory, which gave electricity discrete quantities such as we measure today, was first proposed by H. Lorentz in 1892.

41. Hopkins, *Sermons and Devotional Writings,* 238–39.

sudden change at "flame," and the sizzling build a sense of foreboding, abruptly crushed and followed by a stern warning posed as a question. The reader ends the quatrain panting, with the line stopped short by a rhyme to "God": "then . . . men . . . reck . . . rod."

The second quatrain begins to treat of human history rather than the sacramental nature of the world. "Generations" has an emphatic vowel sound much like that in "flame" and "greatness," but distinguished from them by the Oxford pronunciation of the day.[42] The repetitions following the word serve to point up the oddity of its sound, which is further emphasized, as we shall see, in the meter. The flame has left its destruction: "seared" with "trade"—another sharp, harsh vowel sound—the soil is "bare," connected by sound to "wear" and "shares." "L" relates "all" "bleared" and "toil" to "soil" and "smell" and "feel." Soil retains its proper denotation of earth, but its subjection to mankind has made its associations unclean, as if the word were construed as a verb. The earth screams in "seared" and "bleared" and "smeared." There is an undercurrent of snakelike hissing in the alliteration on "s" and the soil does not escape it; nor does its imprisoned inhabitant.

Likewise, the meter serves the argument, though more subtly. My own construction of appropriate speech emphases for "God's Grandeur" I have printed in boldface. The poem can be scanned as iambic pentameter; there are in fact ten syllables in every line, except for the single license Hopkins marked in the third line (a slur on "gathers to a"). The speech emphases, however, create an effect that is not that of iambic pentameter. In the first line, the third and fourth feet are reversed, fulfilling the conditions for counterpoint. The line sounds rather like tetrameter to the ear, yet it is ten syllables. There are four strong voice stresses in the next line as well, and the next, but neither is counterpointed. They strongly establish the "natural" rhythm, a measured pentameter, but continue to suggest the variation—a heard

42. The first version of the *Oxford English Dictionary* reproduces the pronunciation Hopkins expected his readers to hear, one rather different from the flat Hoosier vowels and sharp "r" with which I recited his poetry in childhood. The investigation of pronunciation rewards study in Hopkins.

tetrameter mounted on it. The fourth line is regular, though "crushed" is an uncomfortably strong word for a slack syllable. At the beginning of the fifth line, Hopkins marked two reversed feet in a row, trochees replacing iambs: "Génerátions." Hopkins says that that effect serves to counterpoint a line. This counterpoint puts a tremendous amount of emphatic stress on the third syllable, the main stress of the word "generations." The vowel sound of the third syllable blares as if it were the only stress in the word. The first syllable would ordinarily carry something close to the same amount of emphasis, but its position is one lightly stressed in the heretofore iambic pattern. When the iambs reassert themselves—"have trod, have trod, have trod"—we have again, in effect, a heard tetrameter. It is not necessarily the case that the mounted rhythm must be merely the reverse of the corresponding rhythm—trochees for iambs. The power of it is in suggesting an entirely different scansion—in this case, tetrameter that sounds like two anapests and two iambs.

The octave mainly laments that man, hard of heart, batters the earth; in its last three lines man overpowers and spoils its complex gorgeousness. Pentameter asserts itself and trudges along until its numbed foot stumbles into the rising hope of the sestet. One may perhaps make a connection between the wild earth's imagined corners and the irregular tetrameter mounted upon the decasyllabic human artifice of pentameter.[43]

The imagery of light and motion in the sestet is tranquil and the connections of sounds are associated with soothing words. The reader is panting at first—nature is never spent, but then that combination of "n" and that panting "e" comes to be associated with freshness even as Hopkins alliteratively associates "dearest" with "deep down." The black of the west is not allowed to remain dark. It is connected with the "brown brink" of the east—Hopkins well knew the color of the air in a polluted town—and the sounds in "brown" are in their turn associated with the brooding action of the Holy Spirit over the waste and void

43. Hopkins associated the number 5 with the Incarnation in a long passage of *The Wreck of the Deutschland.* See *Poetical Works,* 124.

of creation at the beginning. The vowel sounds in "Holy Ghost" chime with those in the "oh" before the "morning" (which had, according to the *Oxford English Dictionary,* a related but distinct vowel sound). The sestet reveals the activity of God in the world. In it, tension remains between the spoken rhythm and the written rhythm, especially in the first and last lines. The first line takes advantage of both the "permissible" licenses of iambic pentameter: the first foot and the foot following the caesura are both reversed. This results in a swinging rhythm that approximates a three-syllable foot; in Hopkins's terms, stress-slack-slack-stress: stress-slack-slack-stress, slack-stress. Some of the same tension exists, without so much formal justification, in the fourth line of the sestet; but the most remarkable example is in the final line, which scans as ordinary pentameter with the third foot reversed—very respectable. But the caesura would sit very uncomfortably between "warm" and "breast," since a conjunction follows the noun. The caesura falls between "breast" and "and," which means that it breaks a foot of ordinary scansion, and urges a new scansion. The phrase "with warm breast" is a single foot to the ear.

I scan the poem's last line thus, with five heavy stresses: stress-stress-slack-slack-stress: slack-slack-stress, slack-stress. There are three-syllable feet drawing attention to themselves in the midst of the final line, a line that could be scanned in iambs—but for the sense of the words. Hopkins recommended continuous "rove over" scansion within a stanza. "World" at the beginning of the last line requires more stress than iambic scansion gives it. A noun following an adjective, it completes a phrase from the preceding line. The effect is like the hemiola of a baroque dance in triple meter, except that the cross-rhythm is more complex; the three consecutive stresses, "Bent/World broods," slow the pace, preparing us for a gasp after two anapests have flowed by, and we relax into a final iamb. There are at least two kinds of sense to be made of this at once, besides the sense of the words. It is a grand culminating effect, two simultaneous rhythms, two simultaneous realities: man's reckless ravaging and the tender care of God.

This careful attention to multiplicity springs from Hopkins's philosophical stance about multiplicity of meaning available but unnoticed in the world—"the beholder wanting"—which is indeed the theme of this poem. Certainly divine meaning is imposed on human action in a liturgical sacrament, such as a wedding—but here Hopkins sees the same incarnational presence in the detritus of a society that has abandoned God. God remains immanent in the world whether human beings regard him or not. Hopkins's metrical theme echoes his argument; another rhythm is mounted on the artifice of iambic pentameter, which he preserves in all its decasyllabic strictness. His metrical complexities manifest his opinion that God's word exists in all patterns, even in things without human significance. In language, the perceiving mind can find multiple patterns, multiple inscapes in a single unified object, each present, and none displacing the others. Hopkins's prosody, as compressed and full of conscious pattern as his syntax, offers to the perceiving mind a grand field of interrelationships to be enjoyed and explored. They are not mere rhetorical devices; this poet's lasting power and influence come from his deep understanding of language as a mystery to be appreciated in itself—in its phonetic qualities as much as in its ability to convey meaning. The meaning of language is only part of its mystery, and Hopkins, consciously reveling in its richness, creates the opportunity for his readers to do the same.

CHAPTER 7

DUNS SCOTUS
Formalitas and Inscape

IN 1872, Hopkins found a volume of the *Opus Oxoniense* of John Duns Scotus in his seminary library. As he dipped into it, he scarcely dared to trust his own delight; he had fallen in love. "It may come to nothing or it may be a great mercy of God. But just then when I took in any inscape of the sea or sky I thought of Scotus."[1] Later, he praised Scotus above Aquinas or Aristotle[2] in his poem "Duns Scotus' Oxford," where he calls the philosopher, "Of realty the rarest-veinèd unraveller; a not / Rívalled insight, be rival Italy or Greece."[3] Hopkins's delight is in the way Scotus "unravels"—perceives, classifies, defines—a world outside the mind. Hopkins worked lovingly to reveal that world in his poems. Many critics have searched far afield for the philosophical foundations of Hopkins's art—in particular, inscape, which Hopkins called "the very soul of art."[4] To explain the term in its context of philosophical theology demands attention to the very difficult work of John Duns Scotus.

Philosophical theology will allow us to eschew two opposite camps of critics who agree on treating inscape as beyond the scope of human communication: the one because they believe that mystical religious experience defeats words, the other because they believe that language defeats itself. Recognizing Hopkins's conviction that art requires both

1. Hopkins, *Journals and Papers,* 221.

2. Norman MacKenzie, *A Reader's Guide to Gerard Manley Hopkins* (Ithaca, N.Y.: Cornell University Press, 1981), 113.

3. Hopkins, "Duns Scotus' Oxford," in *Poetical Works,* 156.

4. Hopkins, *Correspondence with Dixon,* 135 (30 June 1886).

faith and love, some religious critics make it therefore a religious experience that draws the poet away from created multiplicity to divine unity. Flirting with monism, they unguardedly open a way for poststructuralist critics, who construe individuality and distinction in Hopkins as tragic negations rather than as good existences in themselves. The poststructuralists rightly recognize that Hopkins's art is based not so much in divine unity as in created heterogeneity, but, unable or unwilling to take seriously the Christian postulate that creation is good, they succumb to corrosive nihilism. Poststructuralists unquestioningly reject the notion that love, especially love of God, can be anyone's primary motive. To them, inscape—indeed, all literature—reveals only that the multitudinousness of language undermines authority and reference. Such ideology had its parallels in the fourteenth century; Scotus contemned its manifestations. Hopkins's Scotist epistemology reveals that he was not seriously tempted by its nineteenth-century analogues. True to his Romantic intellectual ancestry, he does not quail before the unruly variety of nature. Rather, he seeks the conscious wellspring of his art in the multiplicity that confronts us in language and in the world.

Closer to Hopkins are critics who treat him as a serious student of philosophy. Yet because Hopkins's private notes are more than a little cryptic, and the work of John Duns Scotus is notoriously difficult, for centuries little read and less translated, Hopkins's use of Scotus has been a difficult study. Before Allan Wolter's monumental editing and translation project made Scotus's texts accessible, a critical tradition had already arisen that linked the philosopher to Hopkins's Romantic apprehension of the singular self. Critics tended to assume that Hopkins's most famous neologism, "inscape," corresponded to Scotus's best known innovation, *haecceitas,* the very extreme of each creature's particularity. Patricia Ball's great contributions with regard to the Ruskinian perspectivism of Hopkins, and the precision and experiential richness of his language, are the foundation of her argument that inscape is the "individual essence" of a thing.[5] But, for the sake of precision, "essence" must be distinguished from the individuating princi-

5. Ball, *The Science of Aspects,* 107, 109.

ple, *haecceitas.* The essence of a thing or an accident can be identified with its "quiddity," answering the question "What is it?" As an ontological term, essence means the nature of a thing.[6] It is "the foundation and cause of whatever other things are in that thing."[7] But, although Hopkins believed in such essences, as Ong has demonstrated, he believed the deepest selves of other creatures inaccessible to anyone but God. We shall see in the next chapter how those inaccessible selves may be manifested.

Moreover, inscape is not singular for any given thing. Note the plurality of inscapes in sea and sky where Hopkins records his first encounter with Scotus:

> I thought how sadly the beauty of inscape was unknown and buried away from simple people and yet how near at hand if they had eyes to see it and could be called out everywhere again. . . . At this time I had first begun to get hold of the copy of Scotus on the Sentences in the Baddley Library and was flush with a new stroke of enthusiasm. It may come to nothing or it may be a mercy of God. But just then when I took in any inscape of the sky or sea I thought of Scotus.[8]

Nevertheless, Gardner and Pick, with a host of followers, conceive inscape as an attempt to put Scotist *haecceitas* into words. These critics understand something crucial: Hopkins's fascination with the particular. But while Hopkins knew and appropriated the notion of *haecceitas,* it is not inscape; *haecceitas* is unintelligible in this life, and what he says in defending his poem on Saint Alphonsus Rodriguez applies to all his work: "[T]he sonnet (I say it snorting) aims at being intelligible."[9]

Some critics seek the meaning of inscape in universals rather than in particulars. Alan Heuser based his approach to inscape on the Platonic leanings of Hopkins's college circle and the Pre-Raphaelites whom Hopkins admired. Despite some fine, sensitive readings of ma-

6. Bernard Wuellner, S.J., *Dictionary of Scholastic Philosophy* (Milwaukee: Bruce, 1956), 42.

7. R. McKeon, *Selections from Medieval Philosophers,* Vol. 2: *Roger Bacon to William of Ockham* (New York: Scribner's, 1930), 453 (glossary).

8. Hopkins, *Journals and Papers,* 221.

9. Hopkins, *Letters to Bridges,* 293 (3 Oct. 1888).

terial from the journals, Heuser defined inscape as a "fixed type between natural form and essential idea."[10] James Collins, discussing Hopkins's Scotist philosophical grounding, associates inscape with "common nature," a sort of characteristic essence of a species.[11] Scotus indeed discusses such a concept, which can be intellectually constructed from individuals, but it is "indifferent to multiplication"—meaning not particular to any single thing, but capable of appearing in many distinct things. The concept that Collins is discussing is what Hopkins actually called the "make or species."[12] J. Hillis Miller, in his early *The Disappearance of God,* defined inscape as "generic form repeated," though later he changed his opinion about the nature of inscape, indeed about the nature of language. Hopkins did use "inscape" to refer to universals: horses, Spanish chestnuts, or rushing streams in general; he likewise used it to refer to particulars, such as a single bluebell or a singular work of art. Hopkins was a moderate philosophical realist, like Scotus or Aquinas; he considered both particular things and the general principles of their classification to have reality. "Inscape" can be implicit in any worldly thing, be it physical or abstract. The crux of the difficulty of understanding inscape is the way that the word is not limited in reference either exclusively to particular things or exclusively to general ideas. It exists neither entirely in the observed object—although it "governs the behavior" of that object—nor in the observer—although not everyone can see it and sometimes a single object's inscape "multiplies" in the mind of its discoverer.[13] Hopkins cherishes abstract general laws as assiduously as he does the riotous variety of things existing in matter rather than thought. His insights were simultaneously colored through by religion and rigorously aimed at intelligibility; he has definite views and yet invites a trusting collaboration between poet and reader.

10. Heuser, *Shaping Vision of Gerard Manley Hopkins,* 38.

11. Collins, "Philosophical Themes in G. M. Hopkins," 101.

12. Hopkins, *Poetical Works,* 157. Here Hopkins uses the second medieval meaning of "species," a classification in the definitional scheme. A narrowing of that definition has descended to us as the technical term in biology.

13. Hopkins, *Journals and Papers,* 211.

We must sift Hopkins criticism through the philosophical theology that Hopkins studied and loved, especially the work of Scotus, whose mind is yet closer to Hopkins's than Newman's. Scotus acknowledges that a shaping imagination molds the experiences recorded by anyone's senses, and yet affirms that people do know the world outside themselves. The mind organizes experiences not by fictions but by what Scotus calls *formalitates*, aspects of a thing perceived that are separable realities and yet do not violate the unity that makes that entity a single thing.[14] Being real, *formalitates* are independent of individual perceivers, but they require for their existence the possibility of a perceiving intellect. No two people perceive the same things; we therefore must trust, and not demand the single vision that is impossible for wayfarers with separate bodies. Nevertheless, we can say enough to open up truths to one another. If this epistemology is taken seriously, the task of art, of all communication, is to bring these understandings into full reality in human discourse. Hopkins's idea of inscape predates his first encounter with Scotus, but inscapes correspond nearly exactly to Scotus's *formalitates.*

Discovering *formalitates* is a natural human act; and inscape, "the soul of art," animates something that is for Hopkins not supernatural but human. Yet some religious critics, and some Ruskinian romanticists, consider Hopkins's very human artistic inspiration a spiritual ascent. Alison Sulloway, in *Gerard Manley Hopkins and the Victorian Temper,* finds Hopkins looking for "something mystical" in aesthetics. Nathan Cervo, who says "it would be a mistake to think of Hopkins as a philosopher," judges that "poetry and systematic religion of any kind are so radically inimical to each other that the one habitually finds the other heretical or insufficiently articulate."[15] Free of Cervo's allergy to

14. Hopkins did not use the word *formalitates* in any currently published writings. Scotus himself used it interchangeably with various other terms, such as *realitates,* to designate the concept of various identified realities in an object. This concept will be more fully explained in the text. "Formalities" has become the standard term among twentieth-century Scotists writing in English, such as Wolter, Gelber, and Gracjewski, and I follow their usage here. Hopkins's use of "realty" may indicate a preference for *realitates* instead.

15. Cervo, "'The ooze of oil/Crushed,'" 147–48.

system in religion, Maria Lichtmann instead follows James Finn Cotter in pointing readers to the organized gnosis of negative theology.[16] Saying in 1989 that "[i]nscape was in effect a religious experience," Lichtmann makes Hopkins a mystical "proficient" on the "purgative way"[17] of Saint John of the Cross, and thereby distorts her otherwise excellent treatment of parallelism and chiming in Hopkins's poetry; she takes it for a suppression of reasoning for the purpose of "kenosis of the intellect."[18] Cotter's *Inscape: The Christology and Poetry of Gerard Manley Hopkins*, after speculating on a possible patristic background for Hopkins's spirituality, discusses mystical ascent as a systematic retreat from the state of separate being into the self-forgetfulness of union with God. This Cotter associates with inscape, and he warns that "only the pure of heart attain to inscape,"[19] a statement the poet could not approve. Hopkins believed one could be a very good artist and a very bad man (Milton is his example).[20] Donald Walhout, who neither considers Hopkins a mystic nor an example of the opposition of religion to poetic expression, provides a substantial list of other mid-twentieth-century critics who do.[21] As we saw in our discussion of Hopkins's undergraduate musings about Ruskin, Hopkins was familiar with the notion of art as "something mystical" but did not accept it; for Hopkins, art was not the achievement of holiness but an intellectual pursuit, with its moral and religious content dependent on the will of the artist.

16. "Negative" refers to a theology that involves emptying one's understanding of all that applies to creatures. Such theologians are called negative only in reference to their conviction that one must negate, one must not allow oneself to rest in, images of God drawn from the erroneous impressions we get from our senses. As such a technical term "negative" indicates only the theoretical stance, not a value judgment on the technique or any of its putative psychological effects.

17. Lichtmann, *Contemplative Poetry*, 147–49.

18. Lichtmann, *Contemplative Poetry*, 140. As we have seen in the chapter on his relationship to the Oxford Movement, Hopkins was deeply suspicious of religious anti-intellectualism and worshipped "Logos or Reason" as his Savior. For a more dependable understanding of kenosis in Hopkins, see Downes, *The Great Sacrifice*.

19. Cotter, *Inscape*, 24.

20. Hopkins, *Letters to Bridges*, 39 (3 April 1877).

21. Walhout, *Send My Roots Rain*, 131–37.

Hopkins wanted to bring his readers to know God, but, as we saw in Chapter 5, he certainly did not advocate negating either one's own thought or one's knowledge of creatures to encounter God. His letters to his father and Canon Liddon upon his conversion resist ideas about mystical illumination; he attributes his conversion to "(i) simple and strictly drawn arguments partly my own, partly others', (ii) common sense (iii) reading the Bible . . . (iv) an increasing knowledge of the Catholic system."[22] The notion that religious knowledge depends upon special experiences inaccessible to rationality has become a commonplace; indeed, it grounds much twentieth-century political and moral rhetoric which relegates anything labeled "religious" to a twilight zone inaccessible to rational thought.[23] Hopkins acknowledged that natural approaches to God were not fully adequate, but approved of them:

> Let me be to Thee as the circling bird,
> Or bat with tender and air-crisping wings,
> That shapes in half-light his departing rings,
> From both of whom a changeless note is heard.
> I have found my music in a common word . . .
> Love, oh my God, to call thee love and love.[24]

The "common" here is natural, like the cry of bird or bat, yet stable and changeless. The way to knowledge may be obscure, in half-light (as Hopkins wrote to Bridges about his political ignorance, "I live in bat-light").[25] Still, the fully enlightened and those who must live in partial darkness both acknowledge some single thing that leaves "other science all gone out of date."

Mystics pursuing union with God purge their minds of human reason and creaturely concepts because creaturely perfections tell of God only dimly, by analogy, and earthly beauty is a distraction from the divine. Scotus and Hopkins both acknowledge the validity of mystical

22. Hopkins, *Further Letters*, 93 (16 Oct. 1866).

23. Cf. current debate on similar matters among philosophical theologians in Norman Kretzmann, "Evidence against Anti-Evidentialism," in *Our Knowledge of God*, ed. K. J. Clark (Netherlands: Kluwer Academic Publishers, 1992); see esp. 20.

24. Hopkins, *Poetical Works*, 84.

25. Hopkins, *Letters to Bridges*, 27 (2 Aug. 1871).

insights; nevertheless, one could hardly defend the position that Hopkins points his readers away from the beauty of creatures. Hopkins did not disdain imperfect knowledge; he sought to know God in the natural world approached sacramentally, as a philosopher rather than as a mystic. Hopkins finds dignity in the physical world for its own sake, not merely for what it symbolizes.

Hopkins first encountered Scotus in Scotus's *Ordinatio (Commentary on the Sentences).*[26] The prologue to that work features a long argument to prove that theology is a science, not in the term's modern empirical sense, but in the older sense in which mathematics is a science: a body of knowledge that can be pursued by natural means with intellectual certainty. Natural means demanded terms that could be used for both natural and supernatural matters; Scotus claimed that

26. Hopkins had access to the version associated with Scotus's teaching at Oxford and thus called the "Oxford Work," *Opus Oxoniense.* Scholars now call this the *Ordinatio,* a name that refers to the work's place in the Subtle Doctor's academic accreditation. That work I will hereafter refer to as *Ord.* It is divided into four books, in each of which are numerous "distinctions"; many of these are divided into "parts," and finally "quaestiones," which have conventionally numbered paragraphs. The decisive edition is the Vaticanis Polyglottis, which has been underway since 1950; this edition of the *Ordinatio* is not yet complete, but where possible I refer to it as "Vat." by volume and page number after the conventional citation to Scotus's own divisions of the work. I will discuss Scotus with scant regard to the development of his ideas over time; the relevant ideas can be explained without reference to chronology, and Hopkins had no way to date Scotus's works. The works Hopkins had available to him at the Baddely library consisted of an edition of the *Ordinatio* and the *Quaestiones Quodlibetales.* These indeed are considered Scotus's most important works. As late as 1944, when Wolter wrote his study of the transcendentals, there was some confusion about the dependability of the various Scotist texts and how close each was to the master's hand. Charles Balíc's article seems to have been definitive on the subject; he discusses how confusion had reigned for centuries about the authority and dating of the various texts. See "The Life and Work of John Duns Scotus," in *John Duns Scotus, 1265–1965,* Studies in Philosophy and the History of Philosophy, Vol. 3, ed. John Ryan and Bernardine Bonansea (Washington, D.C.: The Catholic University of America Press, 1965), 1–27. Balíc's research allowed Hester Gelber to argue that the formal nonidentity (which will be discussed below) is an early solution to the Trinitarian problem and that Scotus's thought developed beyond it ("Logic and the Trinity" [Ph.D. diss., University of Wisconsin, 1974], passim). Marilyn McCord Adams's "Ockham on Identity and Distinction," *Franciscan Studies* 36 Annual 14 (1976): 5–75, builds on Gelber's conclusion. This is a recent development in Scotus scholarship; Hopkins had not the resources to consider such an idea.

one term applied not analogically but "univocally" to God and naturally accessible creatures alike.

Univocity has occasioned some undue enthusiasm. "Univocal" is a very technical, limited adjective, used in logic rather than metaphysics; it indicates that a term "suffices as a syllogistic middle term," one "whose unity suffices for contradiction when it is affirmed and denied of the same thing."[27] The major premise of a syllogism ordinarily defines some category: "A man is an animal." The minor premise classifies something under the category: "Hopkins is a man." The conclusion follows: "Hopkins is an animal." Predicates that are not definitions also function in syllogisms, though they must cover the entire category to which they are applied: "All men shall die; Hopkins is a man; Hopkins shall die." The terms in the major and the minor premise must be "univocal" rather than "equivocal." The following syllogism is invalid because of equivocal terms:

> Major premise: To deliberately end someone's life is evil.
> Minor premise: Hopkins has a life in Dublin.
> Conclusion: It is evil to deliberately end Hopkins's life in Dublin.

"Life" cannot legitimately mean "heartbeat and brain function" in the first term and "a place in the social and economic world" in the second—though both meanings are old and respectable.[28] A superior could have ended the second kind of life by posting Hopkins to Wales instead of Dublin—and no doubt done plenty of good.

Scotus claims that "being" applies univocally to God and creatures because one can peel away all distinctions and still assert "it is a being" of anything. The term "being" is not merely logical or epistemological; it names something real. However, like logical terms, "being" is "transcendental" to Aristotle's ten categories, which classify assertions

27. John Duns Scotus, *Ord.* 1, d. 3, p. 1, qq. 1–2, no. 26 (Vat. 3:26), trans. Arthur Hyman and James Walsh, in *Philosophy in the Middle Ages: The Christian, Islamic, and Jewish Traditions* (Indianapolis, Ind.: Hackett, 1973), 562.

28. See the chapter "Life," in C. S. Lewis, *Studies in Words*, 2d ed. (Cambridge, U.K.: Cambridge University Press, 1967), 269–305. This particular equivocation has fueled the debate over legal abortion in twentieth-century America.

about things in the contingent, created world.[29] Scotus claims that transcendentals apply not only to creation but to the necessary being, God. In other words, if "being" can be used of God and creatures, one can reason one's way, syllogistically, to other sorts of information about God; thus, natural experience and reason make it possible to say some true things about God. Scotus's position on univocity was unusual, but it was uncontroversial to accept that "goodness," "unicity," and "truth" are transcendental terms "coextensive with being." If something *is*, it is accurate to say that it is good, that it is true, and that it has unicity.[30]

We shall examine Hopkins's poetic outworking of this common philosophical idea in his sonnet "Ribbesdale." The terms "unicity," "goodness," and "truth," while they apply to all the same things, do differ in the ways that they refer to the things' meanings—to being as it is known. (That is, they differ in intension rather than in extension.) *Unicity* refers to being considered in relation to itself; *truth* refers to being considered in relation to the intellect; *goodness* refers to being considered in relation to the will.[31] Now the consideration of a plum, say, in relation to one's will, is real enough—"I really like that plum"—but still that consideration is not as real as the plum. There is a radical asymmetry between being in itself and being as known. Being as known, while various, is greatly diminished in comparison to being in itself. Hyperbole about the tension between being in itself and being as known might stimulate Cotter's expression when he says that inscape "defines this unity of tension between the creature's holding back in nothingness and multiplicity, and its flight toward the center:

29. For further explanation, see Peter Coffey, *Ontology, or the Theory of Being* (1912; reprint, Gloucester, Mass.: Peter Smith, 1970), 207–46.

30. The preceding discussion owes most of its substance to Allan Wolter's classic study, *The Transcendentals and Their Function in the Metaphysics of Duns Scotus* (Washington, D.C.: The Catholic University of America Press, 1946), where Wolter discusses two other classes of metaphysical transcendentals—"pure perfections" and "disjunctive transcendentals"—at length. (Hans Urs von Balthasar follows ancient practice in adding "beauty" to the list of transcendentals coextensive with being, but this can be subsumed under "goodness.")

31. Discussed helpfully in Coffey, *Ontology, or the Theory of Being*, 114.

Being, the One."[32] But if this notion of the nothingness of creation is taken as serious epistemology rather than as rhetorical flourish, only analogical knowledge of God is possible in this life, where information comes through the senses.

A strictly analogical view of human concepts of God was part of the Tractarian intellectual package, and indeed the young poet for a while deprecated the world of sensual reality. But Hopkins's stiff Tractarian analogies give way to the "realer . . . rounder replies" of his priesthood. A univocal approach to being in God and the world stands behind the arresting intimacy of Hopkins's addresses to God in the Terrible Sonnets—"sir," "thou terrible," "thou my friend"—and such odd expressions as "Forth Christ from cupboard fetched" in "The Bugler Boy's First Communion." Hopkins is acknowledging that at least some of what he has learned from his senses applies directly to God. We understand being—and Being—by abstraction. Art, and its "soul," inscape, involves the intelligibility of being as perceived, and perception is not entirely abstract. We have our perceptions, as a rule, from the being of physical creatures. Being as perceived is good, true, and one.

"Intelligibility" is a good definition for transcendental truth, *verum*. A true thing is intelligible to the mind that made it, the mind that perceives it, or both. Although the Latin word is simply *unum*, "one," unicity does not refer to numerical unity, but rather to being "undivided in itself and divided from all else."[33] Perceiving unicity means finding what unifies a thing and distinguishes it from other things. Scotus's favorite example is whiteness. A detectable sameness in white things defines them as white rather than as yellow or green. This paper, a snowfield, and a puddle of milk have such a sameness.[34] Unicity applies to being because, as the simplest of concepts, "being" cannot be divided.[35] By experience, people can distinguish being from not-be-

32. Cotter, *Inscape*, 129–30.

33. Duns Scotus, *Ord.* 4, d. 6, q. 1, n. 4, cited and explained in Wolter, *The Transcendentals*, 103ff.

34. Duns Scotus, *Ord.* 1, d. 3, p. 1, q. 4, no. 230 (Vat. 3:138–39), in *Philosophical Writings*, trans. Allan Wolter (Indianapolis, Ind.: Hackett, 1987), 107.

35. Duns Scotus, *Ord.* 1, d. 3, p. 1, qq. 1–2, no. 80 (Vat. 3:54–55). I am grateful to William Frank for pointing out this reference. A French translation exists in *Jean Duns*

ing, or illusion. (Scotus discounts the exceptional experiences of delusional people.)

Long before he read Scotus, Hopkins discussed unicity in his notes on Parmenides, who compares Being to a ball "rounded and true." Hopkins says non-being is "seen as a want of oneness, all that is unforedrawn"; his Greek translations equate "foredraw" with συνέχω—that is, "to hold (ἔχω) together (σύν)."[36] Non-being he calls "waste space which offers either nothing to the eye to foredraw or many things foredrawing away from one another." It is the observer that must foredraw, pull together, the unicity of being. Not-being is not multiplicity per se but multiplicity that does not cohere. Recall where Hopkins translates Parmenides: "[T]o be and to know or being and thought are the same. The truth in thought is Being." But Hopkins distinguishes being and its attributes, unlike "pantheist" Parmenides. Preserving the priority of being to knowing allows Scotus also to escape "pantheist" monism.[37]

Scotus accepts Saint Augustine's declaration on being in relation to the will: being is the desirable, the good.[38] If truth and unicity are kept formally distinct from being—that is, truly present in being but manifested only in a knower—aesthetic and moral goodness meet. According to Hopkins's early art theory, the goodness in aesthetics is its truth; good art lets us know something. Being is "true," intelligible, so the knower can and must be true, in the sense of "faithful to the object

Scot sur la conaissance de Dieu et l'univocité de l'Étant, trans. Olivier Boulnois (Paris: Presses Universitaires de France, 1988).

36. Hopkins, *Journals and Papers,* 129 and n. fragment 8.33, in Kirk, Raven, and Schofield, *Presocratic Philosophers,* 252.

37. Rachel Salmon, working from a deconstructionist perspective, criticizes Cotter for making being and knowing "one" in "'Wording it How': The Possibilities of Utterance in *The Wreck of the Deutschland,*" *Hopkins Quarterly* 10, no. 3 (Fall 1983): 106, n5. She is accurate in her characterization of his argument, but mistakes this Parmenidean "pantheism," as Hopkins called it, for "incarnationist" theology. The asymmetry of being and knowing is absolutely fundamental to the most ancient expositions of the doctrine of the Trinity (such as Tertullian's). Trinitarian dogma is foundational to any orthodox doctrine of the Incarnation, and certainly to Hopkins's theology. A similar error infects Culler's work, to which she refers.

38. Augustine, *De Civitate Dei* 11.10, 16, 17. *Concerning the City of God, Against the Pagans,* trans. Henry Bettenson (Harmondsworth, Middlesex, England: Penguin Books, 1984), 440, 447–48.

known." Knowledge is desirable but must be responsible. The will, recall, desires what is good about being; with regard to truth, the will binds faithful knowledge to intelligible being and fulfills their unity in goodness. Here is the place where two senses of "true" meet.

Since everything that exists is true and has unicity—that is to say, each thing is distinguishable from other things and from fictions—we can exercise our wills to abstract unicities from experience and remember them. We attach labels to them and thus we can talk truthfully to one another. Of course, if truth were not coextensive with being, language would be inescapably equivocal even though unicity and being could be attributed to God and creatures alike. The transcendental categories coextensive with being stand or fall together; if being lacks goodness, intelligibility or unicity, then the universe as a whole is in fact duplicitous, unintelligible, evil; and a despairing nihilism is the only rational response.[39] But if all being is good, one, and true, then this despair and nihilism is no innocent error, but an evil choice.

Language is, of course, mostly about knowledge of creatures. Morally certain that God means all truth to be accessible, Scotus resisted a common notion that made language a matter of communicating about purely mental entities. He wrote in a section of the *Ordinatio* that Hopkins read: "What is properly signified by a spoken word is a thing."[40] Dominik Perler points out that for Scotus, "a relation (whether real or conceptual) is a peculiar being."[41] Hopkins's 1868 "Notes on Greek thought" anticipate his encounter with Scotus: "All words mean either things or relations of things; you may also say then substances or attributes or again wholes and parts."[42] These declarations are not so naive as they may appear. Hopkins brings to the question an acute sense of the isolation of individuals within their own perceptions; Scotus writes in the midst of the great medieval dispute over the nature of language and memory (which prefigures the positions of some of

39. Duns Scotus, *Ord.* 1, d. 3, p. 1, q. 4, nn. 218–19 (Vat. 3:132–33), trans. McKeon, *Selections from Medieval Philosophers,* 2:320, 324–25.

40. Duns Scotus, *Ord.* 1, d. 27, qq. 1–3, no. 83 (Vat. 6:97), in Dominik Perler, "Duns Scotus on Signification," *Medieval Philosophy and Theology* 3 (1993): 97.

41. Perler, "Duns Scotus on Signification," 99.

42. Hopkins, *Journals and Papers,* 125.

Hopkins's twentieth-century critics). Scotus's work on signification attacked a variant form of Hopkins's pet problem: how to reconcile the evident isolation of each person within the peculiar world of his own senses with the fact that we can communicate.

In 1868, Hopkins traces language to "the idea in the mind" and says "[t]hat idea itself has two terms, the image (of sight or sound or *scapes* of the other senses) which is in fact physical" and "secondly the conception."[43] Not surprisingly, the young Aristotelian's two terms correspond to the two "species" (interior images) in medieval cognition theory, the "sensible species" of sense data and its abstraction into the "intelligible species." But how does one trace a connection between these mental events—"in propriety the word"—and experience outside of discourse? In short, can words mean not ideas of things but *things?* Scotus, another Aristotelian, believed that all information comes from the senses; though logic is simply inherent in the way the mind works, all occasions for its exercise must come from sense data.[44] That information enters the memory through the sensible species, and therefore never without interpretation. But spectres of the future's poststructuralist *ecriture* grin here like skulls; how can we judge the truth if everything is interpreted already? As Scotus puts it, rather ponderously:

> If the species [that is, the concept] abstracted from the thing is a concurrent factor in all knowledge, and if we cannot judge when such a species represents itself as such and when it represents itself as object, then it makes no difference what concurs with such a species. We shall never have a norm for distinguishing the true from what merely appears to be true. These arguments then seem to lead to the conclusion that all is uncertain, the opinion of the Academicians.[45]

It is at least the opinion of many academicians today; but neither Scotus nor Hopkins accepted it. Scotus discussed "the certitude of those

43. Hopkins, *Journals and Papers*, 125.

44. Duns Scotus, *Ord.* 1, d. 3, p. 1, q. 4, no. 234 (Vat. 3:140–41), trans. Wolter, *Philosophical Writings*, 108.

45. Duns Scotus, *Ord.* 1, d. 3, p. 1, q. 4, no. 222 (Vat. 3:134–35), trans. Wolter, *Philosophical Writings*, 104.

things known through sense experience"[46] with characteristic subtlety. First of all, a wayfarer can ordinarily recognize impediments to the senses. To disallow sense experience when we sense no impediment is morally bad-faith argumentation: "If therefore we do not doubt their truth and we are not deceived, as is clear, then we are certain of things known by way of sense. . . . a power [that is, one of the senses] does not err concerning the object proper and proportional to it unless it is indisposed."[47] Scotus argues that some basic information is "known through itself," most importantly our own willed actions, such as accepting or recalling sense data. Our willed actions we know "intuitively," in "the technical sense of knowledge of an object as existing and present."[48] He disapproves of people's refusal to acknowledge the truths they live by: "[I]f you contend against me that *no* proposition is *known through itself*, I do not wish to dispute with you: for it is shown that you are shameless, because you are not persuaded, as is evident in your actions."[49] Then he points out that when awake, people know that their dreams were only dreams, and do not act as if they were real; therefore they know the state of their own faculties. Scotus observes that memory, the foundation of language, has two objects: the *thing* we remember and our mental act of creating a "species," an image of it. No one can recall a *thing* with intuitive certainty. The action of one's own soul in receiving the information and creating the image is what one knows intuitively.[50] We then analyze our experiences and

46. Duns Scotus, *Ord.* 1, d. 3, p. 1, q. 4, no. 225 (Vat. 3:136), trans. Wolter, *Philosophical Writings*, 105.

47. Duns Scotus, *Ord.* 1, d. 3, p. 1, q. 4, no. 253 (Vat. 3:154), trans. Wolter, *Philosophical Writings*, 118.

48. Stephen Dumont, "Theology as a Science and Duns Scotus's Distinction between Intuitive and Abstractive Cognition," *Speculum* 64 (1989): 579–99 (580). Scotus establishes four kinds of knowledge "of which we are necessarily certain, viz. (1) things knowable in an unqualified sense, (2) things knowable through experience, (3) our actions, (4) things known at the present time through the senses." Cf. Duns Scotus, *Ord.* 1, d. 3, p. 1, q. 4, no. 228, *adnotatio* (Vat. 3:137), trans. Wolter, *Philosophical Writings*, 105–6.

49. Duns Scotus, *Ord.* 1, d. 3, p. 1, q. 4, no. 256 (Vat. 3:155–56), trans. McKeon, *Selections from Medieval Philosophers*, 2:336. Wolter's translation, *Philosophical Writings*, 119, is good but less colorful.

50. Dumont, "Theology as a Science," passim, and Wolter, "Duns Scotus on Intuition, Memory, and Our Knowledge of Individuals," in *The Philosophical Theology of*

reason about what it was that we received. We also know enough of time intuitively to understand the present state of our powers, receiving or recalling.

This is a very small window on reality: that we have experienced some intrusion of information is the entire content of intuitive knowledge. Analysis is secondary; however useful it might be to know whether the animal in the bush is a rabbit or a bear, it is nevertheless knowledge to recognize that something *is* in the bush. To know that something truly exists out there is actually to know a great deal. That single intuitive recognition establishes the vital difference between truth and self-deception. We can avoid deceiving ourselves. We can know things. The window of unmediated experience, however small, is an escape route from the prison house of language, an opportunity for meaningful communication: there's a world out there to talk about.

How does Hopkins's poetry work in conjunction with these Scotist doctrines? It is important to Hopkins's technique to allow his readers to experience unanalyzed perception, which Christopher Devlin mistakes for inscape, and gives the Scotist name of *species specialissima*.[51] Inscape does not leave the intellect fallow, but Hopkins does rely heavily upon his reader's memory and associated analytical powers to make a poem "explode" into meaning. Such blind trust can look like

John Duns Scotus, ed. Marilyn McCord Adams (Ithaca, N.Y.: Cornell University Press, 1990), 98 124.

51. Hopkins is likely to have come across the concept, which is discussed in *Ord.* 1, d. 3, qq. 1–2, nn. 3, 76–78 (Vat. 3:50–55). See Christopher Devlin, "The Image and the Word, Parts 1 and 2," *The Month,* n.s., 3 (1950): 120 (1) and 197 (2). Devlin describes Hopkins's Scotism cautiously in his editorial notes, but here errs first in identifying unanalyzed perception with inscape and second in making it a spiritual insight. According to William Frank, "*species specialissima*" is simply the moment's impression ("species") upon the senses, called "specialissima" because it has not yet been made general or indeed analyzed in any way (Frank, personal correspondence). Heuser, building on Devlin's article, did not take the term as epistemological. Heuser linked inscape to "nature being created, nature in search of or on the verge of self, called the *species specialissima*"; see *Shaping Vision of Gerard Manley Hopkins,* 37. Hopkins sometimes uses terms from Scotus's epistemological analysis as a basis for his ontological speculations (see Chapter 8 below at notes 37ff.), so Devlin's error in fusing real and logical terms is not uncommon in Hopkins studies.

an attempt to overwhelm mere intellectual comprehension, but Hopkins respected intellectual comprehension. Sometimes he just gets carried away with his confidence that his reader will be able to follow. Bridges was simply unable to interpret

His rash-fresh re-winded new-skeinèd score
In crisps of curl off wild winch whirl, and pour
And pelt músic, till none's to spill nor spend.[52]

Hopkins told Bridges, somewhat shamefacedly, that he did mean the lines to be intelligible.

I was fascinated with *cynghannedd* or consonant-chime, and as in Welsh *englyns*, "the sense" as one of themselves said, "gets the worst of it." In this case it exists but is far from glaring. . . . Rash-fresh . . . (it is dreadful to explain these things in cold blood) means a headlong and exciting new snatch of singing, resumption by the lark of his song. . . . The skein and the coil are the lark's song, which from his height gives the impression (not to me only) of something falling to earth and not vertically quite but tricklingly or wavingly, something as a skein of silk ribbed by having been tightly wound.[53]

Hopkins is not offended, though he is embarrassed, by having to explain. The experience was not beyond normal understanding; it was just put together in "a mood of great, in fact abnormal, mental acuteness," in which metaphorical relationships could be more easily forged.

Scotus points out that with no socially recognized definition—a "relation of reason"—there is no language, only noise.[54] Abstract and articulate definitions, based on voluntary faith in the linguistic community, can only unfold once there is a sensory conception in the memory; to be language, the physical reality of the noise (or other sign) must wed the social reality of the definition. Hopkins read Sco-

52. Hopkins, "The Sea and the Skylark," in *Poetical Works*, 143 and note, 374.

53. Hopkins, *Letters to Bridges*, 163–64 (26 Nov. 1882).

54. Daniel O. Dahlstrom, "Signification and Logic: Scotus on Universals from a Logical Point of View," *Vivarium* 18 (1980): 84. In note 11, Dahlstrom points out that even a natural sign, such as smoke for fire or darkness for an eclipse, requires the working of a rational mind to make it a sign. Cf. Perler, "Duns Scotus on Signification," 99. Dahlstrom calls the reality of the sound or other physical sign the "foundation."

tus in 1872; for his 1872–1873 lectures on rhetoric, he calls poetry "speech framed to be heard for its own sake and interest even over and above its interest of meaning." He distinguishes the purely formal—verse—from the actual communication which is poetry. Verse without meaning is not language; even if musically lovely, it isn't poetry. Yet poetry is meant to draw our attention to physical aspects of language, "the shape which is contemplated for its own sake," as well as to its meaning:

> Verse is (inscape of spoken sound, not spoken words, or speech employed to carry the inscape of spoken sound—or in the usual words) speech wholly or partially repeating the same figure of sound. Now there is speech which wholly or partially repeats the same figure of grammar and this may be framed to be heard for its own sake over and above its interest of meaning. . . . Verse . . . might be composed without meaning. . . . and then *alone* it would not be poetry but might be part of a poem. But if it has meaning and is meant to be heard for its own sake it will be poetry.[55]

In choice of word and image, a poet attends to the making of good symbols, but also to the sounds and structures of language, interesting for their own sake, which Hopkins trusts can lead us further into meaning. For "subtle and recondite" meanings, the sounds and structures may become so complex that not all can be immediately apprehended but must "explode" later. As Culler demonstrates in reading "The Golden Echo," primitive predefinitional knowledge of the poem comes through its aural qualities, and the poem hangs upon them in the memory, awaiting understanding.

All that we know intuitively is being; from that we can reason to speak of God and creatures. The concept of being is one, and the separate knowledge of God and creatures must be disentangled from this fused state—"confused knowledge" as Scotus called it. And all that we know of a poem is sound—like being, common to many objects of knowledge.

Indeed, Hopkins cares most deeply about opening for his readers, through the knowledge of undifferentiated being, a way into encoun-

55. Hopkins, *Journals and Papers,* 289.

tering truths about God in creatures. Building on his Tractarian conceptions of analogy, Hopkins considered the physical sounds of words themselves as information about the Creator for those who choose to believe—as indeed, words reveal other knowledge to believers in language. Hopkins's preoccupation with the foundations of language (recall his youthful enthusiasm for the onomatopoetic theory) had a different history than that of Scotus, who was concerned with defending natural theology from a relapse into mere fideism;[56] coming of age in the wake of Romanticism, Hopkins felt the need for rational confidence and direction in dealing with an intuitive religious commitment. By locating the root of rationality in the prerational experience of being, Scotus was putting his finger on the point where the rational and the intuitive meet, forging a unified epistemology in which the knowledge of creation finds its proper end in the knowledge of God. Hopkins found his deepest insights about language echoed in Scotist epistemology.

But instead of grappling with Hopkins's yearning for a philosophy that would put him in contact with meaning and being, J. Hillis Miller attributes to Hopkins the rarefied hedonism of his Oxford tutor Walter Pater, an isolating cocoon of "quickened, multiplied consciousness" cultivated in order to get "as many pulsations as possible into the given time."[57] As Pater's brand of consciousness immerses a person in "impressions, unstable, flickering, inconsistent, which burn and are extinguished with our consciousness of them, it contracts still further: the whole scope of observation is dwarfed into the narrow chamber of the individual mind . . . each mind keeping as solitary prisoner its dream of a world."[58] Miller grafts Hopkins's art onto the Hegelian

56. Stephen Dumont delineates the subtleties of medieval ideas about intuitition and abstraction in the knowledge of God. He demonstrates how Scotus argued that angels naturally know the nature of God through abstraction, and are granted intuitive knowledge of God only by grace. Intuitive knowledge is *visio existens ut existens*—direct sight of that which is as it is. It cannot be identiied with the "confused knowledge" of undifferentiated being which J. Hillis Miller associates with instress on pp. 321–23 of *The Disappearance of God* (Cambridge, Mass.: Harvard University Press, 1963).

57. Walter Pater, *The Renaissance: Studies in Art and Poetry,* ed. Donald Hill (Berkeley and Los Angeles: University of California Press, 1980), 190.

58. Pater, *The Renaissance,* 187–88.

roots of Pater's "Aesthetic Poetry," and Pater's inescapable "dream of a world" grows drearily like poststructuralism's encrusting morass of *ecriture,* which completely engulfs the consciousness. Miller gloats, "Each word leads to another of which it is the displacement, in a movement without origin or end."[59] Miller's linguistic quicksand becomes an eternal being, more sinister and mechanical than Hegel's *geist,* though Miller perhaps rightly claims Hegel as the notion's progenitor. But neither Pater nor Bridges could budge Hopkins in the direction of Hegel. When Bridges tried to share his own Hegelian enthusiasms, Hopkins demurred: "After all I can, at all events a little, read Duns Scotus and I care for him far more than even Aristotle and more *pace tua* than a dozen Hegels."[60]

Hopkins considered Hegel a modern representative of exploded theories about consciousness revived from the twelfth century. In dense notes made as a mature Jesuit, Hopkins refutes "the Hegelians" as he considers whether a human being can be self-existent, or whether there is some universal Humanity that might be self-existent and of which he could be a part.[61] He has already settled that neither his body nor his sensations are self-existent:

> But is it as a last alternative possible that, though neither my body nor the faculties and functions of my soul exist of themselves, there should be one thing in the soul or mind, as if compounded or selved-up with these, which does? a most spiritual principle in some manner the form of the mind as the mind or the soul is said to be of the body; so that my mind would be one selving or pitch of the universal mind, working in others too besides mine, and even in all other things according to their natures and powers and becoming conscious in man. And this would be that very/distinctive self that was spoken of. Here we touch the *intellectus agens* of the Averrhoists and the doctrine of the Hegelians and others.[62]

59. Miller, *Linguistic Moment,* 11, 264.

60. Hopkins, *Letters to Bridges,* 31 (20 Feb. 1875).

61. Inexplicably, Daniel Brown (*Hopkins's Idealism,* 42, 193, 197) reads this passage and the following page to mean the opposite of the plain sense of the words, and proclaims Hopkins a Hegelian. Brown's thesis about Hegelian influences on Hopkins's language could be argued without asserting such a commitment. Had he accepted Hegel's ideas, Hopkins, being a man of firm consistency, and philosophically aware of the difference between Christianity and monism, would have at least quit the Jesuits.

62. Hopkins, *Sermons and Devotional Writings,* 125.

He concludes, after some pages of careful argument, that "there is no such universal."[63] This "*intellectus agens*" originated with the Islamic thinker Averroes, who[64] introduced Aristotle's philosophy to the West. Aristotle, finding perceptions mutable and believing Form changeless, holds that the human mind cannot be pure, active Form. Averroes proposed a passive "material intellect" to receive and store sense data[65] and an immaterial active—or "agent"—intellect to abstract the perceptions organizing Forms.[66] The active intellect may be compared to the Romantic concreating intellect, though it does not bear the emotional weight of Coleridge's enthusiasm.[67] Twentieth-century scholars think Aristotle's "agent intellect" is an impersonal pro-

63. Hopkins, *Sermons and Devotional Writings*, 127.

64. Averroes was an enormously important commentator on Aristotle; cf. Stephen Tempier, Bishop of Paris, "Condemnation of 277 Propositions," trans. in Hyman and Walsh, *Philosophy in the Middle Ages*, 549. All humanity, Averroes believed, exists for the sake of those few who can attain to the Agent Intellect, a sort of universal human mind. Averroes states this most frankly in his important commentary on *The Republic* of Plato, translated by Ralph Lerner in *Averroes on Plato's "Republic"* (Ithaca, N.Y.: Cornell University Press, 1974) but also discusses it in *The Decisive Treatise on the Relation between Religion and Philosophy*, in *On the Harmony of Religions and Philosophy, A Translation, with introduction and notes, of Ibn-Rushd's Kitab fasl al-maqal, with its appendix (Damina) and an Extract from Kitab al-kashf 'an manahij al-adilla*, by George Faldo Hourani. (UNESCO Collection of Great Works. Arabic Series.) ("E. J. W. Gibb Memorial" Series. New Series, 21) (London: Luzac and Co., 1961). Averroes frankly despised the poor and simple, who were to be deceived and pacified so they could better serve the philosophers; his divinization of philosophy and philosophers presented theological problems to the Christians (as it had to the Muslims, who burned Averroes's works and imprisoned him).

65. Bernardo Carlos Bazan, "*Intellectum Speculativum:* Averroes, Thomas Aquinas, and Siger of Brabant on the Intelligible Object," *Journal of the History of Philosophy* 19 (1981): 425–46, 426. Bazan refers his readers to the texts in Averroes. Arthur Hyman points out that commentators differ on whether the passive intellect is indeed material; see his "Averroes as Commentator on Aristotle's Theory of the Intellect," in *Studies in Aristotle*, Studies in Philosophy and the History of Philosophy, Vol. 9, ed. Dominic J. O'Meara (Washington, D.C.: The Catholic University of America Press, 1981), 161–91 (173).

66. Hyman, "Averroes as Commentator on Aristotle's Theory of the Intellect," 170–73.

67. We have seen how the understanding of sensation as a psychological event was also important to Hopkins and Newman. See Newman, "On the Punishment of the Wicked Having No Termination," in *Grammar of Assent*, 389–92; also cf. his *Discourses Addressed to Mixed Congregations* (Westminster, Md.: Christian Classics, 1966), as well

cess for understanding anything; indeed, in its lack of any personal aspect, the Agent Intellect seems to resemble the discursive world of human understanding.[68] If the nihilism of *ecriture* is, as Miller believes, a version of Hegelianism, then perhaps Hopkins has completed the circle by connecting Hegel's concept with Aristotle's linguistic Agent Intellect. But it is important to understand how Averroes shapes the arc of this idea.

Averroes considered the Agent Intellect a spiritual entity, the universal Form of the human mind, instantiated to some degree in human beings. The purified abstractions of philosophy can free the mind from corrupt matter and return it to the immortal, eternal Agent Intellect, clearly a god substitute for Averroes.[69] Scotus, following Thomas Aquinas, calls Aristotle's Agent Intellect a power of the soul.[70] He therefore denies that wayfarers should seek union with it as a "separated substance." Aquinas argued that if the means of knowledge is a single separated substance, then there can be only one knower; individual human beings would be separated from that other, percipient

as Hopkins, *Sermons and Devotional Writings,* 241 and note 3, which refers the reader to Scotus. Then again, the idea was a medieval commonplace.

68. This interpretation is implied in the arguments of Stuart MacClintock, "Heresy and Epithet: An Approach to the Problem of Latin Averroism, Part 2," *Review of Metaphysics* 8 (Dec. 1954): 343–56 (345ff.), and Roland J. Teske, "The End of Man in the Philosophy of Averroes," *New Scholasticism* 37 (1963): 431–61 (440ff.). The phrase that is used to communicate the Agent Intellect being a process, or form, rather than a composite of form and matter, is "all act"—a description also used for God in medieval philosophy, though God is not considered impersonal like the Agent Intellect.

69. *Averroes on Plato's "Republic,"* trans. Ralph Lerner, 21–22. Bazan, *"Intellectum Speculativum,"* 435. Some philosophers tried to Christianize Averroes's Agent Intellect into being the light of the Holy Spirit, who makes knowledge possible. Cf. Dominique Salman, O.P., "Note sur la premiere influence de Averroes," *Revue Neoscolastique de Philosophie* 40 (1937): 203–12. See also Stuart MacClintock, "Heresy and Epithet: An Approach to the Problem of Latin Averroism, Parts 1, 2, and 3," *Review of Metaphysics* 8 (Sept., 1954; Dec. 1954; March 1955): 526–45, 342–56, and 176–99, respectively. By Scotus's time few philosophers held this doctrine. See Steven P. Marrone, *Truth and Scientific Knowledge in the Thought of Henry of Ghent,* Speculum Anniversary Monographs 11 (Cambridge, Mass.: Mediaeval Society of America, 1985), 136–39 and nn.

70. Duns Scotus, *Ord.* 1, d. 3, p. 1, q. 4, no. 260 (Vat. 3:158–59), trans. Allan Wolter, *Philosophical Writings,* 122. The Vaticanis Polyglottis edition adds a "textus interpolatus," which displays some likeness to Hopkins's argument against the existence of the Averroist Agent Intellect; then again, the argument was used by Thomists too.

entity. Though Hopkins speaks more personally, he follows Aquinas's form of argument in critiquing the Hegelian idea of an evolving process of universal consciousness—"the doctrine of the Hegelians."[71] We shall see in Chapter 8 how, good disciple of Newman that he is, Hopkins in a thought experiment contrasts his own experience of incommunicable personality with the experience of existence for a spiritual entity like Hegel's *geist* or Averroes's *intellectus agens.* All Hopkins's perceptions, bound up with his particular existence, are perceived by this projected universal self not as Hopkins perceives them but differently, if at all. In the turn of phrase to which Hillis Miller alludes when he pronounces the deconstructionist verdict on Hopkins—"there is no such [primal] word"—Hopkins is only denying that there is any Agent Intellect, or self-sustaining world of discourse, to subsume individual intellects: "In other words the universal is not really identified with everything else nor with anything else, which was supposed; that is/ there is no such universal."[72] And it is Averroes, not, as Miller thinks, Hopkins, who found, "this splitting apart [i.e., the world's sensual variety] intolerable, and . . . attempted to use language to bring the fragmented pieces back together."[73]

Miller alludes to Hopkins's refusal to identify with the Agent Intellect in his explication of *The Wreck of the Deutschland:*

> "The Wreck of the Deutschland," like all the great poems of Hopkins' maturity, turns on a recognition of the ultimate failure of all poetic language. Its failure is never to be able to express the inconceivable and unsayable mystery of how something that is as unique as a single word—that is, a created soul—may be transformed into the one Word, Christ, which is its model, without ceasing to be a unique and individual self. The theological thought depends on the notion of an initial unity that has been divided or fragmented and so could conceivably be reunified. The linguistic underthought depends on the notion of an initial bifurcation that could not by any conceivable series of lin-

71. Hopkins, *Sermons and Devotional Writings,* 125–27. Thomas Aquinas, *Summa Contra Gentiles* 2:59.9–10, 60.4–5, 73.4–5, 76.2.

72. Hopkins, *Sermons and Devotional Writings,* 127. The Scotist turn of phrase, which Miller appropriates to make the world of discourse indeed into the nonexistent Universal Man, is used by Hopkins to distinguish this fiction from God.

73. Miller, *Linguistic Moment,* 243.

guistic transformations . . . reach back to any primal word. There is no such word. Hopkins' linguistic underthought undoes his Christian overthought.[74]

Hopkins's work thus becomes mere formalistic preciosity—an exercise in increasing undecidability in the text.[75] Miller ignores Hopkins's own linguistic theory and attributes unconscious poststructuralism to him instead: "Hopkins's underthought is a thought about language itself. It recognizes that there is no word for the Word, that all words are metaphors. Each word leads to another of which it is the displacement, in a movement without origin or end."[76] Hopkins had thought too deeply about language to believe that "all words are metaphors," but he loved both puns and metaphors, the former for their multiplicity, the latter because metaphor ferries (θέρειν) across (μετα) difference. Miller's Derridean vocabulary rests on an irrational poststructuralist article of faith: that all language is founded in distinctions. Ferdinand de Saussure noted reasonable distinctions necessary for telling one sign from another; it is the deconstructionists who deny words any communicative basis. Since Miller's words refer, insanely, only to words, a grounding would have to be, not experience, but a primal word. Miller's language becomes a pointless, unwinnable game played in isolation, a "principle of difference and differentiation," which disintegrates the unity that it appears to serve.

The atheistic poststructuralist delectation over the linguistically circumscribed emptiness of all things has elements of an odd similarity to the ineffable deity envisioned by those critics who imply that Hopkins writes of the creature's longing for undifferentiated fusion with God. The idea that multiplicity is a disastrous "initial bifurcation" sparks a certain amount of poststructuralist posturing about tragedy at the heart of Christianity. Using Catholic philosophical vocabulary as irresponsibly as his colleague Culler, Miller consistently misrepresents Christianity as a sort of failed monism. For him, not all being is, as in Christian theology, good; the creation of "the individual

74. Miller, *Linguistic Moment*, 264–65.
75. Miller, *Linguistic Moment*, 248ff.
76. Miller, *Linguistic Moment*, 11, 264.

natural object," and even the Trinity, spring from "the principle of distance or differentiation," a merely lamentable "principle of splitting or punning which is discovered to have already occurred, however far back toward the primal unity one goes, even within the bosom of the Trinity itself."[77] In Hopkins's conception, man as eye, tongue, heart, of the "sweet earth," can indeed speak the One Word in the riotous variety of the world, rejoicing rather than lamenting that in the "series of linguistic transformations,"[78] as Miller puts it, "there is no word for the Word"—at least no single word. Among creatures, individual distinction is, at least in one way, limitation: I am myself because (or partly because) I am not you.[79] But the uniqueness of God does not depend upon distinction from others. Ignorant of this Scotist notion underlying Hopkins's position, Miller strikes a tragic pose:

> The individual natural object and the individual self, by the fact of their individuality, are incapable of being more than a metaphor for Christ—that is, split off from Christ. . . . The more a man affirms himself, the more he affirms his eccentricity, his individuality, his failure to be Christ.[80]

Contrast this to Hopkins's Scotist meditation on the distinction between God and creatures:

> I mean/ a being so intimately present as God is to other things would be identified with them were it not for God's infinity or were it not for God's infinity he could not be so intimately present to things.[81]

77. Miller's implied association of the principles of unity and diversity with the Father and Son respectively has nothing to do with the theology either in its basic catechetical form of distinct persons with equal identity with the Godhead, nor in its more sophisticated outworking in Scotist theology as Hopkins studied it.

78. Miller, *Linguistic Moment,* 265.

79. Allan Wolter argues that this privative sense of nonidentity is important among the contemporaries of Scotus, but that Scotus thinks the individuating principle of creatures is more positive; see his *Philosophical Theology of John Duns Scotus,* 84. In that chapter Wolter discusses individuation with the example of cloned cells. Hopkins thought the individuality of identical organisms without free will could be questionable, while the individuality of cloned humans (as monozygotic twins are) he would not question. See his remarks on the individuality of animals in *Sermons and Devotional Writings,* 128 and 147. I will discuss identity and personality more fully in Chapter 8.

80. Miller, *Linguistic Moment,* 264–65.

81. Hopkins, *Sermons and Devotional Writings,* 128.

Good, in other words, does not flee from all objects that are not Goodness Itself. Miller's analysis, of course, serves the usual poststructuralist conclusion that literature is about the self-referentiality of language.

As we shall see, Hopkins opaquely entwines rhyme, rhythm, and syntax not desperately, to hide the dissolution of a world where nothing is sufficiently like Christ, but because through these physical realities human beings encounter Christ in many ways. How this variety comes to be seen as revelation of the One is the secret of inscape. What Miller calls "Hopkins's darker insight" about multiplicity is in fact "the uncreated light" in its millions of brilliant colors. Hopkins's God treasures, rather than annihilates, all the individual details of his beloved, not despising even the most fleeting graces: "[W]hatever's prized and passes of us, everything that's fresh / and fast flying of us, seems to us sweet of us and swiftly away . . . ," Hopkins says, is in God's love

> kept with fő̋nder a care,
> Fonder a ca̋re kept than we could have kept it, ke̋pt
> Fa̋r with fonder a care (and we, we̋ should have lost it)[82]

And when in his curtal-sonnet Hopkins cries:

> All things counter, original, spáre, stránge;
> Whatever is fickle, frecklèd (who knows how?)
> With swíft, slów; sweet, sőur; adázzle, dím;
> He fathers-forth whose beauty is pást chánge:
> Práise hím.[83]

the poet is giving life to the Scholastic commonplace about the goodness of creation.

Critics who treat Hopkins's poetry as a celebration of absolute individuality and look to *haecceitas* to define inscape are closer to Hopkins, philosophically. It is perverse to imagine Hopkins, with his love of the odd and singular, believing that to be some individual other than God is an evil; and Scotus honored created individuality perhaps even excessively with his theory of *haecceitas*. Nevertheless, inscape is

82. Hopkins, *Poetical Works*, 170–71.
83. Hopkins, *Poetical Works*, 144.

doubly irreconcilable with the concept of *haecceitas.* First, there can be multiple inscapes of a single thing, but only one individuating principle; and, second, it is possible to apprehend and describe inscape, while to do either with *haecceitas* is impossible. A thing's *haecceitas* cannot be described, for *haecceitas* is independent of matter and thus the material accidents that are all that our senses can detect in this life.

Most of Scotus's contemporaries considered matter the source of a thing's individuality, following Aristotle's hypothesis that matter was the changeable, corruptible medium in which changeless, immortal Form was instantiated. Scotus argues that things can be individual without being material; he thinks angels have individual personalities.[84] He observes that since the Form of a species, say "oak tree," is one, then the interaction with matter, which will accept any Form, should not produce trees that differ. Similarly, no aggregation of accidents or qualities could converge to the individuality of one particular thing, such that a clone of that thing (that is, a different thing with all the same accidental features) could be seen as distinct from it.[85] Allan Wolter summarizes: individuality, "that most perfect of unities," is "not privative, but positive, not something accidental like quantity, or contingent like actual existence." He concludes: "Therefore, it must be something intrinsic, pertaining to the category of substance."[86] Thus

84. Wolter, *Philosophical Theology of John Duns Scotus,* 69–71.

85. Timothy B. Noone, "Individuation in Scotus," *American Catholic Philosophical Quarterly* 69 (1995): 527–42, 535; Wolter, *Philosophical Theology of John Duns Scotus,* 81 (what Wolter calls Scotus's fifth argument), 88.

86. Wolter, *Philosophical Theology of John Duns Scotus,* 90. Even a possibility without a nature has *being,* in Scotus's paradigm, in that it contains no internal contradictions (*Quod.* 3; see Perler, "Duns Scotus on Signification," 99 and note 6). Individuality, that aspect of a thing that makes it "incapable of being duplicated" (Wolter, *Philosophical Theology of John Duns Scotus,* 84), is formally distinct from the individual; to consider it is like considering a human without regard to sex or age. It can be done, although no human really exists without sex or age. Real, as opposed to formal, distinctions, allow the distinct things to be separated—like the soul and the body, which death sunders. (Technically, in the theology Hopkins studied, neither a corpse nor a separated soul is a human person; to be fully human, one must have a body. Cf. Ott, *Fundamentals of Catholic Dogma,* 98.) "Formal" distinctions cannot be separated from the object in which they inhere. *Haecceitas* is a formality in any actual creature—that aspect which separates *(repugnare)* creatures from one another when God calls them into being.

Scotus's notion of the real individuating principle is the exact opposite of equating multiplicity with nothingness: multiplicity is intrinsic to created being, and created being, although it is contingent, is nonetheless real—it is true, it is good, and it is one (in a sense that in no way contradicts its multiplicity).

It was W. H. Gardner, in his monumental 1944 study—very early for Hopkins criticism—who tentatively, but very influentially, identified *haecceitas* and inscape.[87] In 1948, W. A. M. Peters discussed Scotus's concepts of *formalitas* and undifferentiated knowledge, but nevertheless identified inscape, as Gardner had, with *haecceitas*.[88] John Pick continued the tradition of treating "inscape" as an ontological term in his introduction to the popular pocket edition, *A Hopkins Reader;* there inscapes are "sharply individuated selves" such that "each thing was almost a separate species."[89] Norman MacKenzie in 1964 attributes intelligibility to *haecceitas,* and conflates it with the undifferentiated experience of being that Scotus did find intelligible, though in his 1981 commentary on Hopkins's sonnets he is more cautious, merely calling Scotus's work "very complicated."[90] Even so acute a critic as Walter Ong connected inscape to the individuating principle.[91]

If a critic thinks that Hopkins seeks to represent the *haecceitas* of a thing and also recognizes that individual essences are inaccessible to our knowledge, then Hopkins's art must seem hopeless and nihilistic. One might try to escape the dilemma by imagining that Hopkins felt

87. W. H. Gardner, *Gerard Manley Hopkins: A Study of Poetic Idiosyncrasy in Relation to Poetic Tradition,* 2 vols. (London: Oxford University Press, 1944), 26.

88. W. A. M. Peters, *Gerard Manley Hopkins: A Critical Essay Towards the Understanding of His Poetry* (1948; reprint, Oxford, U.K.: Basil Blackwell and Johnson Reprint, 1970), 23.

89. John Pick, *A Hopkins Reader* (Garden City, N.Y.: Doubleday Image Books, 1966), 19–20. Pick is using "species" not in the sense of image but in the related sense of a category of classification, whence it has come from the medievals into our biology textbooks.

90. Norman MacKenzie, "Introduction" to *Poems and Prose of Gerard Manley Hopkins* (Baltimore: Penguin Books, 1964), xxiv; *A Reader's Guide to Gerard Manley Hopkins,* note 2, 113.

91. Walter Ong, S.J., *Hopkins, the Self, and God* (Toronto: University of Toronto, 1986), 17, 106–8.

himself to be gifted with special insights, inaccessible to ordinary experience; but everything we know of Hopkins's personality and writings argues against this. It is much better to divorce inscape from *haecceitas,* but not with such haste as to lose sight of the valuable insights of many who have made this mistaken identification.

Catherine Phillips's excellent introduction to the Oxford Authors edition of Hopkins's poems recognizes that Hopkins applies "inscape" to universals, such as species of animals, and that even when inscape is conceived in its most particular manifestations, *haecceitas* refers to an "individuality . . . more fundamental and abstract than that covered by inscape."[92] More importantly, she recognizes both the role of the perceiver in catching inscapes—it is an "artist's analysis"—and the grounding of inscapes in the object seen, at least in those references to inscape that she finds the most significant: "[O]n . . . occasions it is used of the crucial features that form or communicate the inner character, essence or 'personality' of something."[93] Phillips understands that inscape refers to the perceiver drawing out of the thing perceived something that already lies latent within it. Hence Hopkins's use of inscape as a verb: rushing streams are "inscaped" in pillows and troughs[94] because pillows and troughs may offer us an occasion to catch an inscape of rushing streams. Phillips is unable to find a single meaning for inscape, because while sometimes Hopkins seems to use it for the "inner character" of a thing, or the secret law of its growth and decay, sometimes the inscapes of a thing can be multiple: there can be transient inscape, such as that of the sweepings of snow by a door;[95] there can be an inscape of a single thing over time, as in the case of a flower withering. Thus one must actively exert one's mind sometimes to work it out, as in the curves and whorls by which a horse may be "inscaped very simply." Phillips concludes that the term is "not applied with philosophical rigor." However, the term may quite properly have a range that covers all these uses. Phillips has not escaped the

92. Phillips, *Gerard Manley Hopkins,* xxiii.
93. Phillips, *Gerard Manley Hopkins,* xx.
94. Hopkins, *Journals,* 176.
95. Hopkins, *Journals and Papers,* 230.

notion that a thing's inscape must be singular: "the [not "a"] characteristic shape of a thing or species."[96] Some features, Phillips believes, are unimportant, while others reveal "essence or 'personality'"; but Hopkins notices everything. If inscapes must reveal a single, ideal vision of the thing, then we will perhaps undervalue the uniqueness of these humble or fleeting beauties of sweepings or tumbling clouds. But if the deepest uniqueness of each thing is inaccessible to us in this life, then we are free to appreciate the intrinsic value of each of the infinite number of inscapes of a thing, each real and true.

It is not unreasonable to associate inscape and *haecceitas.* Both concepts touch on the special concern with particularity that Hopkins and Scotus shared. However, misunderstandings arise from confusing the two. *Haecceitas* reifies the uniqueness of each individual thing; inscape grounds in the reality of a thing each of the many ways of understanding it. Though critics most often have identified inscape as Scotus's *haecceitas,* in its characteristics of multiplicity and intelligibility, inscape corresponds far more closely to Scotus's epistemological term *formalitas.*[97]

96. Phillips, *Gerard Manley Hopkins,* xx.

97. There also textual reasons for holding this opinion. Perhaps Hopkins studied the *quaestiones* in which Scotus develops the idea of *haecceitas,* but his excitement over his first reading of Scotus can scarcely have come from such an encounter. Scotus invoked the formal distinction and the idea of *formalitates* literally hundreds of times, but wrote in very few places of *haecceitas,* and rarely used the word. On the single occasion when Hopkins used the word he spelt it *ecceitas*—which indicates that his source for it was not Scotus but some Italian commentator. But early in the *Ordinatio,* in which Hopkins first read him, Scotus discussed what Scotists call "formal nonidentity," which is the basis for the reality of *formalitates* (*Ord.* 1, d. 2, p. 2, qq. 1–4, nos. 388–410 [Vat. 2:349–62]). See Wolter, *The Transcendentals and Their Function in the Metaphysics of Duns Scotus,* 21–24. Hopkins almost certainly read this section. Christopher Devlin, in Appendix 2 (338–51) of *Sermons and Devotional Writings,* identifies Hopkins's allusions to things Scotus discussed there. Two of the other more important loci for the discussion of the formal nonidentity were also in questions Hopkins almost certainly read: *Ord.* 1, d. 8, p. 1, q. 3, nos. 103–7 (Vat. 4:200–202), and *Ord.* 1, d. 8, p. 1, q. 4, nos. 186–217 (Vat. 4:254–74), available in French, trans. Boulnois, 237–39 and 279–94; Devlin (editorial matter in *Sermons and Devotional Writings,* 342) argues convincingly that Hopkins refers to material from *Ord.* 1, d. 8. Maurice Grajewski lists major loci for the discussions of the formal nonidentity in *The Formal Distinction of Duns Scotus: A Study in Metaphysics,* Philosophical Series 90 (Washington, D.C.: The Catholic University of America Press, 1944),

The idea of *formalitas* arose in the midst of the medieval controversy over universal terms, with which Hopkins was familiar even while at the Oratory. Put simply, the dispute is about whether we are referring to anything real by using common nouns. If not, then the basis for our concepts becomes purely arbitrary and fictional. The problem can be posed as a series of dilemmas. If universal terms name realities, how can we explain multiple concepts of single things?[98] If they are real, must not the multiple concepts of a single thing imply different beings? But if our concepts are ultimately fictional creations, all logic, every syllogism fails,[99] and no moral obligation can bind one to tell the truth, because the truth cannot be told. Hillis Miller professed in 1985, "Epistemology should take precedence over ethics";[100] certainly, with no logical basis for epistemology or language, ethics would be meaningless. Nothing could securely be called good. But if experience is intelligible—if truth is coextensive with being, as Hopkins believed—language has a foundation. If goodness is coextensive with being, epistemology cannot take precedence over ethics, even in literary criticism, because it is good to know the truth, and, as Hopkins notes, sane to prefer it.[101]

Scotus accords universal concepts a basis in reality, but does not confuse reference with reproduction. A generation before Ockham, he applies "Ockham's razor" (which he attributes to Aristotle) and refuses to needlessly multiply entities. Common nouns mark recognized simi-

---

68–71. His citation from *Quod.* 6, while not an especially clear discussion of the formal nonidentity (appearing in the argument only as an implication), is interesting because according to Devlin Hopkins appears to have read much in the *Quodlibet* as well, and in *Quod.* 6:77, Scotus discusses Philippians 2.5–11 much the way Hopkins does in his letter to Bridges, cited below.

98. S. Y. Watson, "A Problem for Realism: Our Multiple Concepts of Individual Things and the Solution of Duns Scotus," in Ryan and Bonansea, *John Duns Scotus,* 63.

99. Daniel O. Dahlstrom also identifies the logical concerns driving "what for Scotus is properly the problem of universals. viz. the question of the status of predicables within the domain of logic," in "Signification and Logic," 82.

100. Miller, *Linguistic Moment,* 54. The unmasking of the Nazism of his colleague Paul DeMan, to whose memory *The Linguistic Moment* was dedicated, reveals the sinister implications of this claim perhaps more than Miller intended.

101. Hopkins, *Journals and Papers,* 126.

larities among groups, not separable beings. Crucially, the concept underlying a common noun is not a fiction simply because it does not point to some single object; it is an epistemological relation, and thus, in a diminished sense, it is real. More importantly for Hopkins's aesthetic, a single thing can be truthfully known by many names, each firmly grounded in the experience that produced it—in Scholastic terms, each formally distinct from the other but not really distinct from the thing itself.

Scotus's solution to the dilemma of multiple reference, the idea of *formalitates*, must have struck Hopkins with the joy of finding an alter ego; someone else understood, in quite a different form, his dearest and oddest ideas. Scotus asserted that various organizing relations in things can each be real, nonidentical, and existent in the same single object.[102] These various relations Scotus calls *formalitates*, ways of understanding with a real basis. "Form," an ordinary term in Scholastic philosophy, names a mental construct abstracted from similar objects. *Formalitates*, "little forms," are organizing relations within a single object. Scotus explained that his *formalitates* are not separable from one another as one thing *(res)* is from another, but that nevertheless the mind detects rather than invents them, and with the diminished, dependent reality of relations they do nevertheless inhere, with a reality they have in themselves, in individual creatures. They depend for their realization, but not for their potentiality, on a perceiving intellect. Hopkins inscapes the concept more simply: "These things, these things were here, and but the beholder/Wanting."

The controversy over the Universals was, in a way, a dispute over various kinds of reductionism. A nation, for instance, can be conceived of as a collection of atoms being acted upon by physical forces, or a group of animals in a particular ecosystem, or an example of mass psychology, or a legal construct. An easy way to deal with the problem is to call each of these accounts a fiction, but Scotus rejected this epistemologically bankrupt tactic. Even before human beings talked about ecosystems, or about atoms, a Scotist could argue, a nation was the

102. Grajewski, *Formal Distinction of Duns Scotus*, 45–55.

sort of thing that could be perceived in each of those ways, were there a mind to detect that understanding. *Formalitates* depend not upon the act of the perceiving mind, but upon the possibility that there can be such a mind.[103] To recognize a defining quality making up the whole—say, to see a nation as linguistic entity or as collection of kinship groups—is knowledge. A thing potentially has as many *formalitates* as there are truthful ways of looking at it. Truth is not a one-to-one correspondence between thing and word. Such a correspondence is impossible, but it is also not the point of language. People use language to share their diverse insights and understandings, because the world is too rich for a single account of it to suffice. Lying is wrong, but difference enriches; only contradiction indicates illusion. The potentially infinite multiplicity of understandings is not the spinning of fictions but the serial revelation of the actual structure of truth, in the only way it can be perceived by temporal creatures.

Inscape applies to various subjectively perceived, yet true, understandings of the same object. Like *formalitates*, inscapes are present in the object and available to the intellect. Hopkins often mentions "catching" or "calling out" the inscapes of something. An inscape is one of an intensive infinity of *formalitates*, "scapes," really contained in the object, and available to the perceptive intellect. It must be said that *formalitas* and inscape are not quite identical. Scotus was thinking of a formal scheme of classifying epistemological concepts. Hopkins, heir to the romantics, contemplates his "real knowledge" in Newman's sense. This means he attends to the abundance of selving in individual things—the blacksmith who became "Felix Randal"; the Binsey poplars; Oxford. His inscapes amount to different views of different minds—or even of the same mind at different moments—encountering the particularities of the world. Scotus theorized; Hopkins wants us to taste.

Hopkins believes that every being proclaims God's truth in the infinity of its inscapes. The world itself speaks, whether we understand it or not. A word is foremost a humanly intended sign, but its human

103. Allan Wolter, "The Formal Distinction of Duns Scotus," in Ryan and Bonansea, *John Duns Scotus*, 45–60 (52).

meaning is another inscape grafted onto the sound. Just as Hopkins's "inchoate word" is formed of associated sensations, a word is always received by means of sensations. Because the sounds of language are things, and therefore intelligible, they have an intelligible shape whether they are words or not; it is an enrichment of them, a new *formalitas*, that noises have a human meaning. The implications for Hopkins's poetry are far-ranging. Hopkins's design, as a poet, is that every word, every phrase, every sentence, every poem, in all of its being should proclaim, on as many levels as possible, the infinite glory of God. The very pattern of the noises in English, which would seem to be the result of chance and choice and ancient invasion, is a mine of *formalitates* to be unearthed and enjoyed for God's praise. All unity, even the unity of rhyme, has intelligibility and goodness. Poetry is about the unities and intelligibilities in every aspect of language itself: "Poetry is in fact speech only employed to carry the inscape of speech for the inscape's sake—and therefore the inscape must be dwelt on. . . . repetition, oftening, over-and-overing, aftering of the inscape must take place in order to detach it to the mind."[104] Hopkins's chiming sounds are signs of God not only because Hopkins intends them to be but in themselves. Still, the repetitions serve to make us aware of the signs.

On every layer of structure, he finds what Scotus would call a *formalitas*—as ordered sound, as symbolic structure, as sensation in the memory. On each level Hopkins finds meaning. It takes effort to call out inscape, both on the part of the poet and on the part of the reader. Bridges described his friend's efforts sympathetically, but with some dismay, as an attempt at

> an unattainable perfection of language, as if words—each with its twofold value in sense and sound—could be arranged like so many separate gems to compose a whole expression of thought, in which the force of grammar and the beauty of rhythm absolutely correspond.[105]

Hopkins made bold to attempt it because of his conviction that all being is indeed intelligible, right down to the level of noises. One has

104. Hopkins, *Journals and Papers*, 289.
105. Quoted in the introduction to Hopkins, *Letters to Bridges*, xxii.

only to "look, look," or to "read not slovenly with the eyes but take a deep breath and read it with the ears." Hopkins trusts that his reader will understand the poetry of sensation that he writes, attending at least as much to sound and rhythm as to argument. He and his reader share a physical world to which they can both refer through language. They can judge and understand one another's references because of the intelligibility of their common experience of the world. If poetry is to accurately inscape speech for the inscape's sake, the poet and readers cannot attend solely to sound. Human speech has meaning; Hopkins removes nonsense verse from his definition of poetry as the inscaping of speech. So the grammar and the thought—philosophical depth of meaning, emotional nuance, and psychological association included—must, like the sound, be "the elevation of ordinary modern speech . . . heightened, to any degree heightened and unlike itself" so that it may startle the reader into perceiving things anew.[106]

Hopkins's sonnet "Ribbesdale" demonstrates this poetic. It is, like his other sonnets, a score for a performance to be heard in time, though written to allow "study." Consider its structures in the light of the Scotist philosophy that Hopkins illustrates rather than explains in the poem.[107] The octave should be read aloud:

> Earth, sweet Earth, sweet lándscape, with leavés throng
> And louchèd low grass, heaven that dost appeal
> To, with no tongue to plead, no heart to feel;
> That canst but only be, but dost that long—
>
> Thou canst but be, but that thou well dost; strong
> Thy plea with him who dealt, nay does now deal
> Thy lovely dale down thus and thus bids reel
> Thy river, and o'er gives all to rack or wrong.

The lush alliteration and rhythm are beautiful in themselves, but the performer must interact intellectually with the text to deliver a mean-

106. Hopkins, *Letters to Bridges*, 89 (14 Aug. 1879).

107. Ellis's brief comment on "Ribbesdale" (*Language of Mystery*, 148) is just, and Peter Milward (*A Commentary on the Sonnets of G. M. Hopkins* [Chicago: Loyola University Press, 1969], 119–23) and Norman MacKenzie (*A Reader's Guide*) have both written fine commentaries on it, but neither has considered the poem's Scotist aspects.

ing to the hearer, deciding about pauses, emphases, and even what syntactical function to assign a word. It is as if we, Hopkins's audience, suddenly tumble into a landscape seen for a moment as an unclassified entity of movement and color; with another look, shapes and directions leap into perspective. Detail by detail, the landscape becomes more intelligible as the perceiving mind acts upon it. Hopkins's inversions, calculated to call attention to rhythmical effects, alliteration, and rhyme, force interpretive reading. For an audience to understand, the reader must communicate by performance what part of speech "throng" is meant to be, or whether it is heaven or earth that is appealing.

A person speaks with disordered words when under the stress of some emotional or intellectual impediment to the easy expression of his thought. In conversation, a well-ordered Johnsonian sentence would create an aura of effortfully assumed authority. The dislocation of words in this poem is an atmospheric device, and a brilliant one; it distances the poem from the realm of oratory and puts it closer to the realm of conversation, presuming mutual trust and intimacy. The interlocutor is expected to come half-way, to mend the expression of the speaker by reference to their shared knowledge of the language and the subject matter. Hopkins presumes such familiarity with his reader because they are creatures in a common world.

The earth Hopkins addresses is the ordinary earth. It does protest against human depredations, but not like a Wordsworthian wood full of spirits out to teach poets a lesson. The earth makes its appeal not to the poet but to God; it has no tongue. Lacking tongue or heart, the earth has being; its being is what it "well dost." In his commentary on this poem, Milward notes Hopkins's reference to the "Scholastic axiom that all being is good."[108] He is right; in fact, Hopkins writes here in terms of all the convertible transcendentals. The earth is also true, that is, intelligible; its Creator finds the wordless appeal not only intelligible but "strong." Its Creator also commands that "thus"—and in no other way—the dale will be dealt, spread out, and "thus"—in one sin-

108. Milward, *Commentary on the Sonnets of G. M. Hopkins,* 121–22.

gular way—the river will run. Dale and river each have unicity, each having one particular way of being in itself, and differing from anything that is not "thus." At least this much of their being should be intelligible to man, but Hopkins mourns that it is given over to human "rack or wrong."

As he investigates the inscapes of speech, Hopkins makes his reader acutely conscious of process in the poem—not just in the musical time of the rhythm, but through the historical time in which understanding grows. Quibbles on an incomplete sentence are the stuff of farce, but rare in sonnets. They invite the reader into the place of an interlocutor in a conversation, who leaps to fill the meaning as her friend gropes for a word, but must continue listening in order to check her hunch. Hear it in action as the sestet begins:

> And what is earth's eye, tongue or heart else, where
> Else, but in dear and dogged man? Ah, the heir
> To his own selfbent so bound, so tied to his turn . . .

The lovely inquiry about "dear and dogged man" prepares the reader for something glorious after "heir," especially because the line break mandates a pause. In a moment, as if in correction of the thought, man becomes heir to a "selfbent," which at first seems to be shackled. The high artistry of "heir / to his own selfbent so bound" is not only in its alliteration but in its ambiguities. Normal English would phrase it unambiguously as either "The heir so bound to his selfbent" or "the heir to a selfwill in such bondage." It is only after the verb "tied" is introduced in parallel to "bound" that the fetter's application to the heir is discovered. The landscape, as it were, begins to show patterns of hill and gully and brush; it becomes possible to gather things into groups and patterns, to detect unities. Hopkins's complicated phrasing invites a constant rethinking of sentences as they unfold in time rather than merely a Miltonic suspension of the understanding. It is not only that one waits a long time for the verb (though not nearly as long as one must in the first sentence of *Paradise Lost*) but that there is an effect of successive understandings. Each level of understanding has its applications to the unfolding meanings of the poem, its *formalitates* of inscape and experience.

The manuscript draft of "Ribbesdale" has as an epigraph Romans 8.19–20, about how the earth groans awaiting "the redemption of our bodies." Unredeemed man has not attended to the inherent intelligibility of the earth, but instead to his own "self-being," destructively.[109] As Christ is the creaturely articulation of God, so man is the articulation of his own nature as a creature. Although fallen now, man should be the speaking self-consciousness of creation—a tongue or heart for the earth. According to the Scotist theory of the Incarnation, a human being is the proper vehicle for God's self-consciousness manifested in time and space. Christopher Devlin says that Hopkins's chief aesthetic delight is the Son as "God's design or inscape,"[110] in creation, for Scotus speculated that God elected to create in order to be both a creature and God at once. The multiplicity of *formalitates* would indeed apply a fortiori, to the eternal Son "in whom all things hold together." Rightly Devlin says that "Scotus' theory that the decree of the Incarnation was prior to that of the creation of angels and men"[111] is central to Hopkins as artist. If the "Word" is God's self-conception,[112] then God's act of creation is the decision to see himself as a being with limitations even while he upholds all things in existence through his ubiquitous immanence. Christ the Man is the "first in order of intention" or "firstborn" of creation. As the Word made flesh manifests God, so do other creatures, in their own way, and human beings can understand God in creation as God understands himself: in the many inscapes he offers as *formalitates* in the things of the world. But man has sinned; intended for glory, the "heir" instead has chosen

> To thriftless reave both our rich round world bare
> And none reck of the world after, this bids wear
> Earth brows of such care, care and dear concern.

109. Gardner, *Poems*, 160 and nn.

110. Devlin's notes to *Sermons and Devotional Writings*, 109.

111. Devlin mentions in his editorial material in Hopkins's *Sermons and Devotional Writings* (111) a theory of an angelic Incarnation, but, for Hopkins, the rationality of human beings is emphatically the image of the divine Word.

112. This idea is very ancient, at least as old as Tertullian's *Against Praxeas*, 5. See translation in *The Ante-Nicene Fathers*, ed. A. Roberts and J. Donaldson (New York: Charles Scribner's Sons, 1903), 3:600–601. The concept has roots in the personification of Wisdom in Proverbs 8.12–31 and Wisdom 7.22–27.

His own glory long lost, man destroys the world's. The ecological complaint is only the most obvious of the inscapes of meaning in "Ribbesdale." Scotus and Hopkins both posit man as the head of creation. Man's fall from his proper position among creatures has subjected the earth to hostile ugliness. An inscape of theology underlies the inscape of argument in this poem as the geological structure underlies the shape of the land. One can, for instance, make sense of the landscape around the San Andreas Fault without knowing the geology. Cloud and hillside and bush retain their colors; rise and ravine mark shapes suitable for mapping; the arrangements of forest, grassland, and undergrowth remain. Nevertheless, the ancient fault, once understood, gives meaning to the whole and endows the patterns with new intelligibility. Layer upon layer of meaning is unconcealed.

A metrical analysis of the poem yields the same result. Hopkins said it was in "common rhythm counterpointed," and the counterpoint especially in the sestet yields the impression of hexameters imposed upon the pentameter.[113] As in other sonnets, his fascination for layered multiplicity of meaning permeates even his rhythms. He provides not just one pattern of rhythm, but two in the same line or stanza. In the last four lines of the poem, where Hopkins turns to man after speaking so long of the earth, the speech emphases grow more thick; the odd word "selfbent" seems to need strong stress on both syllables; in the next line, both "both" and "rich" seem to require stress; and "none reck" can hardly be said save as a sprung phrase, with no slack in it; nor is it possible to remove the stress from either "Earth" or "brows." Yet can it be doubted that there are four stresses in "care, care and dear concern"? Man adds stress to the system of the sonnet, in perhaps all the senses of stress that Hopkins used; and the stress is at points of moral significance. Man adds inscape to the world.

Scotus's *formalitas* illuminates inscape, "the very soul of art," as an infinitude of meanings that can be shared because they refer to a world whose real intelligibility makes a common language possible. Hopkins did not seek a transparent medium of language to display

113. Phillips, *Gerard Manley Hopkins,* 369.

some single essence for the thing he described. Neither did he wish to beguile his readers—still less himself!—from seeing the howling wilderness of an infinite regress of words in the human consciousness. Poetic language is, to Hopkins, a resource for the revelation of the order that is real in the world. He wrote his poems as opportunities for the discovery of the *formalitates* of language, infinite in truth and goodness. Confident that he and his audience shared an intelligible world, he believed that, if not in his day, then in a generation or so, they would be able to waken in his work the various inscapes awaiting them there.

CHAPTER 8

INSTRESS

CATCHING INSCAPES IS A GOOD THING; to understand exactly how it is good, we must investigate another word Hopkins coined: instress. Here again Scotus will serve us. Instress is an action of the will—a moral action, for good or evil. Instress is assent, to use Newman's term, to an inscape. To call out an inscape is a pleasure, though not one necessarily leading to God; Hopkins saw Satan's sin as instressing his own inscape.[1] But the ability to see and instress inscapes is the imaginative faculty that makes love possible. Scotus shows how in order to rise to the perfection of charity and justice, one must exercise this imaginative capacity that enables a person to see another thing (much more another person) in truth and unicity—to inscape it as, in some sense, another self. We exercise in art the generosity of imagination that engenders disinterested love.

The full meaning of "instress" best emerges by following Hopkins through his speculations on the nature of the self, moral freedom, the will, and, finally, justice. At the foundation for many poems is the idea that perfect freedom is the fullest manifestation of a self—which is always love and sacrifice. The self is predestined to an incommunicable moral individuality: "pitch," a concept so close to Scotus's *haecceitas* that Hopkins once conflates them, but that is more specific to human rationality and imaginative capacity than Scotus's concept. "As kingfishers catch fire" illustrates perfect selving, which, for the "just man" constitutes identification with Christ. The Scotist understanding of damnation, the journey away from generosity and sacrifice into imperfect selving, explains "The dark-out Lucifer detesting this." Hop-

1. Hopkins, *Sermons and Devotional Writings*, 201.

kins vividly narrates, and yet escapes, the failure to selve in his Terrible Sonnets; "I wake and feel the fell of dark" applies Scotist ethics to his own spiritual life.

Hopkins himself defines "instress" once: "[I]t is choice as when in English we say 'because I choose' which means no more (and with precision does mean)/ I instress my will to so-and-so."[2] However, its range of meaning does not seem to be exhausted by that definition. Hopkins uses the word in a variety of situations that more than one critic has found bewildering.[3] Sometimes it appears to be a characteristic of some natural thing: "an instress about this place," "instress and charm of Wales."[4] Sometimes it appears to be the capacity of a piece of art to elicit feeling: "not quite the spirit or instress the poem conveys"; "Millais, *Scotch Firs* . . . instress absent, fir trunks ungrouped"; "three-light lancets . . . which dwell on the mind with a simple direct instress of trinity."[5] Sometimes it seems to be the will: "all that energy or instress by which the soul animates and otherwise acts in the body"; "compliance of the sovereign to the subject's instress of initiation"; "Body no longer swayed as a piece by the nervous and muscular instress seems to fall in and hang like a dead weight."[6] Then again, it seems to have philosophical overtones: in the notes on Parmenides, Hopkins amends his translation, "Being is and not-being is not—which one perhaps one can say, a little over-defining his meaning, means that all things are upheld by instress and are meaningless without it."[7] However, all of these seemingly various meanings have a single root; while the semantic field may at first resemble a gerrymandered voting district, it is, upon examination, actually quite orderly.

In the notes on Parmenides Hopkins first mentions instress and

2. Hopkins, *Sermons and Devotional Writings*, 150.

3. It does make one rather fear to tread in places found so thorny by W. H. Gardner, *A Study of Poetic Idiosyncrasy in Relation to Poetic Tradition*, 1:12; Sulloway, *Gerard Manley Hopkins and the Victorian Temper*, 46; and Elizabeth Schneider, *The Dragon in the Gate: Studies in the Poetry of G. M. Hopkins* (Berkeley and Los Angeles: University of California Press, 1968), 118–19.

4. Hopkins, *Journals and Papers*, 253, 258.

5. Hopkins, *Further Letters*, 319 (to Patmore, 25 Oct. 1883); *Journals*, 244, 215.

6. Hopkins, *Sermons and Devotional Writings*, 137, 168; *Journals*, 238.

7. Hopkins, *Journals and Papers*, 127.

connects it to inscape. Observe its relation both to epistemology and to moral choice: "But indeed I have often felt when I have been in this mood and felt the depth of an instress or how fast the inscape holds a thing that nothing is so pregnant and straightforward to the truth as simple *yes* and *is*."[8] Inscape is being as being is recognized; instress is being as its intelligibility is upheld by the affirmation of the observer—the "yes" that accompanies the "is."

Christopher Devlin thought that in Hopkins's notes on instress, the poet confused two different things. Devlin observes that Hopkins actually equated the term with the Scholastic philosophical term *intentio,* the word for the mind's grasping something; but also, he used the word for the act of a person in selving.[9] However, Hopkins's use of a single term for both is proper. It is by grasping or understanding other things that a rational creature actualizes its self. The divine commission to love, "pitch," is given to each person in potential—at "neap," as Hopkins puts it.[10] To properly exercise this ultimate individuality, logically prior to one's nature and one's actual existence, one must justly judge and rightly honor the things that one is suited to judge. Making a self requires both the intellectual faculty for judging and the activity of judgment; instress is that activity, pitch "at splay," in Hopkins's terms.

And Hopkins has theological tradition on his side; the wide semantic field of "instress" is nearly coextensive with that of the Scholastic term *intentio.* According to Bernard Wuellner's *Dictionary of Scholastic Philosophy,*[11] the meaning of the Scholastics' "intention" most likely expands from "the direction or application of a causal power to an effect," which "shows the notion of directing or tending on the part of a being or power." Wuellner distinguishes two clusters of meanings; each of these has a range determined by the degree of relative emphasis on the power or on the effect. The first cluster matches the modern,

8. Hopkins, *Journals and Papers,* 127.

9. Hopkins, *Sermons and Devotional Writings,* 288–89.

10. See Walter Ong's magnificent *Hopkins, the Self, and God* (Toronto: University of Toronto Press, 1986).

11. Wuellner, *Dictionary of Scholastic Philosophy,* 63.

nontechnical "intention": "the act of the will toward an end that is or is thought to be obtainable." A shift in emphasis from the act to the end gives the term the meaning of "the purpose of an act," or "the good sought in this present act." The second cluster of meanings focuses on acts of knowing. When the emphasis is on the knower, "intention" comes to mean "the mental representation" of a thing. When the emphasis shifts to the thing known (but without losing sight of its relation to the knower), another meaning arises: "the object or being that is represented in knowledge; the objective concept, and especially the universal." This epistemological category produces some idiosyncratic Scholastic uses: "first" and "second" intention, which correspond roughly to "language" and "metalanguage" in modern terminology, except that the notion of second intention was conceived of within a philosophical framework that recognized the reality of sublinguistic mental objects (for example, sensible species). First intention is "mental attention to the thing itself as the object of its knowing"; or, shifting emphasis to the thing attended to, "the formal object or being that is directly known." Second intention refers to "mental attention to and representing an object as it exists in the mind." Again, the emphasis can shift to "the object as it exists in the knower."

Because Hopkins does not share the Aristotelian presumption that the mind only knows universals, he does not particularly associate "instress" with universals, but barring that one caveat about emphasis, every known usage of "instress" in his writing inhabits the territory defined by the Scholastic *intentio.* Hopkins does use the noun as a verb, as in "His mercy must be instressed, stressed," but the nominal form already implies action. Indeed, the Scholastic use of the verb *intendere* means not only "to intend, as the understanding or will intends;" but also "to intensify." Hopkins's philological interest probably alerted him to the common origin of the English words *intend* and *intense* in the Latin *intendere,* whose root meaning is "to stretch toward." The kinship of *tend* and *tension* nurtures the word "instress."

Wuellner divides definitions of *intentio* carefully, as a good lexicographer should; Hopkins, a poet, holds the whole semantic field in his mind, playing over its territory, which lies between the knower and the object known. We have already seen Hopkins's incessant attention to this subtle tension in the case of inscape. The way in which instress seems inherent in the object itself has its origin in the will of the observer. His "in looking far up the valley I felt an instress and charm of Wales," bespeaks not only a mental image of Wales but a bending of Hopkins's will toward it. It is not easy to tell whether that instress belongs to Wales or to Hopkins's feelings; instress lies poised between the subject and the object—as indeed does the charm also. The charm may be in Wales—but, without Hopkins, not *this* charm. The primary locus of instress is the will, though it reposes in the object; just as inscape is fundamentally a latency in the object itself, yet is only realized in the intellect.

But most importantly, instress is to the will what inscape is to the intellect. To bend one's will toward one perception does not prevent or demean the instressing of other inscapes. An observer can detect several inscapes in one thing, and even experience more than one instress at a time, if several perceptions strike the senses at once: "[T]he eye seemed to fall perpendicular from level to level along our trees, the nearer and further Park; all things hitting the sense with double but direct instress."[12] The same thing can elicit different instresses at different times:

> On this walk I came to a cross road I had been at in the morning carrying it in another "running instress." I was surprised to recognise it and the moment I did it lost its present instress, breaking off from what had immediately gone before, and fell into the morning's. . . . And what is this running instress, so independent of at least the immediate scape of a thing, which unmistakeably distinguishes and individualises things? Not imposed outwards from the mind as for instance by melancholy or strong feeling; I easily distinguish that instress.[13]

The "running instress," like a sort of internal narrative, occupies his mind as Hopkins rambles. That ongoing understanding can interact freely with memory, as in this incident. Instress is independent of the "immediate scape" of a thing. "Scape" is best defined as intellectual—

12. Hopkins, *Journals and Papers,* 199.
13. Hopkins, *Journals and Papers,* 215.

here a casual perception, of which an inscape would be the intellectually committed intensification in the way that an insight is the intensification of sight. Similarly, instress would be an intensification of stress, deriving from commitment of the will. Hopkins is interested in the nuances of intellectual commitment. One can of course attach one's will to some object for many reasons, some of which may be purely sentimental—to love, say, a silver cup because it was your mother's. Such emotional attachments are easily recognized for what they are, though; and what happened at this crossroads was not that. Hopkins continues:

> I think it is this same running instress by which we identify or, better, test and refuse to identify with our various suggestions / a thought which has just slipped from the mind at an interruption.[14]

Instress seems to be a kind of moral commitment to an insight, like Newman's certitude.

Commitment is the connection between the purely cognitive and the moral; and here morality enters the arts proper (as opposed to the artist's subject matter). The artist might show evidence of instress—or not; Hopkins suspects that Millais made no interpretive commitment in his painting *Scotch Firs.* Or the piece observed might call forth that sort of commitment in the audience, with all its emotional associations, and the commitment will shape the inscape caught: "an instress which only the true old work gives from the strong and noble inscape of the pointed arch."[15] The observer engages in the same active intellectual shaping with the inscapes of natural objects, as when Hopkins saw a lake of the "richest opaque green modulated with an emotional instress to blue."[16]

It seems to be possible that a will may be drawn to a perception without conscious choice; Hopkins once hypnotized a duck with, he speculated, the "fascinating instress of the straight white stroke" of a chalk line.[17] Often the will inclines to one focus of attention without conscious affirmation. However, it is possible to consciously commit

14. Hopkins, *Journals and Papers,* 215.
15. Hopkins, *Journals and Papers,* 263.
16. Hopkins, *Journals and Papers,* 176.
17. Hopkins, *Journals and Papers,* 207.

oneself to an instress and choose among intellectual impressions, as when Hopkins finds among bluebells "a notable glare the eye may abstract and sever from the blue color/ of light beating up from so many glassy heads, which like water is good to float their deeper instress in upon the mind."[18] In his journal he warns against letting fancy intrude upon the truth of the recognition that underlies the affirmation: "What you look hard at seems to look hard at you, hence the true and false instress of nature"; and, after some cloud observations, he advises himself to attend carefully: "Unless you refresh the mind from time to time you cannot always remember or believe how deep the inscape in things is."[19] Freely affirmed instress requires moral effort: a commitment to prepare oneself for encountering it, and an effort of willed attention that might best be called "faith." Distraction hinders instress: "I saw the inscape though freshly, as if my eye were still growing, although with a companion the eye and the ear are for the most part shut and instress cannot come."[20]

Leonard Cochran's meticulous study of the term "instress" proposes that the kernel of the definition can be found in Hopkins's note on Parmenides' "great text . . . that Being is and Not-being is not—which perhaps one can say, a little overdefining his meaning, means that all things are upheld by instress and are meaningless without it." Cochran therefore calls instress the "force which holds being in existence."[21] However, the notes on Parmenides describe the views of Parmenides, which are not precisely those of Hopkins. As I noted in Chapter 5, Hopkins did not embrace Parmenides' "undetermined Pantheist idealism," though he was clearly much intrigued by it. Now, one might properly speak of God holding things in existence by instressing them, by being faithful to the commitment implicit in "Let there be . . ."—but we have no such power or responsibility. The human action of instress holds in existence not being itself but the fulfillment of being in

18. Hopkins, *Journals and Papers*, 231.

19. Hopkins, *Journals and Papers*, 204–5.

20. Hopkins, *Journals and Papers*, 228.

21. Leonard Cochran, "Instress and Its Place," 152–53, quoting Hopkins, *Journals and Papers*, 127. Although my conclusions differ from his, I owe a great debt to his systematic presentation of instress in this article.

intellectual recognition. "And what is Earth's eye, tongue, or heart but dear and dogged man?"

Cochran connects Hopkins's "stress" to universality as "the mind's recognition of the fact of universality," and goes on to elaborate: "If we understand being as universal, recognized as such, and dynamic, then we may define stress as a synonym for *being*."[22] He then opposes "stress" to "instress," associating "instress" with particularity, although he does note a case in which "stress" evidently refers to a very particular self.[23] As we have seen, Hopkins's interest in the multiplicity of inscapes stems from a far different epistemology than one that would try to grasp the unique essence of a thing. So, too, instress is not a singular affirmation of the actuality of a thing, not a mere confirmation of objective reality impressing itself upon the mind—because knowledge does not come to us in such a direct, objective form. The multiplicity of instress reflects the multiplicity of vantage points, that is, the uniqueness of perspective characteristic of each rational self. And as we saw in Chapter 5, in the very notes on Parmenides from which Cochran derives his definition, Hopkins is arguing that without "stress" we would lose not only the recognition of universals, but the recognition of particulars as well. We have seen part of this key passage before, where Hopkins theorizes that if not-being "existed," so to speak,

> There would be no bridge, no stem of stress between us and things to bear us out and carry the mind over: without stress we might not and could not say Blood is red/but only/this blood is red/or/The last blood I saw was red/ nor even that, for in later language not only universals would not be true but the copula would break down even in particular judgments.[24]

Hopkins supports Parmenides' affirmation that there must be some bridge between the mind and external reality because without it cog-

22. Cochran, "Instress and Its Place," 151.

23. "Nothing in nature comes near this unspeakable stress of pitch, distinctiveness and selving, this self-being of my own"; *Sermons and Devotional Writings*, 123, discussed in Cochran, "Instress and Its Place," 149–50. He calls this "a departure in Hopkins's usage."

24. Hopkins, *Journals and Papers*, 127.

nition collapses, for universals and particulars alike. Cochran rightly emphasizes that stress refers to the recognition of being rather than to being itself; "being" and "stress" are not synonyms, and, to distinguish Hopkins's Christianity from Parmenides' monism, they must be kept separate.

To the extent that instress is more than just an intensification of stress, we might do well to distinguish stress from instress by saying that stress inheres in the object and instress in the subject. Stress could be equated with the intrinsic intelligibility of being, that is, with transcendental truth, which is coextensive with being but not identical with it, since they differ intensively. If we recall that truth refers to being as it is considered in relation to the intellect, we can see that stress is still related to the perceiving subject, even as it informs the object. By instress the will binds itself to the object in the relation of perceiver to thing recognized.

As we discuss the significance for "instress" of Hopkins's equating "stress" with ἐνέργεια, that Greek term so laden with suggestions of vigor and force, a caveat is in order. Hopkins has been faulted for simple adoration of power when he praises the (vividly re-created) "stress" of the shipwreck in *The Wreck of the Deutschland* as somehow merciful.[25] But there Hopkins is working from a consistent philosophical position: if we choose to attend to God's love of the world only under its gentle aspect, we do not understand it. Part the First of The *Wreck of the Deutschland* celebrates, in the "fire of stress," a recognition of the otherness of God mercifully doing violence upon Hopkins's own selfwill, as Part the Second vividly re-creates the same action suffered by the shipwreck's victims. To affirm being in itself as good is to affirm it even in its infringements on human pleasure—indeed, to glory in them, to see the inscape of Christ their creator "lionlike," "more dangerous," in them. "His mystery must be instressed, stressed," because to recognize the good is to be able to praise it, and that praise Hopkins conceives as the whole duty of "dear and dogged man."

W. A. M. Peters notes where Hopkins coalesces stress with ἐνέργεια; then, wisely, he associates the Saxon "stress" with the

25. Robinson, *In Extremity,* 110–20.

Scholastic concept of "act" (as contrasted philosophically to "potency").[26] The identification that Peters cites appears in Hopkins's sketches toward a commentary on Loyola's *Spiritual Exercises.* There, scattered over many pages, is Hopkins's most complete attempt at a theory of the will and the self. Chapter 1 at first appears to be an extended digression on the first three words of Ignatius's "Principle and Foundation" section: "Man is created to praise, reverence and serve God." At issue is to what extent a human being is freely self-determining and to what extent made by something external. We can distinguish (delicately) two questions: how the human self came to exist at all; and how, or whether, the will can be free. Hopkins treats the first question in Chapter 1 of the commentary, and the second in Chapter 3 as well as in isolated passages elsewhere. Hopkins mounts a case for the existence of a creating God by the elimination of other alternatives: the human being is neither created by chance nor self-created and therefore must be created by another.

> Chance then is the ἐνέργεια, the stress, of the intrinsic possibility which things have. A chance is an event come about by its own intrinsic possibility. And as mere possibility, passive power, is not power proper and has no activity it cannot of itself come to stress, cannot instress itself. And in fact chance existence is a self-existence. Chance is incredible or impossible by this *a priori* consideration.[27]

Passive, "mere possibility" is unable to instress itself because nothing inclines it to actualize any particular intrinsic possibility it has; in other words, it lacks a will. It is natural that thoughts concerning the nature of the will might arise in a Jesuit's reflections on the *Spiritual Exercises,* an intensely practical handbook for turning the will toward personal, concrete, and immediate decisions to follow Christ.[28] The

26. Peters, *Gerard Manley Hopkins,* 13.

27. Hopkins, *Sermons and Devotional Writings,* 123–24. Note: it is risky to translate ἐνέργεια with its cognate "energy," as Cochran does.

28. In his first prefatory annotation to the *Spiritual Exercises,* Ignatius speaks of how "one might seek and find the divine will in regard to the dispositon of one's life." In the third annotation Ignatius writes: "In all the spiritual exercises that follow we bring the intellect into action in order to think and the will in order to stir the deeper affections. We should therefore note that the activity of the will, when we are speaking vocally or

book would not normally lead anyone (but Hopkins!) to a theoretical investigation of the nature of the soul, but the *Spiritual Exercises* do encourage piercing examination of conscience and cultivation of feelings. It is the heightened sense of his own sin evoked by the exercises of the first week that impressed on Hopkins the utter distinctiveness of his own "self-taste," which dominates his theory of the importance of will to personality.

It is perhaps a bit jarring for admirers of Hopkins's nature poetry to find that when he seeks evidences of God as creator, he scants the observed world in favor of the self, "more distinctive and higher pitched than anything else I see."[29] In the shape of its argument, the proof follows Aquinas, as I observed in the last chapter; but Devlin notes that Scotus's proof that God exists also rests not on the evidence of design in nature generally, but on the existence of a finite self with a mind and will.[30] However, Hopkins's discussion is colored through with a romantic susceptibility to questions of the ultimate value of feeling and personality that is unknown to his medieval predecessors (or to Ignatius). His romantically perceived self "is more distinctive than the taste of ale or alum, more distinctive than the taste of walnut-leaf or camphor, and is incommunicable by any means to any other man. . . . when I compare my self, my being-myself, with anything else whatever, all things alike, all in the same degree, rebuff me with blank unlikeness."[31]

What strikes him as the most "unmistakeable" evidence of the existence of the self is the awareness of sin and merit, which Hopkins

mentally with God Our Lord or with His saints, requires greater reverence on our part than when we are using the intellect to understand" (*Saint Ignatius: Personal Writings*, trans. Joseph A. Munitz and Philip Endean [New York: Penguin Books, 1996], 283). Hopkins, the incorrigible theoretician, could only follow such greater reverence with probing analysis.

29. Hopkins, *Sermons and Devotional Writings*, 122.

30. Hopkins, *Sermons and Devotional Writings*, 283 (note 122.2).

31. Hopkins, *Sermons and Devotional Writings*, 123. It seems Hopkins's use of "incommunicable" here is primarily in the informal modern sense of "ineffable"; he has not yet established that it cannot be shared, as the Scholastic use of the term implies, though he does so later in the commentary.

pointedly discusses in terms of his own life. In other words, what is most central to the self is will. It is on the basis of this moral observation that Hopkins rejects the Hegelian or Averroistic notion of a universal self from which we come and into which our minds are all absorbed. Individual human beings are morally responsible for themselves, and do not share that responsibility with some all-encompassing being: "[T]he universal cannot taste this taste of self as I taste it, for it is not to it, let us say/ it is not to him, that the guilt or shame, the fatal consequence, the fate, comes home."[32] If there is a universal being, the universal being too "must have its self, its distinctive being and distinctive more than mine."[33] Hopkins reasons upon the analogy of a body and one of its parts:

> [I]f I have freely put my finger into the flame and the finger is unwilling, but unable to resist, then I am guilty of my folly and self-mutilation but my finger is innocent; if on the other hand my finger is willing, then it is more guilty than I, for to me the loss of a finger is but mutilation, but to my finger itself it is selfmurder. Or if again it were selfsacrifice the sacrifice would be nobler in the finger, to which it was a holocaust, than in me, in whom it was the consuming of a part only. . . . I do not share its feeling of self at all and share little, if I share any, of its guilt or merit.[34]

The self is an inviolable entity, which cannot be subsumed into some greater whole. This is the heart of Hopkins's categorical rejection of monism.

Hopkins considers self concretely, "not merely in logic or grammar," but in terms of the way in which "[p]art of this world of objects, this object-world, is also part of the very self."[35] Nevertheless, the linguistic and logical concerns of Scotus lurk in the background as Hopkins struggles with the relationship between the individual self and the "nature"—what an individual man holds in common with other humans. Hopkins emphatically asserts that the self is a thing that exists, at least in the conception of its Creator, before the nature: "[S]elf be-

32. Hopkins, *Sermons and Devotional Writings,* 125.
33. Hopkins, *Sermons and Devotional Writings,* 126.
34. Hopkins, *Sermons and Devotional Writings,* 126.
35. Hopkins, *Sermons and Devotional Writings,* 127.

fore nature is no thing as yet but only possible; with the accession of a nature it becomes properly a self, for instance a person."[36]

Yet the possibility of existence of any creature is logically prior to its actual existence: "Self is the intrinsic oneness of a thing, which is prior to its being and does not result from it *ipso facto,* does not result, I mean, from its having independent being." Scotus also in his theory of personality denied that the mere accident of existence gave a thing its individuality.[37] Nevertheless, priority of self to nature seems to have been less of a concern for Scotus, whose interest in individuation centered on the epistemological question of how we move conceptually from the common nature to the individual.[38] Scotus observes that the primary notion of a nature in the intellect is not universal. We see something and find out that it is called a horse; only later do we abstract from many horses some ideal universal notion of "equinity," which, say, excludes mules and zebras. That wider construction of quiddity "accrues only incidentally" to a notion. A thing's nature, as an epistemological category, is "naturally prior to that characteristic contracting it to this unique singularity."[39] Once a classification is established, questions might arise about what individualizes members of it. Contrary to some popular misconceptions, Scotus was not a nominalist. He was a moderate realist, accepting the reality of universal con-

36. Hopkins, *Sermons and Devotional Writings,* 148.

37. Timothy B. Noone, in "Individuation in Scotus," *American Catholic Philosophical Quarterly* 69 (1995): 527–42, gives a clear account of how Scotus could argue that actual existence, no less than matter, location, and quantity, is accidental. Therefore none of these things constitute the individuating principle. "Accident" is distinguished from "substance"; an accident is something that could be changed (such as color, location, and other qualities available to the senses) without making something really turn into a different thing. One can have a horse of a different color, but one can't give it wings and still consider it the same animal. Substance is what makes a thing what it really is.

38. Frank and Wolter, *Duns Scotus Metaphysician* (West Lafayette, Ind.: Purdue University Press, 1995), 196–97. See also the opening pages of Noone, "Individuation in Scotus," 527–42.

39. Duns Scotus, *Ord.* 2, d. 3, p. 1, q. 4, nos. 31–34 (Vat. 7:402–5), trans., quotation from Wolter, *Philosophical Theology of John Duns Scotus,* 83; the quotation itself is from no. 34, Vat. 7:404. The following phrases are also of interest, since they refer to what Hopkins might have taken as the "priority" of the "self" to the "nature." I begin with the matter Wolter quotes, which ends at the asterisk: *est prior naturaliter ipsa ratione contrahente ipsam ad singularitatem illam,* * *et in quantam est prior nautraliter illo contrahente non repugnat sibi esse sine illo contrahente.*

cepts (such as that of the common nature) through which the mind comprehends individual things. The individuating difference distinguishes this individual from another that falls into the same class (say, the horse Secretariat from the horse Bucephalus). Scotus was concerned to locate the individuating difference in the substance of the thing, rather than in any accidents. Nature or quiddity (what a thing is), he claimed, is neither many nor one, but in any particular real instance there is an individuating difference, *haecceitas* or "thisness," that is singular, and, while inseparable from the nature, is yet formally distinct from it.

When Hopkins writes of a self, he means a being with intrinsic unicity, beyond that in which he sometimes detects inscape: "[A]ccidental being, such as that of broken fragments of things or things purely artificial or chance 'installs,' has no true and intrinsic oneness." The real union of the singularity with a nature (for the pattern of a nature is real) brings a thing from possibility into actuality. "Now a bare self, to which no nature has yet been added, which is not yet clothed in or overlaid with a nature, is indeed nothing, a zero, in the score or account of existence," Hopkins says, but adds that "as possible it is positive, like a positive infinitesimal, and intrinsically different from every other self." Bear in mind that in Hopkins's theory it is, strictly speaking, not self that is prior to nature, but "pitch"; it is only "with the accession of a nature that it becomes properly a self." Hopkins's "self" is the whole package: the outworking of some nature joined to an individualizing "pitch" in particular circumstances. Of self before nature he says:

> [O]nly so far as it is prior to nature, that is to say/so far as it is a definite self, the possibility of a definite self (and not merely the possibility of a number or fetch of nature) it is identified with pitch, moral pitch, determination of right and wrong.[40]

"Fetch" is his term for the Scholastic "instantiation."[41] "Nature" refers to the common nature of a species—what makes something a human or a horse or an angel, for instance. Yet Hopkins's sense of the priority

40. Hopkins, *Sermons and Devotional Writings,* 146, 148. See also 151, quoted below (at note 49), 148.

41. Hopkins, *Sermons and Devotional Writings,* 146, where persons are said to "wear and 'fetch' or instance" natures or essences or inscapes.

of self to nature begins with a fundamentally romantic experience, the "blank unlikeness" of all else to himself, and especially with his sense of sin.

Hopkins is not here discussing individuation in general but human individuality, especially as he experiences it—in moral terms, as moral freedom and responsibility. Recall that the question at the center of Hopkins's work on the *Spiritual Exercises* is to what extent a human being is freely self-determining and to what extent made by something external. Hopkins was still working on his commentary in 1883, so we know something of his sources from an 1883 letter wherein Hopkins says that Duns Scotus "shews that freedom is compatible with necessity."[42] Nevertheless, he refers to Thomas Aquinas and Suarez as he begins his discussion of free will. The Thomists, he says, make the will absolutely arbitrary; they posit an indifference to alternatives, which makes it free. Hopkins disagrees.

> The indifference, the absence of pitch, is in the nature to be superadded. And when the nature is superadded, then it cannot be believed, as the Thomists think, that in every circumstance of free choice the person is of himself indifferent towards the alternatives and that God determines which he shall, though freely, choose. The difficulty does not lie so much in his being determined by God and yet choosing freely, for on one side that may and must happen, but in his being supposed equally disposed or pitched towards both at once. This is impossible and destroys the notion of freedom and of pitch.[43]

Recall that Hopkins is speaking of "nature" not as an epistemological term but as a state of being in which an entity can exist. A nature can be rational or irrational. Freedom accompanies rationality: "Now if self begins to manifest its freedom with the rise from an irrational to a rational nature it is according to analogy to expect it will manifest more freedom with further rise in nature."[44] Angels, for instance, have more freedom than humans; hence the fate of fallen angels is worse than that of fallen men. In other words, we cannot equate freedom with pitch, yet pitch is the ground of human freedom.

42. Hopkins, *Letters to Bridges*, 169 (4 Jan. 1883).
43. Hopkins, *Sermons and Devotional Writings*, 148–49.
44. Hopkins, *Sermons and Devotional Writings*, 147.

But, as he shows in his resistance to "the Thomists," Hopkins does not think of free will as a faculty of arbitrary decision; it is rather, as in Scotus, a capacity to incline to the good without the force of necessity. Pitch subsists in the delicate interplay of desire and choice that characterizes the operation of the will. He embarks first on a long discussion of the subtle workings of grace, through which God may steer one's affections toward a certain good, yet without removing one's freedom to give consent or refusal. Then Hopkins adds that "choice in the sense of the taking of one and leaving of another real alternative is not what freedom of pitch really and strictly lies in. It is choice as when in English we say 'because I choose,' which means no more than (and with precision does mean)/ I instress my will to so-and-so." In other words, this freedom of pitch is, above all, the freedom to commit oneself to something, a freedom that one would retain even if there were no alternatives—or, to use Hopkins's phrase, if there were no freedom of field. This, he says, is the freedom the divine will has toward God's own necessary acts. These definitions give context to a passage we have seen before:

> And no freedom is more perfect; for freedom of field is only an accident. So also *pitch* is ultimately simple positiveness, that by which being differs from and is more than nothing and not-being, and it is with precision expressed by the English *do* (the simple auxiliary), which when we employ or emphasise, as "he said it, he did say it," we do not mean the fact is any more a fact but that we the more state it (it is also at bottom the copula in logic and the Welsh *a* in "Efe a ddywedodd.") So that this pitch might be expressed, if it were good English, *the doing* be, *the doing* choose, *the doing* so-and-so in that sense. Where there was no question of will it would become mere fact; where there is will it is free action, moral action. And such "doing-be" and the thread or chain of such pitches or "doing-bes's" prior to nature's being overlaid is self, personality; but it is not truly self; self or personality then truly comes into being when the self, the person, comes into being with the accession of nature.
>
> Is not this pitch or whatever we call it then the same as Scotus's *ecceitas?*[45]

Actually, it isn't, quite. *Haecceitas* is the individuating principle for *any* individual thing. It would apply equally to creatures without free

45. Hopkins, *Sermons and Devotional Writings*, 150, 151.

will, mere "fetches" which in Hopkins's eyes have only a shadow of will in the "mere fact" that their proclivities are set, in some manner, prior to their existence. Hopkins conceives of pitch as the yearning for some particular aspect of the good. This yearning shapes the separate selves of individual rational beings, creating self out of a series or "chain" of moral affirmations. An angel might have a similar setting of the will to some desire, but would of course enact it differently than a man or a woman. And a human nature confronted with living in different circumstances of history would work out its pitch differently; pitch is only the center of a "circle" of personality.

In order to conflate the concepts of *haecceitas* and pitch, as Hopkins does, it is necessary to equate the individuating principle with the final cause of each thing. The final cause—that for love of which the efficient cause brings something about—is, as Scotus never tires of saying, first in the order of intention. In particular, the final cause of some being, its divinely envisioned destiny, is prior to nature of that being. And the final cause, is, finally, love.

The conflation of pitch and *haecceitas* may not reflect exactly what Scotus had in mind, but in Hopkins's most Scotist poems it bears abundant fruit. The ineffable and yet decisive quality of pitch is the subject matter of these lines from "On the Portrait of Two Beautiful Young People":

> Man lives that list, that leaning in the will
> No wisdom can forecast by gauge or guess,
> The selfless self of self, most strange, most still,
> Fast furled and all foredrawn to No or Yes.

In his nature poems, Hopkins gives the things of the world a self like his own moral self, needing to be recognized and loved as a manifestation of Christ: "God's utterance of himself within himself is God the Word, outside himself is this world. The world then is word, expression, news of God. Therefore its end, its purpose, its purport, its meaning, is God and its life or work to name and praise him. Therefore praise is put before reverence and service."[46] "Ribbesdale" and

46. Hopkins, *Sermons and Devotional Writings*, 129.

"The Windhover" show all creation, each thing in its particular excellences, revealing Christ to the beholder. More fully than his warning to the beautiful young people, "As Kingfishers catch fire" addresses the question of pitch and its unfurling; God sees Christ, sees himself incarnate, in the person of the just man, yet the just man retains an individual self.

These revelations of God in creation are not just metaphors. Sacramentally, creation is God's utterance of himself at the same time that it is itself, outside God. Recall that Hopkins rejected as nonsense the idea that God is some universal self or mind; about two years after drafting his proof "shewing there is no universal a true self which is 'fetched' or 'pitched' or 'selved' in every other self," Hopkins added a remark that to assume oneself part of such a universal self "is to assume oneself in a hypostatic union."[47] That technical term refers to the divine nature united with the human nature in the Incarnation; Christian theology asserts that such a union is a single person, Jesus Christ. And the theologian whom Hopkins followed in theories about the nature of the Incarnation was Scotus.

All creation of course comes from God, but human nature, Scotus speculates, was created as the particular vehicle by which God could enact the Word, the Second Person of the Trinity, in a creature. The Incarnation of God as a person required a rational nature for its vehicle, because personhood requires free will. However, rationality is not the same as personality; a soul is rational, according to Catholic theology, but it is not a person. A soul is oriented toward not its own separate existence but the existence of the soul-body composite; *dependere* is the Latin word Scotus uses to describe this relation, the orientation of one being (in this case, the soul) toward the good of some other entity (in this case, the whole human being). Created persons cannot be oriented toward the existence of each other; each has its particularity,

47. Hopkins, *Sermons and Devotional Writings,* 128, 129. It is *de fide* doctrine—the strongest form of obligatory belief on the part of Catholics—that the union of God and man in Jesus is unique and complete. All the attributes of deity are his, as well as all those of humanity; but Christ is only one person, a person being an entity able to act with free will.

its "thisness" *(haecceitas)* which makes it "repugnant to" sharing its self with another. But God can have a rational created nature "depending" on Divine Personality—oriented toward God, rather than the created existence, as its primary good—because nothing in a creature can repel God's being. God does not have that "repugnant" individuating principle *(haecceitas)* to distinguish him from others of his kind, because there is no other.

God made human nature, Scotus says, with the "aptitude" to "depend" on the Second Person of the Trinity, so that it would be naturally inclined to seek the good not of itself but of God's Personality—in other words, to be one Person with God. This Scotus calls "aptitudinal dependency on the Word," and the aptitude can be put into play or not. Only in Jesus is this dependency actualized; this is the Hypostatic Union, the Incarnation. If the aptitude for complete union with God is not actualized, a person actualizes the lower aptitude: to be inclined to seek its own good. A holy person that is not in the Hypostatic Union—in other words, one who isn't Jesus—can actually orient all its actions toward the will of God. That is the state of holiness called the Beatific Vision. However, even such a holy person nevertheless is inclined first to his or her own limited good; the saint is not the same person as Christ, even if the person's will is wholly given over to serve Christ through the sacrament of Baptism and perfection of life. The limited orientation toward its own good and being in a creature constitutes its personhood, just as the orientation toward the good of the Second Person of the Trinity (which is all good) constitutes Christ's personality.[48] Christ gets his individuality through his uniquely full relationship with God; everyone else "achieves personhood formally by virtue of that negation" of "aptitudinal dependency" toward the Second Person of the Trinity—a limitation that prevents the individual from being swallowed up by the infinite One.[49] The creating God is present immanently in all things, but is identified with only one.

48. Duns Scotus, *Ord.* 3, d. 1, q. 1, trans. Allan Wolter, "John Duns Scotus on the Primacy and Personality of Christ," in *Franciscan Christology,* ed. Damian McElrath (St. Bonaventure, N.Y.: Franciscan Institute, 1980), 139–82, quotation from 179.

49. The argument of this paragraph is an attempt to explain in the context of Hop-

The distinction between an actual sacramental union and an aptitudinal dependency is crucial to avoiding monistic implications in the "Kingfishers" sonnet, where Hopkins writes that the just man "Acts in God's eye what in God's eye he is— / Christ." The distinction also explains the otherwise paradoxical subsequent line speaking of Christ in limbs and "eyes not his." The union of other persons with Christ, the manner in which the just man is Christ, "in God's eye," is a sacramental, not a hypostatic, union. Unlimited by *haecceitas,* God is really present in the sacrament, and in the believer sacramentally; he is not limited to being only *this thing* and nothing else. More than a metaphor, but less than divinity, the *res* of the sacrament transforms the will without negating the personality.

All things declare Christ in their beauty and goodness.

> God is so deeply present to everything *("Tu autem, O bone omnipotens, eras superior summo meo et interior intimo meo")* that it would be impossible for him but for his infinity not to be identified with them, or, from the other side, impossible but for his infinity so to be present to them.[50]

Hopkins's gloss on Augustine here confirms the concept of multiplicity of being, which was so important to Hopkins's understanding of the sacraments, in a wider application. When in a poem he speaks of a human being declaring Christ, inscapes multiply into sacrament. That is the burden of "As kingfishers catch fire." In that poem, Hopkins employs the concepts underlying pitch; muses on the inanimate world having *haecceitas,* and God needing none; and, through the portrait of the just man in relation to these things, begins to reveal a Scotist concept of justice.

As kingfishers catch fire, dragonflies draw flame;
  As tumbled over rim in roundy wells
  Stones ring; like each tucked string tells, each hung bell's
Bow swung finds tongue to fling out bold its name;

kins's poetry the argument of *Ord.* 1, d. 23, q. un. (Vat. 5:355–57), and *Quodlibetal Questions* q. 19 a. 3 as edited, discussed, and translated by Wolter in "John Duns Scotus on the Primacy and Personality of Christ" (169–79).

50. Hopkins, *Sermons and Devotional Writings,* 128.

Each mortal thing does one thing and the same:
Deals out that being indoors each one dwells;
Selves—goes its self; *myself* it speaks and spells,
Crying *What I do is me: for that I came.*

Í say more: the just man justices;
Keeps gráce: thát keeps all his goings graces;
Ácts in God's eye what in God's eye he is—
Chríst. For Christ plays in ten thousand places,
Lovely in limbs and lovely in eyes not his
To the Father through the features of men's faces.[51]

The poem starts with miniature inscapes of bird and insect life; meter, like the stone, which we only see falling from the rim of the well, upholds the poem's activity. The natural excellences of kingfishers and dragonflies, stones and bells, are variously beautiful, and, for the sorts of beings that they are, the bird and insect do their ultimate. Their activity reveals their deepest purposes: to seek good and manifest God. Even stones have characteristic, revealing actions. The basic metrical pattern is iambic pentameter, with sprung lines introduced for special effects—some of which happen unnervingly early. The second foot of the first line is a stress followed by three slack syllables. Hopkins called this a "First Paeon";[52] among the Greek meters, the paeon is associated with songs of triumph and thanksgiving. The intent of praise proclaimed, all in terms of fire and action, the meter settles down to a comfortable five iambs per line—for one line. In the sprung third line, the second foot is a paeon once again, as an assembly of beings unites in praise.

Already an intricate pattern of parallelisms, both aural and grammatical, emerges. Words keep their own syntactical places and meanings and take on yet more meaning through the relations of their sounds. The meaning of each pattern echoes others. The first line's alliteration points to the sameness of the activity of selving in different characteristic modes of being. A sameness or rhyme exists between

51. Hopkins, "As kingfishers catch fire," *Poetical Works*, 141.

52. See "Author's Preface on Rhythm," *Poetical Works*, 115–17 (116), for definitions of these metrical terms.

suggested activity and the names of things: a string can ring the bell that tells, whose bow swung finds tongue. Metrical length links nouns to verbs. A slur over the first syllables of "dragonflies" removes an intermediate stress so that the final foot of the line (like the second, a "sensitive" foot) is sprung: "dráw fláme." The slur also allows it to have the same timing as "kingfishers," so that the animal world is unanimous in the way it catches fire for the observer, as the falcon does in "The Windhover." And, though as in Psalm 19 (Vulgate 18) it is without words that the irrational creature "uttereth knowledge," it speaks with tongues of flame.

Iambic pentameter reasserts itself in the fourth line, and the one thing that is inverted in the fifth line is "óne thíng." In order to make those two syllables both strong, the word "one" must be emphasized with unusual force; the emphasis reinforces the underlying unity of the action. The "name" is not a human word but the very self of a thing, laden with divine significance. No common noun can express such particularity; it is *haecceitas,* utterly unlike anything else. "Indoors" is inverted in the next line, drawing the reader's attention to the difficulty of accenting the oddly chosen word; the being that dwells in each one colors its whole activity as Hopkins's "selftaste" colors his own experience.

"Selves" here is a verb, soon matched with the nouns "itself" and "myself," more fully illustrating how being and act are one. The initial stresses on "Deals" and "selves" begin lines strongly with inverted feet. The rhyme of "same" to "name" emphasizes that action and existence are one for all things. Vowel sounds subtly unite particularity, action, and being in "deals," "speaks," "each," and "being." The next line has two extra syllables, one of them evidently stressed, but Hopkins marked "Crying" as he did the first syllables of "dragonflies"; the word should be read with the weight of a single syllable. Thus lengthened and marked, it draws attention to the straightforward statement of the central idea of the octave, which Hopkins underlined for further emphasis: *What I do is me.* John's Gospel provides context for the phrase "for that I came." The phrase is what the Λόγος said when he became a creature and was on trial, about to be sacrificed on the cross: "To this end was I born, and for this cause came I into the world, that I should bear witness to the truth" (John 18.37).

In this poem, as in "Ribbesdale," the very stones cry out. Yet who can hear them dealing out their being? We, who have language, know that our inmost name remains secret even when most fully lived, as in the life of Saint Alphonsus Rodriguez. *Haecceitas* is unavailable to the senses and therefore impossible to articulate. Yet every bird or bell outstresses toward utterance of the silent interior word in a way that can be interpreted, the way a spelled word can be. Like the exterior acts, that indicate but do not constitute the interior being, a spelling is not a word itself, but the sign of a word.

The sestet begins with a marked emphasis on "I." The repeated "I" is conjoined with "crying" and "myself" by assonance, and with Christ by the allusion to his words at the trial before Pilate. A bird or bug may say itself; a man says more, because he can know more. A just man does with his freedom what the dumb beasts do with their inclinations toward their own good. By properly instressing the things he encounters, he too fulfills the utmost of his being—and of theirs. "Just" should take the full weight of Scotus's definition: giving each thing its due, loving each thing for its own sake.

Scotus finds two "affections" in the will; one, the *affectio commodi,* inclines toward one's own particular delight; and the other, *affectio iustitiae,* the affection for justice, inclines to give everything, including oneself, its due. Both, properly applied, are virtuous: "[C]harity perfects the will insofar as it is inclined to, or subject to, the affection for justice, whereas hope perfects the will insofar as it is inclined to, or subject to, the affection for what is advantageous."[53] It is possible to love oneself with charity—to desire, for instance, to be chastised for moral failings, when one's desire for pleasure would draw one to shirk. Scotus is solicitous to communicate that both one's own pleasure and justice itself are real goods and therefore both attractive to the will. The practice of justice consists of being able to restrain the compelling

53. Duns Scotus, *Ord.* 3, suppl. d. 26, trans. (facing Latin text), ed. Allan Wolter, in *Duns Scotus on the Will and Morality* (Washington, D.C.: The Catholic University of America Press, 1986), 179.

importunity of the default setting of desire: the desire for one's own good. A rational mind can change the setting and turn the attention of the intellect away from its own pleasures, so as to allow justice to exercise its attraction. (Justice can, properly, involve seeking one's own benefit; the giving of what is due does not exclude the self.) But either desire can pull the whole being into action. Rationality is the capacity for making comparisons. Rationality allows one to compare goods, to see equalities, and to distinguish the greater from the lesser. Therefore it is naturally the precondition for practicing justice and charity. Justice and charity both name the quality of perception that allows the just man to regard the other like the self and to seek the other's good. I cannot prefer the good of another if I am unable to see what that good is. As we shall see, one of Hopkins's sermons on charity reveals that he read this bit of Scotus; he follows Scotus's general lines of argument, and, like Scotus, calls charity and justice by the name of "friendship."

In the poem, Hopkins, with Scotus in the background, writes an abrupt, active nine-syllable line on the just man after the octave's contemplative pattern of long lines. The use of "justice" as a verb gives the word two unaccented syllables, so three strong accents fall together: "júst mán jústices." Hopkins marked stresses in the next line to make sure that "grace," not "Keeps," would be the focus of the hearer's attention. He put a "great colon" to mark a strong pause after "grace"; both the punctuation and the meter require that "that" be a relative pronoun, rather than a subordinating conjunction. The action of grace, not a particular kind of grace, is the thing that "keeps all his goings graces." What the just man does is justice, giving its due to everything; and that action is God's action, grace. Similarly, in "The Windhover," the plow and the falling embers, in apparent destruction, open the earth to fruitfulness and release again the light caught from the heavens as the tree grew.

Hopkins's notes on the *Spiritual Exercises* speculate on grace and salvation: since pitch is not a single, unitary essence but involves a chain of choices, God can make a new creation of someone by changing the person's pitch through grace. Without losing the continuity of personal identity found in the chain of pitches, God replaces a wayfarer's "faulty pitch of will" with an "uprighter and more perfect one." The creature can fail to affirm this, to instress it; then the old pitch remains. But the creature whose pitch has been made anew perceives not only all that he could before but also God's act, God's being, in the act of another self. This newness is new freedom, new opportunity for charity. Hopkins quotes Ephesians 3.17–19 (in Greek) to describe the action of grace on the "inward man";[54] in order "[t]hat Christ may dwell by faith in your hearts." Hopkins leaves implicit the rest of the passage, which speaks of the knowledge of the depth and breadth of God's love, and the love that surpasses knowledge, "that you may be filled unto all the fulness of God." Grace makes it possible to appreciate formerly unperceived *formalitates* in the world—to see with the charity, the justness, of God. Hopkins says the "fulness" of God, the πλήρωμα τοῦ Θεοῦ of Ephesians 3.19, is "the burl of being in Christ."

In "Kingfishers," the lavish pattern of syntactical and aural echoing multiplies the fullness of significance in Hopkins's language. A crescendo of repeated words, "just" and "justices," "grace" and "graces," culminates in "lovely"; the limbs and eyes of Christ are lovely in God's eyes and are lovely in eyes not his. Since even in Christ God is not limited by *haecceitas,* Christ identifies with the particularity of his creatures: "That is Christ playing at me and me playing at Christ, only that it is no play but truth; that is Christ being me and me being Christ."[55] The proper pitching of the self is to the tone of Christ, so that one's own will is Christ's, acted out in all the particularities of one's life. This might seem to destroy the individuality essential to pitch; but Christ's infinity allows for every particularity, and the resolution is sacramental. The just man is himself, always himself in all his particularity; and in his fullest selving is Christ too, and all his merits Christ's, and all his sins overwhelmed by that fullness.

Thus, the just man is a *res et sacramentum:* himself, inimitably himself, but also a symbol and a vehicle for the relationship of Christ to the world. To be fully human is to be grace and justice, to be Christ in

54. Hopkins, *Sermons and Devotional Writings,* 156.
55. Hopkins, *Sermons and Devotional Writings,* 154.

the world, to be "God's eye." A slant rhyme acknowledges nevertheless a difference between the human perceiver and God; "eyes not his" both affirms and denies likeness with "eye he is." That phrase has a slur, too, so the line is in two repeating figures. Then, with stresses read thus, with "Acts" and "is" in the strongest rhetorical positions, so as to hang in the mind together:

Ácts in Gód's eye whát in Gód's eye he ís—

"Christ" is marked for heavy emphasis. God not only understands but inhabits the just man. For a Christian, "to live is Christ" (Phil. 1.21).

So here we see the Scotist concept of justice tied to sacramentality: the just man, attending to the good of all creation, acts the part of Christ, and is both symbol and reality of the Great Sacrifice. Justice depends on grace, but it is not merely ascribed to the just man on Christ's merit. It is a reality. The creature is indeed transformed into the Just One, not in being but through the justice of God working in him. In a sermon he preached in Liverpool, Hopkins spoke in such terms, and invoked Scotus's concept of original justice. He talked of how God made a covenant with Adam, that is, the unfallen human race, so that "while man did his duty, for God could not fail in his, both sides would be just, equally just—unspeakable stately dignity of man! man as just as God, just with God's own justice!"[56] This "kingdom" of God, Hopkins says, "was so at the beginning, then it must have ceased to be, and now it is again."[57] Its renascence is the Church; and the "just man" of the poem is the Church in act and is, like the Church itself, a sacrament.[58]

Justice is both a state and an activity. As a state, the just man's justice is his sacramental identity with Christ. To see how this individual creature's justice is not merely swallowed up by the universal justice of

56. Hopkins, *Sermons and Devotional Writings*, 57. A note on page 280 discusses how Hopkins follows Scotus in distinguishing sanctifying grace from original justice, and in what ways Hopkins differs from Scotus in the sermon.

57. Hopkins, *Sermons and Devotional Writings*, 55.

58. *Catechism of the Catholic Church* (London: Geoffrey Chapman, 1994), sec. 1111, p. 288. cf. *Lumen Gentium* l. l.

God we should recall the way in which Hopkins invoked his concept of pitch to prove that there is no agent intellect, or universal self. His key evidence came from his sense of guilt and shame: the inescapable awareness that it is not to any universal self, but to himself alone that the "fatal consequence" of his sin "comes home" proves that his self it not subsumed by any other, greater self. Of course, the self is only responsible for its actions to the extent that it is free to will and to execute them. But if there is only one universal justice, then it would seem that the freedom of the individual will reduces to an ugly choice: it could either obliterate its individuality by acquiescing to the universal or it could assert itself in rebellion. The solution to this dilemma lies in the uniqueness of each person's perspective—that is, in the relation of one's will to one's pitch.

Scotus's concept of justice is the cornerstone of his theory of the will, so we might expect Hopkins to follow Scotus closely in his own discussion of the workings of the will. However, at the beginning of his fullest analysis of will and personality, he indicates that his immediate impulse for writing that day (while working through the First Week of the *Spiritual Exercises*) came from a reference in Suarez to the doctrine of Aquinas, which rests on "the distinction of the will as *arbitrium* and, so St. Thomas speaks, as nature. . . . Here I may put down some thoughts which throw light on and receive light from the above on personality."[59] When Ignatius advises that we should be "desiring and choosing only those which may better lead us to the end for which we were created," Hopkins comments: "here distinction of affective and elective will."[60] Hopkins uses the terms "elective will" and *arbitrium* interchangeably and gives no indication that he intends his preferred term "affective will" to mean anything different from Aquinas's "nature."

59. Hopkins, *Sermons and Devotional Writings*, 146.

60. Hopkins, *Sermons and Devotional Writings*, 130. According to Devlin, "GMH always notes any sign of this distinction in the *Spiritual Exercises*" (286 [n. 130.2]). There is no question in the mind of any of these thinkers that the will is a single entity. Hopkins writes that "if [the elective and affective will] are both one and the same faculty, then the first is the faculty at pitch, the other not, or it is the faculty at splay" (142). Indeed, even the will and the intellect are not really distinct faculties, though according to Scotus they may be distinguished formally.

> [T]he affective will is well affected towards, likes, desires, chooses, whatever has the quality and look of good, and *cannot choose* but so like and choose; so that the affective will, taken strictly as a faculty of the mind, is really no freer than the understanding or the imagination.[61]

The basic distinction between "affective" and "elective," reflected in the common words "desire" and "choose," is between passive and active aspects of the will; the will is drawn to things, yet it has the power to make choices. For Hopkins, as well as for Aquinas, it is only the *arbitrium,* which is exclusive to rational creatures, that is really free. Its freedom comes into play when it is presented with alternatives, "all of which must have, though in different degrees, the quality of good." Hopkins gives the following, tantalizingly brief, account of this freedom: "[S]elf can in every object it has see another self, personal or not, and taking the whole object . . . can treat any one thing how great or small soever as equal to any other thing how small or great soever."[62]

Here he veers away from Aquinas and heads in a distinctly Scotist direction. For Aquinas, the natural inclination of the will is always directed toward the end, toward the good, toward happiness; thus choice, the activity of the *arbitrium,* is exercised only in regard to means, since "to choose is to desire something for the sake of obtaining something else."[63] Hopkins's *arbitrium,* on the other hand, gains its freedom by a capacity to see other selves as equal, and thus can choose to seek the good of another rather than being bound to seeking only its own happiness. Behind Hopkins's account one can detect a sensitivity to goodness as a transcendental attribute of being. Each thing "how great or small soever" has a goodness of its own in accordance with that "being indoors each one dwells." And each thing cries, "what I do"—my actuality or stress—"is me: for that I came." The intrinsic goodness of a thing, which is coextensive with its being, is its final cause, that for the sake of which the efficient cause acts (in this case, the creation of the object). It is that to which the *arbitrium* is called to do justice.

The highest good is God. It might seem that Hopkins has made his

61. Hopkins, *Sermons and Devotional Writings,* 152.

62. Hopkins, *Sermons and Devotional Writings,* 152.

63. Saint Thomas Aquinas, *Summa Theologica,* I, Q.83, a.4; cf. I–II, Q.10, a.1.

elective will attentive to ends rather than means only by lowering the will's sights from the highest good, God, to created, lesser goods. But Hopkins claims, on the contrary, that the "elective will" gives human beings a natural likeness to God:

> [T]he tendency in the soul towards an infinite object comes from the *arbitrium*. The *arbitrium* in itself is man's personality and individuality and places him on a level of individuality in some sense with God; so that in so far as God is one thing, a self, an individual being, he is an object of apprehension, desire, pursuit to man's *arbitrium*.[64]

Hopkins is determined here not to remove God, insofar as he is a self, to some entirely different sphere from other selves. A created self has a real goodness that makes love of it a proper end in itself (in its aspect as *res*), even though it is at the same time a vehicle or manifestation of God's goodness (as it were, in its aspect as *res et sacramentum*). This ties the freedom of the will to individual perspective: to recognize oneself as one self among many is to see that one's uniqueness is determined by one's particular point of view. Hence the *arbitrium* is the seat of personality and individuality. Within Aquinas's theory one could no doubt make room for differences between individual wills by postulating that each creature's enjoyment of the supreme good (that is, God) has its unique characteristics, but such differences do not seem crucial to the theory.

Hopkins's reasoning and his terminology are not particularly dependent on Scotus here, but the notion of individual perspective also lies at the root of Scotus's theory of created free will. However, Scotus's primary concern was not to explain personality per se, but to secure the faculty of choice within the will itself, rather than to allow that it was shared with, or even subservient to, the intellect, as Thomas's theory would have it.[65] Scotus recognizes the characteristics of inclination and choice in the will, but the distinction that he uses to analyze the will comes not from Scotus's predecessor Thomas, but from Thomas's predecessor, Anselm (1033–1109).[66] Scotus follows Anselm in finding

64. Hopkins, *Sermons and Devotional Writings*, 138–39.

65. Aquinas says that free choice is materially an act of the will, but formally an act of the intellect (*Summa Theologica*, I–II, Q.13, a.1).

66. Wolter, *Duns Scotus on the Will and Morality*, 12–13.

that each rational creature is drawn by two affections: an affection for what is advantageous to itself (the *affectio commodi*) and an affection for justice *(affectio iustitiae)*. Since Scotus finds more than one inclination in the will, the will's choice is not, as in Thomas, restricted to consideration of means. Certainly in one sense there is only one ultimate end, one Final Cause, the Supreme Good; yet there are differences in what that looks like as it is viewed from inside the skins of different creatures.

The *affectio commodi* corresponds closely with Aquinas's "nature," inasmuch as a creature cannot help but be attracted to what is advantageous for itself. However, it differs in two significant ways. First, it is inseparably bound to the creature's perspective: it is "a thing's natural inclination towards its proper perfection."[67] Second, this inclination is not entirely irresistible.

The basis for free will lies in the affection for justice, and especially in what Scotus calls innate justice, "which is the will's congenital liberty by reason of which it is able to will some good not oriented to self."[68] Scotus's theory limits the range, but not the freedom, of choice. Affection for the advantageous is not free, being unable to will anything "save with reference to self," but the affection for justice—the sense that there is some good not oriented to self—introduces free play: many and various possibilities of restraining the affection for the advantageous and being drawn to action for another's good. Affection for justice calls the will to the enjoyment of a very real good. Affection for justice may not have the force of instinctive desire, but it is an affection, and its quiet voice can be heard when the *affectio commodi* is hushed. "To love something in itself [or for its own sake] is more an act of giving or sharing and is a freer act than is desiring that object for oneself. As such it is an act more appropriate to the will."[69] Scotus takes pains to argue that the primary operation of the will is not a choosing between alternatives, but acting or refraining from acting on

67. Duns Scotus, *Ord.* 3, d. 17, trans. Wolter, *Duns Scotus on the Will and Morality*, 181.

68. Duns Scotus, *Ord.* 3, suppl. d. 26, trans. Wolter, *Duns Scotus on the Will and Morality*, 179.

69. Duns Scotus, *Ord.* 3, suppl. d. 26, trans. Wolter, *Duns Scotus on the Will and Morality*, 179.

an inclination. He readily concedes that the will cannot actively desire unhappiness, but insists that it can still refrain from acting on its inclination to seek its own happiness.[70] In Hopkins's language, it is free to instress its natural inclination or not. This is freedom of pitch. Hopkins considered it the most perfect freedom, since freedom of play (the freedom to entertain more than one option) and freedom of field (the freedom to follow through with acting upon different choices) are merely accidental, dependent on circumstance.[71]

Though Scotus's *affectio iustitiae* is not identical with Hopkins's *arbitrium,* the narrow gap between them is readily bridged, and when it is, Hopkins's description of the *arbitrium* offers an apt explanation of how this quieter affection comes into play. To desire the good of another being, one must recognize and respect its likeness to oneself in having a good of its own to be realized. We see Hopkins calling this respect "friendship" in his sermons. Such a desire would be an image of the desire for one's own good, and arises naturally as the *arbitrium* sees in some object another self. Only by attending to this affection for justice can one turn one's attention away from the compulsions of one's own pleasure.

It was a Scholastic commonplace that there could only be freedom in a creation springing from the free act of God; if creation is by necessity, necessity determines everything. Scotus, too, points out that God was under no necessity to create, but that, in creating, God does know the true good of everything, and justly respects it. God loves each thing for its own sake, and he gives to each thing not only its due but more than its due: without owing existence to any thing, God has voluntarily given things intrinsic worth. God freely chooses to define himself as the lord of a world rather than to rest in his necessary and self-sufficient goodness. This idea of God limiting his own delight, in order to create others who may have joy, lies at the heart of Hopkins's notion of the Great Sacrifice. When God creates a world, gives it a

70. Duns Scotus, *Ord.* 4, suppl. d. 49, qq. 9–10, trans. Wolter, *Duns Scotus on the Will and Morality,* 191–97.

71. See chapter 9 at note 10. Cf. Hopkins, *Sermons and Devotional Writings,* 151.

good of its own, and turns his attention to that good, he restrains his own glory, empties himself. Attention to other rather than self is what Hopkins terms the "Great Sacrifice," which creates the world.

Hopkins conceives his notion of the Great Sacrifice as, in first intention, the Incarnation; from that springs a free creation; and thence, the cross. Scotus is famous for proposing this idea about the Incarnation as the very purpose for creation. The sacrifice of redemption follows the same pattern as the sacrifice of creation because it is the outworking of the same sacrifice in the context of a fallen world. God's self-limitation in the Great Sacrifice parallels exactly the restraint of the *affectio commodi* that is the wellspring of man's moral freedom according to Scotus. Vividly paraphrasing the famous kenotic passage of Philippians 2.5–11, Hopkins explained to Bridges:

> This mind [Saint Paul] says, was in Christ Jesus—he means as man: being in the form of God—that is, finding, as in the first instant of his incarnation he did, his human nature informed by the godhead—he thought it nevertheless no snatching-matter for him to be equal with God, but annihilated himself, taking the form of a servant; that is, he could not but see what he was, God, but would see it as if he did not see it. . . . It is this holding of himself back, and not snatching at the truest and highest good, the good that was his right, nay his possession from a past eternity in his other nature, his own being and self, which seems to me the root of all his holiness and the imitation of this the root of all moral good in other men.[72]

The way to achieve one's highest good is not by snatching at it. In fact, to snatch at it is damnation.

On the same scrap of paper on which he wrote "As kingfishers catch fire," Hopkins drafted a poetic fragment that suggests the Scotist theory of damnation, involved with a Scotist-influenced theory of personality and the will that would later emerge more fully in the Terrible Sonnets. Scotus participated in the long tradition of looking to the relatively uncluttered case of the fall of Lucifer for insights into the nature of damnation. Hopkins left clear evidence that he was familiar with the writings of Scotus, as well as other Scholastics, on this topic.

72. Hopkins, *Letters to Bridges,* 175 (3 Feb. 1883).

The First Week of the *Spiritual Exercises,* which focuses on sin and damnation, leads Hopkins into his discussion of the will. Scotist cognitive theory guides his understanding of the metaphor of hellfire, the penalty for actual sins—"Our action leaves in our minds scapes or species, the extreme 'intention' or instressing of which would be painful."[73] Not the scapes but the "instressing" of them causes the pain, because instress involves the will.

The fragment is brief, a prelude to the Fall of Eve with a hint of *Paradise Lost:*

> The dark-out Lucifer detesting this
> Self-trellises the touch-tree in live green twines
> And loops the fruity boughs with beauty-bines

The tree and the serpent entwining it are both resplendent with loveliness; there is yet a kind of glory in the fallen angel. Lucifer appreciates beauty, but not God's beauty.

Hopkins's speculations about the fall of Satan precisely explain the phrase "dark-out Lucifer." This being of pure intellect, having sinned, is blind because "intellectual action is spoken of under the figure of sight" and the will, the power to desire good, is itself frustrated.

> But this constraint and this blindness or darkness will be most painful when it is the main stress or energy of the whole being that is thus balked. This is its strain or tendency toward being, towards good, towards God—being, that is/their own more or continued being, good/their own good, their natural felicity, and God/the God at least of nature, not to speak of grace. This strain must go on after their fall, because it is the strain of creating action as received in the creature and cannot cease without the creature's ceasing to be.[74]

An angel naturally seeks to enjoy, in all the things it contemplates, the fullest being, which flowers only in accord with the will of God. To know any thing fully is to know God's will concerning it—that is, to know the end for which it was made. But this the fallen angel has chosen not to know, or at any rate not to instress; he has chosen not God's will but his own. Detesting this beauty in God's creation, even his own

73. Hopkins, *Sermons and Devotional Writings,* 136.
74. Hopkins, *Sermons and Devotional Writings,* 137.

beauty as God had intended it, Lucifer self-trellises in beauty of his own making, adorning the tree with a counterfeit beauty. Lucifer, the lightbearer, can no longer bear light, no longer reach toward the object that would naturally give him the most joy:

> [T]he understanding open wide like an eye, towards truth in God, towards light, is confronted by that scape, that act of its own, which blotted out God and so put blackness in the place of light; does not see God but sees that. . . . Against these acts of its own the lost spirit dashes itself like a caged bear and is in prison, violently instresses them and burns, stares into them and is the deeper darkened.[75]

Though appetite can be perverted toward things that are not ultimately good—say, addictive street drugs—each thing naturally seeks, and if conscious, recognizes, its proper benefit in nutrition or generation or rest. Since God is of all goods the most desirable, to desire him is right and proper, indeed a virtue: "[H]ope perfects the will insofar as it is inclined to, or subject to, the affection for what is advantageous [*affectio commodi*]."[76] Every creature pursues its own good, whether the principles of its existence be God's laws of physics (Scotus's favorite examples come from this science) or of biological instinct. The chief joy of any rational creature lies in the fulfillment of its rationality through knowing and loving the truth. Mere self-love, indeed, the all-consuming desire for the good of any mere creature, is frustrating for a rational being with free will, because it paralyzes the faculty of innate justice. The ultimate good goes beyond the good oriented to any finite creature. Fullness of joy actually lies in setting that individual good in the context of transcendent good. For this reason, the failure to restrain the inclination of the *affectio commodi* prevents one even from finding one's own joy. Joy in God is what we are made for. The virtue of hope is necessary to train our wills to that desire; hope is the virtue of desiring the particular pleasure for which one is made. Lucifer's damnation from lack of charity is also the loss of hope; he is no

75. Hopkins, *Sermons and Devotional Writings*, 138.

76. Duns Scotus, *Ord.* 3, suppl. d. 26, trans. Wolter in *Duns Scotus on the Will and Morality*, 179.

longer capable of desiring his own joy, and that is despair and damnation.

Scotus says that Satan fell not through desire for his own pleasure but through "inordinate friendship-love"[77] for himself. Friendship-love manifests itself in a special concern for the good of the friend. As such, it involves a restraining of one's *affectio commodi* for the sake of justice. However, any creature's knowledge of justice in any given situation is limited, so the good of the other that friendship seeks is correspondingly limited. Hence, Lucifer's friendship-love for himself would amount to using his rational freedom to restrain his instinctive inclination toward his true good, in order to attend to his own betterment as he perceives it.

Scotus speculates that had Satan been able to seek his own rational happiness somehow without free choice, he would have sought and enjoyed knowing God, the only infinite pleasure. But a rational being, by definition, can attend to something besides pleasure. In order to have "inordinate friendship-love" Lucifer had to restrain his desire for God (which was his own true happiness) and attend to some good that he chose to value more than joy. To resist one's proper joy for one that falsely seems higher (like a child who refuses supper in order to feel power over its parents) is to sin against hope. Hopkins speculates that it was a sort of "selfsacrifice" Satan sought, for he was sinless until he elected to put aside his own pleasure in order to seek some less pleasant glory for himself: the glory of a finite being rather than the Infinite.

Hopkins's view of the sin of Satan resembles but does not precisely reproduce Scotus's severely abstract treatment. Recall where Hopkins called Satan's sin "an instressing of his own inscape."[78] An inscape is a way of understanding a thing, and does not account for the thing in its totality, which is known only to the mind and command of God. Even Satan does not know himself fully. Satan's self-love can only be for that limited aspect of himself that he knows—an inscape, not all his in-

77. Duns Scotus, *Ord.* 2, d. 6, q. 2, trans. Wolter, *Duns Scotus on the Will and Morality,* 465.

78. Hopkins, *Sermons and Devotional Writings,* 201.

scapes. He does not love enough; he does not even desire that he should be loved as God loves him, but is, Hopkins says, like a singer who spoils his song for some lovely note—"ravished by his own sweetness and dazzled, the prophet says, by his beauty, he was involved in spiritual sloth."[79] Sloth is lack of love—in this case, lack of love for the infinite Other. The act of limitation—limiting his love to a creature rather than God, who is infinite—frustrates his intellectual powers, so that the more play Lucifer gives to his will, the more he feels his own resistance to loving anything big enough for his powers: "like a caged bear and in prison."

Hopkins understands well the difference between hope and the direction of the will that Scotus calls the virtue of charity. In his sermons, Hopkins distinguishes between "holy hope" and the highest rational good, "holy charity." When he is trying to reassure anxious parishioners who wish to know, "Do I feel for God love enough to be saved?" Hopkins calls upon Scotist ideas to explain that charity is an act of will. In analyzing what it means to love God "above all," Scotus opposes two ways of considering love: the one according to how "fervent or tender" the feeling, the other according to strength and firmness, "ready to sustain martyrdom" for the sake of the beloved. Scotus maintains that firmness is the true measure of love: "I am speaking here about that love which is an act of the will, and not about that which is a feeling in the sense appetite." He explains the "greater sweetness" felt by some devout persons is not "an act elicited by the will, but a certain rewarding feeling associated with the will-act whereby God nourishes his little ones and draws them to himself lest they fall away."[80]

Hopkins also employs Scotus's diction, in using "friendship" to mean "the most perfect of the moral virtues . . . justice as a whole."[81] Hopkins wishes to reassure his parishioners about their everyday virtue as he preaches:

79. Hopkins, *Sermons and Devotional Writings*, 180.

80. Duns Scotus, *Ord.* 3, suppl. d. 27, trans. in Wolter, *Duns Scotus on the Will and Morality*, 439–41.

81. Duns Scotus, *Ord.* 3, suppl. d. 34, trans. in Wolter, *Duns Scotus on the Will and Morality*, 369.

[C]harity begins at home; true and just selflove lies in wishing and in promoting our own best good and happiness, this is charity toward ourselves. . . . [S]hort-sighted selfish love of ourselves which is selfishness and not true self-love even lies in the consenting to and gratifying the wishes of our lower, our worst, selves. . . . [T]rue and lasting or selfish and short-sighted, all love is seen in doing the beloved's will; to oblige people, to befriend them to be their friends, to shew them love, to love them, is to do their will. So then it is with God: to love him is to do his will.

Then Hopkins describes how even a mere dutifulness is true and firm love of God:

To obey or do God's will from hope or fear is good, is right, but it is not charity: It is holy hope but not holy charity. . . . [T]o act from charity is both easy and common. . . . [A]sk any simple man or woman or child why he does this or that duty . . . the answer will be: Because it is right. . . . [S]ay/ I will do God's will and not my own, because God is God and I am only man and it is right that man should obey God. . . . [T]his state of mind is love of God and divine charity. Nay, my brethren, this is not only love but it is as high as the highest. There is a sweeter, a tenderer love. . . . but . . . none can be higher.[82]

Hopkins's aggressively antisentimental account of charity is heavily influenced by Scotus's assertion that sweetness of emotion is not required for love of God.

Yet, though the preacher calls charity "easy and common," his late poetry and prose often lack the awareness of the attraction offered to the will by another's good—though the luminous nature sonnets are everywhere alive to that call. His Terrible Sonnets make the poet seem lost indeed. If, as I believe, these sonnets are a sort of fragmentary spiritual diary, we can see in them the collapse of the poet's own distorted elective will—in fact, the collapse of his pride. Margaret Ellsberg[83] has assembled a convincing case that by the time of the writing of the Terrible Sonnets, Hopkins knew his chief enemy was his determination to avoid being "imperfect, no master of myself."[84] Hopkins finds it necessary to remind himself of this in the Terrible Sonnets, such as "My own heart."

82. Hopkins, *Sermons and Devotional Writings,* 51–53.

83. Margaret Ellsberg, *Created to Praise,* 39–45.

84. Hopkins, *Sermons and Devotional Writings,* 262.

The Terrible Sonnets are connected verbally, temporally, and thematically to retreat notes in which Hopkins describes how he has been trying to fashion himself into things he thought his Jesuit identity demanded: a scholar, a preacher, a theologian. His superiors, meanwhile, seem to have been at cross-purposes with him, trying to find some place to use this brilliant but most peculiar priest.[85] Hopkins concentrated on fulfilling his conception of the demands of Jesuit obedience so punctiliously that he would not accept a cup of tea without permission. In Dublin, he graded exams until two and three in the morning, creating columns of fractional grades that he was too exhausted to add. He exhibited a tremendous determination to be "master of myself" through this ostensibly humble attempt to strangle his natural desires and form himself into his conception of a perfect Jesuit. In a little moral quatrain of his youth, he admitted "I own a preference for Pride." The next chapter shall discuss how his stubbornness about his artistic vision could not be classified as pride—but his determination to choose the shape of his character certainly could. As he put it to Bridges, "[M]y trouble is not the not being able to write a book; it is the not being fit for my work and the struggling vainly to make myself fitter."[86] If this is, as I suspect, the struggle with God which "Carrion Comfort" records, Hopkins was glad to be the loser. After the despairing 1888 retreat notes in which he calls himself a "eunuch" and reports "helpless loathing," he writes Bridges in a cheerful letter, "I am a eunuch"—and then turns it into a biblical allusion indicating that he no longer claims control over the matter—"but it is for the kingdom of heaven's sake."[87]

The moments of autobiography in the Terrible Sonnets chronicle the breakdown of the poet's ambition and his acceptance of whatever state he had to endure.[88] In "Carrion Comfort," Hopkins observes the

85. Robert Bernard Martin gives a most balanced account of this in his biography, *Gerard Manley Hopkins: A Very Private Life* (London: Harper Collins, 1991).

86. Hopkins, *Letters to Bridges*, 252 (18 Feb. 1887). But cf. the letter of 22 Jan. 1888.

87. Hopkins, *Letters to Bridges*, 270 (12 Jan. 1888).

88. I argue this more fully in my senior honors thesis, "Poet and Priest in the Terrible Sonnets: Gerard Manley Hopkins" (Harvard University, 1981), which is available at Widener Library, but its argument is summarized neatly and more accessibly in the larger argument of Ellsberg, *Created to Praise*, chap. 1.

twofold will in action as his own best good outrages his desire for comfort. He seeks to love God with charity in "*Justus tu es, Domine.*" He reminds himself in "To Seem the Stranger" that "not but at all removes I can / Kind love both give and get." He succeeds, in these sonnets, in removing himself, in loving even himself with charity—an ordinate charity, which meant for him, as his 1883 retreat notes apprehensively record, not success at self-mastery but the helplessness of "being lifted on a higher cross." In "Patience, hard thing," he sees the crucifixion of Christ as heroism, of course, but also, following Scotus, patience; because, as Scotus points out, all willingness to endure suffering for the good, from the courage of a soldier to the most humble act, is alike patience.[89] For patience, Hopkins is willing to "do without, take tosses, and obey."

In "I wake and feel," he explains in human terms the constriction of spirit and inward turning that is damnation in his theology, and his relief at having escaped it. Here we see Hopkins using his reading of Scotus to explore his own internal landscape:

> I wake and feel the fell of dark, not day.
> What hours, O what black hoürs we have spent
> This night! What sights you, heart, saw, ways you went!
> And more must, in yet longer light's delay.
> With witness I speak this. But where I say
> Hours I mean years, mean life. And my lament
> Is cries countless, cries like dead letters sent
> To dearest him that lives alas! away.
> I am gall, I am heartburn. God's most deep decree
> Bitter would have me taste: my taste was me;
> Bones built in me, flesh filled, blood brimmed the curse.
>
> Selfyeast of spirit a dull dough sours. I see
> The lost are like this, and their scourge to be
> As I am mine, their sweating selves; but worse.

Hopkins is in the place of Lucifer; the night is like dying, wherein "all that energy or instress with which the soul animates and otherwise acts upon the body by death is thrown back upon the soul itself."[90]

89. Duns Scotus, *Ord.* 3, suppl. d. 34, trans. Wolter, *Duns Scotus on the Will and Morality,* 361.

90. Hopkins, *Sermons and Devotional Writings,* 137.

Assonance joins the widely separated "Wake" and "day," but strongly emphasized alliterations for "feel the fell" and "dark not day" aurally dominate the first line. The puns on "fell" multiply meaning: Hopkins as speaker indeed feels what it is to be fallen, cruelly and brutally, and the brute's skin foreshadows the allusion to the cursed blood and bones of Adam. (According to Genesis, God clothes Adam and Eve with animal skins after their fall.) Then the poet addresses himself in the plural, as divided from his own heart. "Hours" is to be pronounced like two syllables, according to Hopkins's metrical mark, giving that word particular weight; that license makes the line become regular. There is some distortion in the hours, but they proceed according to the customary order. The monotonous beat continues, lengthened by a deliberately disjointed sentence structure necessitating many punctuated pauses. "W" and "s" carry a burden of alliteration with groaning and hissing. Amidst the sprung syllables and alliterations, the reader cannot miss "must": compulsion marks the darkened future of the wayfarer, whose alliterative delay removes him from "light"; in a poem about damnation, this refers to the intellect.

The second quatrain develops the metaphor: this is a life in darkness. "S" and "w" continue to predominate. "I," repeated thrice in these two lines, assonates with another repetition in line seven: "cries." The quatrain is about speaking; "say" is connected by rhyme to "day," "delay," and "away." Insofar as the role of a human being is to speak the world as word, and to name his deepest self, Hopkins's speech is of distance and endless delay, black hours, sent laments, and cries. Prepared by no related sounds, the phrase "dearest him" imparts a sudden, poignant tenderness to the last line of the octave, as slow and heavily regular as any of the first five. This is not anger; this is a lover suffering abandonment.

The sestet is metrically bolder, but still basically iambic, as if license itself were beyond the poet's strength. However, the verbs in the first two feet of this line twice swallow the personal pronoun "I," as if "I am" were a single syllable. The "gall" of this slack self is connected, strangely, to "God," who in the Incarnation indeed tasted it once (Matt. 27.34), and whose "deep decree" is enforced upon the reader's mind, both by alliteration and the strong end-of-line rhetorical position. Metrical and syntactical inversion combine to reinforce the passion in the first word of the next line: "Bitter." Hopkins associated intensity and intimacy—and isolation—with the sense of taste.

What is the nature, then, of this infinitely personal, most deep decree? It is the decree of Hopkins's very being—that such a "pitch" should be. And when his nature is "superadded," it is flesh, bones, blood: human nature, brimful of Adam's curse. His whole nature is skewed and founded upon sin. When he turns his will upon himself—"selfyeast"—his nature goes bad. The "dull dough," with flawed ingredients, decomposes; one can taste it, and the bubbling yeast hisses in the fermenting mixture. Consuming himself as yeast consumes the dough, puffing himself up, in the biblical phrase, he constructs a self according to a plan of mastery. He cannot find the joys he planned to meet; he confronts only himself, and repeats the cycle of frustration. Hopkins is *capax dei,* a creature capable of enjoying God, but turned in upon himself his spirit "is confronted by that scape, that act of its own, which blotted out God and so put blackness in the place of light; does not see God but sees that." Hence his scourge, like that of the devils and the damned, is his own sweating self. He cannot find love except by standing apart from himself and looking upon himself, not with mastery, but with the same kind of charity with which he is commanded to regard everything else. And indeed, the end of the poem indicates that he does so.

The first hint that he is not truly damned comes early, with the repetition of "you" in the address to his own heart: he treats himself as an other, a companion. The last two lines of the poem again distance the speaker from the desolation he is experiencing. "Lost" alliterates with "like"—a likeness that is not identity—and "this" with "their," reinforcing the idea that the speaker, while he most intimately understands damnation, has escaped it. Hopkins has a tender love and longing for the divine lover; he at least desires the pleasure of knowing God. This is not "divine charity," but it is "holy hope." Although Scotus writes that "the affection for justice is nobler than the affection for the advantageous,"[91] Hopkins does not therefore disregard the virtue of

91. Duns Scotus, *Ord.* 3, suppl. d. 26, trans. Wolter, *Duns Scotus on the Will and Morality,* 179.

Hope, which is the proper function of the affection for the advantageous. In preaching about those who have been sinners for their whole lives, Hopkins urged his congregation to hope: "Hope is an anchor cast in heaven: as long as you do not let it go, hold it must and lost you cannot be."[92] "I wake and feel" is about sin, longing for God, and, ultimately, the salvation of this "sweating self." Like the sinners in Hopkins's sermon, the speaker is among those whose "salvation was due to their never altogether giving over holy hope."[93]

Scotus suffused Hopkins's theology and his art, and indeed, the whole man. In his last years, he confronted his own pride, which focused his attention on the good of the creature he was determined to make himself into, rather than the good of the creation he was to witness. His poems from this dark time enunciate the problem, and signal hope that, his offense known and confessed, he may yet fulfill his vocation. Hopkins said Scotus "most of all men sways my spirits to peace;" and indeed it is in the Scotist ideas about fulfillment of self and about hope that Hopkins finds light in the Terrible Sonnets. The sonnet cycle is not Scotism expounded; it is Scotism lived.

In earlier years, Hopkins had recognized that one must devote one's energy and attention to call forth the inscapes of the world. Hopkins found a comrade in Scotus; the poet's concept of "pitch" found echoes in Scotus's "affection for justice." Hopkins read in the Scotist concern for individuation a sense, like his, of a deep and most particular self, which is divinely predestined to a particular way of understanding the world. God, not bound to so limited an individuality, can participate in his creatures such that they become vehicles and signs of his activity in the world. His grace enables free, rational beings to perceive the real value of things besides themselves, and bring to fruit the goodness understood in those perceptions. Hopkins had early had an intuition that the noblest deed is sacrifice and that somehow art can be sacrifice, too. Scotus taught him that to love things might well mean to speak of them justly, rejoicing in their goodness and drawing forth the *formalitates* he sees. If perception and utterance are the activities in which a human being most resembles the Divine Word, to rejoice in the

92. Hopkins, *Sermons and Devotional Writings*, 251.
93. Hopkins, *Sermons and Devotional Writings*, 250.

world's beauty is sacrificial, as Christ's Incarnation is, and acceptable to God. In Scotus, Hopkins found his sense of incommunicable particularity confirmed in its importance, and yet was confirmed in his yearning to share his love and insight in words.

To be able to love the external world is to have a consciousness, a self; to actually love the world for its own sake is liberty. Scotus saw the most fundamental task of the human being—justice—as an exercise first of all in paying attention to the goodness of the things of the world. Hopkins took to heart both Scotus's understanding of the way in which God can participate in human nature and his images of damnation in the frustration of one's loves. Through this understanding of self, of nature, of grace, and of the importance of knowing and speaking what he sees, Hopkins achieves hope: although he may be "groping round my comfortless," he knows that God promises joy, and invites his readers to the "lovely mile." Even the desolate places he encounters, when he speaks them, are rich with hidden inscapes, full of the measureless beauty of God.

CHAPTER 9

THE USES OF POETRY

LONG BEFORE Hopkins's scholarly ambitions collapsed under the grim imagined weight of his "professional" Jesuit identity, he had, far more freely, given up his professional identity as an artist. After the "slaughter of the innocents," when he burnt his poems and resolved to wait until he had "leave" to write more, he never seriously pursued a literary audience. Although he thought fame the proper atmosphere for poetry, his attempts to publish his poetry were few and feeble, and he forbade his friends even the attempt; he wrote little and took little care to preserve what he did write.[1] Quite deliberately he left his poems to the care of God, perfectly satisfied, he said, if they should be lost. Devlin went so far as to say that the poet "treated his muse in public like a slut and her children as an unwanted and vaguely sinful burden." Devlin continues, "[I]n secret he loved them passionately,"[2] and indeed Hopkins's faith in the merit of his work seems almost arrogant: "I cannot think of altering anything. Why shd. I? I do not write for the public. You are my public and I hope to convert you,"[3] he says to Bridges. His last sonnet, "To R.B.," apologizes for his slim productivity, but proclaims his "hand at work now never wrong." Hopkins's Scotist aesthetic can unravel this apparent tangle of reticence and Olympian pride. We have seen before something of the way he begins to explain it in a letter to Bridges:

1. "All therefore that I think of doing is to keep my verses together in one place—at present I have not even correct copies—, that, if anyone shd. like, they might be published after my death. . . . I cannot in conscience spend time on poetry"; Hopkins, *Letters to Bridges,* 66 (15 Feb. 1879).

2. Devlin, editorial matter, *Sermons and Devotional Writings,* 119.

3. Hopkins, *Letters to Bridges,* 46 (21 Aug. 1877).

> Art and its fame do not really matter, spiritually they are nothing, virtue is the only good; but it is only by bringing in the infinite that to a just judgment they can be made to look infinitesimal or small or less than vastly great; and in this ordinary view of them I apply to them, and it is the true rule for dealing with them, what Christ our Lord said of virtue, let your light shine before men that they may see your good works (say, of art) and glorify yr. Father in heaven (that is, acknowledge that they have an absolute excellence in them and are steps in a scale of infinite and inexhaustible excellence.)[4]

We shall see more of that scale of excellence; it ranges from purely physical beauty through the "beauty of mind" to the "beauty of character" to sainthood—but always it starts with the physical. An artist recognizes the world outside the self through the senses and must work to do it justice, to unfold it into meaning and bring it to completion as a sacrifice of praise. For a Scotist such as Hopkins, the world's profusion of particularity serves the most glorious singularity, the Incarnation of Christ, through whom and in whom it has its being. Anyone who attends to justice in the world—or, like the artist, attends to the world in justice—participates in the divine freedom that is the foundation of creation, seeking not merely the benefit of one creature, which has its limits, but the good of all being, which rests in the goodness of the Infinite Being.

Hopkins had thought more deeply than Ruskin, but never ceased to respect him; for Hopkins, as for the early Ruskin, the practice of true art could only be an act of piety. Yet both Ruskin and Hopkins knew that in this fallen world the arts are not the most urgent good one can do. Post-Christian Ruskin had turned uneasily away from the arts to political economy. Hopkins felt he could not "in conscience" spend time on poetry, and in his twenties turned decisively from poetry to ministry, believing that service there addressed more urgent needs. Nevertheless, he has a high view of art, and his perspective on the function of art is thoroughly religious: a good poem participates in the "Great Sacrifice," which is no less than the creation and salvation of the world.

Hopkins discusses aesthetic theory in poetry as well as in prose. In an 1879 draft of a lyric, Hopkins uses Scotist theories of the self and

4. Hopkins, *Letters to Bridges*, 231 (13 Oct. 1886).

the nature of free will in a meditation upon the moral relationship of an artist to art. The draft has many variants and cancellations, and no finished copy exists; even the order of the stanzas is uncertain.[5] However, the lack of Hopkins's customary polish actually serves to highlight the philosophical groundwork underlying the poem. Bridges thought that the poem was about a piece of music, but I follow Catherine Phillips in believing that the musical metaphors serve an image drawn from architecture. The poem's main idea is that the external expression of the artist's "pitch" shows us something of the range of beauty known by his deepest self, but not whether he has salvific faith or love. Artistic achievement displays a more external kind of beauty: that of the mind.

Who shaped these walls has shewn
The music of his mind,
Made known, though thick through stone,
What beauty beat behind.

How all's to one thing wrought!
The members, how they sit!
O what a tune the thought
Must be that fancied it.

The artist makes unity out of many "members," a word Ruskin commonly used for architectural features in *Seven Lamps of Architecture.* Conscious of the biblical image of the Church as the Body of Christ (1 Cor. 12.14–27), where the word bore the original and literal sense of body parts, Hopkins sets this meaning in tension with its later meaning as "unit in an organization." In building up a harmonious unity, the artist acts the part of Christ, "in whom and through whom all things

5. I follow Norman MacKenzie's sensitive edition of this vexed text in the *Poetical Works*, 159–60. Although my reading here follows that later edition, I would also support one variant, inverting stanzas 3 and 4 of the *Poetical Works* edition, in accord with the arrangement found in the fourth edition of the *Poems*, 104–5, which MacKenzie edited with W. H. Gardner. I have seen the manuscript in facsimile, and agree that it is in a sufficiently confused state that the author's final intentions are not known; see Geoffrey Bliss, "In a Poet's Workshop," *The Month* 167 (Feb. 1936): 160–67. Catherine Phillips arranges it in a different and less theologically pregnant way than either MacKenzie arrangement in *The Oxford Authors Gerard Manley Hopkins*, 145–46, though her notes are, as usual, a rich mine of worthwhile information.

were made." The "tune" of the building is its "design, pattern, or what I am in the habit of calling inscape."[6] Inscape, in a work of art, comes first in the "order of intention" and "fancies" all the elements necessary to execute the perfected work. An artist thinks of a work in its perfection before deciding on the ways to reach that perfection, or, as Scotus put it, "Everyone who wills in a reasonable way, first wills the end, and secondly that which immediately attains the end, and thirdly other things which are more remotely ordered to the attainment of his end."[7]

Though down his being's bent
Like air he changed in choice,
That was an instrument
Which overvaulted voice.

All choices are made within the limits of the creature's pitch, his "being's bent." Hopkins comments elsewhere on "the necessary or constrained affection on the creature's part, to which the *arbitrium* of the creature may give . . . consent or refusal." Choice is possible even within such constraints. When God moves the soul by grace to be attracted to some good action, "in ordinary cases refusal is possible not only physically but morally and often takes place."[8] The unclear pronoun reference in the third line of this stanza gains some clarity from a variant of the fourth line: "That vaulted round his voice."[9] The artist's voice would be his assent to or dissent from his predestined good. "That" instrument is the one God made for the artist's playing: the artist's pitch. It is in an architectural sense that the constraints of the creature's possible desires "vault round" or "overvault" his actual choices: they provide the space in which free choice can function. But the artist is

Not free in this because
His powers seemed free to play:
He swept what scope he was
To sweep and must obey.

6. Hopkins, *Letters to Bridges,* 66 (15 Feb. 1879).

7. Duns Scotus, *Ord.* 3, supp. dis 32, trans. as "How God's Love Extends to All Things," in Wolter, "John Duns Scotus on the Primacy and Personality of Christ," 155.

8. Hopkins, *Sermons and Devotional Writings,* 149.

9. Phillips, *Oxford Authors Gerard Manley Hopkins,* 362.

The word "play" appears here with the force of Hopkins's philosophical language behind it. Hopkins wrote detailed notes on the distinctions between freedom of "pitch" and "play."

> This is the natural order of the three: freedom of pitch, that is/ self determination, is in the chooser himself and his choosing faculty; freedom of play is in the execution; freedom of field is in the object, the field of choice. . . . it is freedom of pitch to be able to choose for yourself which of several doors you will go in by; it is freedom of play to go unhindered to it and through the one you choose; but suppose all were false doors or locked but the very one you happened to choose, there is here wanting freedom of field.[10]

God can allow the elective will to be free (freedom of pitch) and nevertheless determine actions by offering to the affective will nothing so attractive as that which God wills the creature to do. Armed with this philosophy, Hopkins can see art as the fulfillment of a divine commission without accepting Ruskin's infallible artistic imagination. The artist did, within the range of his commission, what he wanted to do; excellence in execution is evidence both of the consent of the will and freedom of play on the artist's part. However, God may not have offered the artist freedom of field; he must obey his desire if nothing else within his knowledge could possibly seem better. The artist, although free, was constrained by his pitch to a particular range of beauty and could not create beauty beyond his scope. We have seen how the fullness of freedom is charity which loves without distinction not only the things one takes particular pleasure in but all things. Art gives no information about whether the artist did that.

Though a work has artistic integrity, a good in itself, this integrity does not tell us of the state of the artist's soul:

> Nor angel insight can
> Learn how the heart is hence:
> Since all the make of man
> Is law's indifference.

No other human being, nor even any angel, knows whether another wayfarer is in grace or in sin during this life. The "make" of man here is "make or species," understood in its sense of essential classification,

10. Hopkins, *Sermons and Devotional Writings*, 149.

as the word appears in Hopkins's epigraph to "Henry Purcell," an earlier poem about art.[11]

Another draft of the last two lines of the stanza reads: "The manners of the man / are all indifference"; and there the "make" more clearly refers to culture. Hopkins included the "object-world" in the self. Hopkins said that whatever can truthfully be called a self, "it is not a mere centre or point of reference for consciousness or action attributed to it, everything else, all it is conscious of or acts upon being its object only and outside it."[12] A person's body is, in a sense, also his self; in a more distant sense, so are his works; yet more distantly, the very culture and surroundings in which one declares one's self become part of that self. When an observer brings things into fuller reality through human recognition, their selves are, in a sense, joined to that of the observer. For example, Monet's water lilies are lilies, but they are also Monet. Yet while self extends to one's actions in the world, a person's whole external self, even the artist's extended body of work, does not necessarily disclose the artist's moral beauty.

Hopkins discusses the "make of man" in general in a letter written in October 1879, at most a few months after writing this draft, and clearly about the same ideas (the poem is partly drafted on a letter sent to Hopkins in May 1879):

> [T]he soul may have no other beauty, so to speak, than that which it expresses in the symmetry of the body—barring those blurs in the cast which wd. not be found in the die or the mould. This needs no illustration, as all know it. But what is more to be remarked is that in like manner the soul may have no further beauty than that which is seen in the mind, that there may be genius uninformed by character. I sometimes wonder at this in a man like Tennyson; his gift of utterance is truly golden, but go further and you come to thoughts commonplace and wanting in nobility.[13]

Genius and elegance of expression are not the same as noble character. The "make" of a man, the design of his personality, is, in one way,

11. Wuellner, *Dictionary of Scholastic Philosophy,* 117, *s.v.* "species." MacKenzie, in his editorial commentary in Hopkins, *Poetical Works,* 410, provides the illuminating earlier draft of the following line, which led me to consider the relevance of the epigraph of "Henry Purcell" with reference to this line.

12. Hopkins, *Sermons and Devotional Writings,* 127.

13. Hopkins, *Letters to Bridges,* 95 (22 Oct. 1879).

indifferent to the internal freedom that determines salvation or damnation; it has, like a work of art, its "inlaw," its internal logic. Recall how Hopkins put it in his private notes: "[T]hough self, as personality, is prior to nature it is not prior to pitch."[14] Personality, in Scholastic terms, is the seeking of one's own good and existence. The execution of the design of one's personality is a matter of moral weight, but the perfection of a work of art according to its inlaw is indifferent to the moral law. One need not attribute moral weight to the excellences, as art, of an artifact of culture—even so complex an artifact as one's external persona.

Therefóre this masterhood,
This piece of perfect song,
This fault-not-found-with good,
Is neither right nor wrong.

No more than red and blue,
No more than Re and Mi,
Or sweet the golden glue
That's built for by the bee.

To create appreciation and inspire love for the things of the world by art is objectively good, and a work may be particularly good in execution; but its goodness is in the order of the goodness of nature. As Ruskin too had observed, early in *Modern Painters,* one cannot morally fault an artist, nor must one overpraise him, as a moral being, for the beauty he perceives and desires. Hopkins now turns to the beauty in itself:

For good grows wild and wide,
Has shades, is nowhere none;
But right must seek a side
And choose for chieftain one.

No being lacks goodness; evil is perverted good, and attracts our desire under the appearance of goodness. But good grows wild; creatures with free will must set in order their apprehensions of beauty so that in their desires the lesser good does not overwhelm the greater.

14. Hopkins, *Sermons and Devotional Writings,* 148.

There is a difference between an artist's "pitch" toward apprehending some beauty and the use he chooses to make of that apprehension.

Hopkins then goes on to consider what the best kind of beauty is:

> What makes the man and what
> The man within that makes:
> Ask whom he serves or not
> Serves and what side he takes.

Another draft of the first two lines of this stanza reads: "What makes the man and what / With that the man shall make." It addresses the tension between work and character that lies at the heart of the poem: that an artist's work, which is a manifestation of the "pitch" at the origin of his being, is not the same as the true work of his life. What a man makes of himself, in the deepest way, can only be known by knowing whom he takes for his Lord. Like a good Jesuit, Hopkins envisions the spiritual life as a war between two armies.

> Who built these walls made known
> The music of his mind,
> Yet here he has but shewn
> His ruder-rounded rind.
> His brightest blooms lie there unblown,
> His sweetest nectar hides behind.

The moral beauty of an artist's soul is the "sweetest nectar," but that lies hidden; beauty as it presents itself in the artist's vision is not moral good, which we know in contradistinction to evil, but simple good. Moral good—Scotus's "nobler" affection, by which we participate in the Great Sacrifice—does not necessarily flower in artistic endeavor.

Sin has so perilously disordered our capacity for joy that the desire for delight in simple good is no longer necessarily the desire for God. Art should teach people to love goodness without disordering their desires; Hopkins wrote: "What are works of art for? to educate, to be standards."[15] The artist, divinely commissioned to do justice to a particular "cleave" of the realities of the world, does an honorable duty.

15. Hopkins, *Letters to Bridges*, 231 (13 Oct. 1886).

Art's function is revelatory, but artistic skill is gear, tackle, not in itself virtuous nor an extraordinary medium of divine grace—in fact, less so than the most ordinary acts of charity. The love of beauty is insufficient if not restrained by charity. An artist must take care that in performing his art, he does not limit himself to wishing well to his own art, which is his own good. He must wish good to the thing to which he attends; and to his audience he must wish virtue, true good. An artist might wish to know human degradation, for instance, in order to make a compelling tale. There might be a temptation to rejoice in evil or dwell on it, not wishing it transformed into good but only wishing to make a vivid canvas. It is good to excel in art, but that is a limited wish; if art excels at the cost of ruined lives, as Ruskin argues in *The Stones of Venice,* the art itself is degraded. In Scotist terms, such a corrupt artist has betrayed a human being's primary commission: charity toward all being. In Hopkins's more vivid image, the chorister murders the greater joy of the song because he is ravished by the beauty of his single note. And in succumbing to irrational desire for the limited good of a creature, rather than to the rational desire for the good of all, the artist loses his intrinsic freedom. Real freedom is compatible with artistic necessity, for freedom resides in the ability not to be mastered by anything less than the fullest good.

In "[Who shaped these walls has shewn]" Hopkins dealt with the beauty of the artist's mind, but human beings possess two other kinds of beauty in his "scale of infinite and inexhaustible excellence":

> I think then no one can admire the beauty of the body more than I do and it is of course a comfort to find beauty in a friend or a friend in beauty. But this kind of beauty is dangerous. Then comes the beauty of the mind, such as genius, and this is greater than the beauty of the body and not to call dangerous. And more beautiful than the beauty of the mind is beauty of character, the "handsome heart."[16]

Hopkins develops the theme of a hierarchical relationship ordering from the beauty of body to virtue in an 1885 sonnet, his most sophisti-

16. *Letters to Bridges,* 95 (22 Oct. 1879).

cated poem on aesthetic theory.[17] The poem is in sprung alexandrines, a meter Hopkins had developed around this time for his verse tragedy (of which fragments exist) *St. Winefred's Well.* He said the rhythm "lends itself to expressing passion."[18] The scansion marks are my own, except caesuras, the circumflex at "See: it," and the pairs of words printed with a ⌐¬ over them, which Hopkins joined with a mark to indicate that "though one has and the other has not the metrical stress, in the recitation-stress they are to be about equal."[19]

To what serves Mortal Beauty?

To whát serves mórtal béauty—́ | dángerous; does sét dánc-
Ing blóod—the o-séal-that-só | féature, flung próuder fórm
Than Púrcell tune léts tréad to? | Sée: it does thís: keeps wárm
Men's wíts to the thíngs that áre; | what góod méans—where a glánce
Máster móre may than gáze, | gáze out of cóuntenánce.
Those lóvely láds once, wét-fresh | wíndfalls of wár's stórm,
Hów then should Grégory, a fáther, | have gléanèd élse from swárm-
Èd Róme? But Gód to a nation | déalt that dáy's dear chánce.
To mán, that néeds would wórship | blóck or bárren stóne,
Our láw says/ lóve what áre | love's wórthiest, were áll knówn;
World's lóveliest—men's sélves. | Sélf fláshes off fráme and fáce.
What dó then? how méet béauty? | Mérely méet it; ówn,
Hóme at héart, heaven's sweet gíft; | then léave, lét that alóne.
Yea, wísh that though, wísh áll, | God's bétter béauty, gráce.

17. See the discussion of this poem in terms of a dialogue between Tractarian versus Paterian "aesthetic" poetry in Maureen F. Moran, "Manl(e)y Mortal Beauty: Hopkins as Tractarian Aesthete," *Hopkins Quarterly* 22, nos. 1–2 (Winter 1994–Spring 1995): 3–29.

18. Hopkins, *Letters to Bridges,* 92 (2 Oct. 1879).

19. Hopkins's note quoted in *Poems,* 4th ed., ed. Gardner and MacKenzie, 285. In the following rendition of the poem I follow the D manuscript as found in Norman MacKenzie, ed., *Gerard Manley Hopkins: The Later Poetic Manuscripts* (New York: Garland, 1991), plate 452, rather than the text in Norman MacKenzie, ed., *Poetical Works.* I concur in Catherine Phillips's choice to leave in more metrical marks, and her editing of the second line, which MacKenzie edits "o-seal-that-so | face, prouder flung the form." I add manuscript D metrical marks which neither editor included. Both readings have the authority of autograph fair copies, and the more compressed form, besides being more typical of Hopkins's excisions of the definite article in his most polished work, creates a grammatical parallel between "feature" and "form" that seems to me better focused than the manuscript A reading that MacKenzie adopts.

In an age dominated by professional psychology, critics have been eager to seize upon the danger Hopkins saw in sensual beauty. Some find, in his decision to live the most strenuous possible spiritual life, an impulse to flee a physical reality he feared but did not love.[20] Hopkins certainly freely acknowledged that he had chosen his way of life to support him in resisting impulses that he consciously considered destructive.[21] He engaged, for instance, in a practice known as "custody of the eyes" which prevented him for six months from seeing much physical beauty; asceticism is not, however, a rejection of beauty, any more than athletic training is a renunciation of bodily pleasure.[22] Vigils do not presume that sleep is an evil; a fast does not proclaim eating a vice, nor is that form of prayer recommended only for gluttons. As-

20. See Claude Colleer Abbott's hostile and reductive notes to his editions of Hopkins's letters. Eleanor Ruggles's sensationalistic accounts of ascetic practices in *Gerard Manley Hopkins: A Life* bore fruit in many attempts to find out why Hopkins was such a masochist as to become a Jesuit. Hot critical battles broke out; worthwhile contributions include two by Austin Warren, "Gerard Manley Hopkins" and "Instress of Inscape," both in *Gerard Manley Hopkins by the Kenyon Critics,* ed. John Crowe Ransom and Cleanth Brooks (Norfolk, Conn.: New Directions, 1945), especially "Gerard Manley Hopkins," 13; and Martin C. Carroll, S.J., "Gerard Manley Hopkins and the Society of Jesus," in *Immortal Diamond: Studies in Gerard Manley Hopkins* (New York: Sheed & Ward, 1949), 3–50. For Sandra Gilbert and Susan Gubar on Hopkins, see their *The Madwoman in the Attic: The Woman Writer and the Nineteenth-Century Literary Imagination* (New Haven, Conn.: Yale University Press, 1979), 3, which cites, without comprehension, a letter in which he uses masculine metaphors for creativity, unbalanced by such material as "To R.B." in which his metaphors are feminine. Hopkins's sexism, which was certainly strong and hidebound, is not actually manifested in an aesthetic nervousness about "power," such as they presume.

21. Hopkins, *Further Letters,* 231 (to A. W. M. Baillie, 12 Feb. 1868). Ruggles, in *Gerard Manley Hopkins: A Life,* passim, and White, in *Hopkins: A Literary Biography* (Oxford, U.K.: Clarendon Press, 1992), 181–82, seem unable to see any motivation in self-restraint except an obscure form of perversion, but the desire to seek out psychological abnormalities, especially sexual, is common among his biographers. Paddy Kitchen, too, in *Gerard Manley Hopkins,* 71, dwells unduly upon Digby Dolben in search of some sort of sexual peculiarity, though Hopkins's fellow Jesuits indicated in his obituaries that his chastity was admired.

22. For a penance so unusual as Hopkins's, however, one may reasonably suppose that he had made some inappropriate use of his eyes, or had found his love of certain kinds of beauty leading him into desires he had determined not to indulge; one can lay claim to freedom from an addiction by removing the occasion of its indulgence.

ceticism is training, one might say, in proper attention to the world—and well-ordered love of the things of the world is the practice of the virtue of hope. Allan Wolter warmly describes Scotus's vision of the significance of worldly delights: "God first intended Christ as King and center of the universe," a doctrine which "makes the human nature of Christ the *motif* the Divine Architect was to carry out in the rest of creation. In Christ's soul God saw mirrored the choirs of angels; after his body the visible world was sculptured. The whole universe is full of Christ."[23]

Three dangers attend "mortal beauty." The "dancing" in the blood is no doubt a sexual temptation,[24] but beauty also provokes something like covetousness. The desire that beauty should defy time and change can ensnare the viewer in a hatred of the very stream of time in which earthly beauty has its existence. The repetition of the sound of "seal-that-so" recalls the situation in *The Golden Echo,* where "soaring sighs deliver" beauty to "beauty's self and beauty's giver," who preserves the "not-by-morning matchéd face, / The flower of beauty, fleece of beauty, too too apt to, ah! to fleet." The third danger is vanity beyond measure, with measure being slyly suggested by the "tread" of a dancing tune. The conjunction of the "prouder form" with the beloved name of Purcell, aided by alliteration, suggests also that art, a form of mortal beauty, is subject to some of the same dangers.

Hopkins will show us, with his own example of mortal artistic beauty, what its good is: "*See.*" We are to enjoy our lesson; it should keep our wits warm to the problem of dealing with the desires aroused by beauty. Hopkins reminds his audience that desire is, on the whole, a good thing. The most primitive desire rouses a creature's interest in things that are good for it: food, air, warmth, comfort. And this *affectio commodi* can awaken disinterested love for things one could otherwise scarcely notice. Hopkins is playing on the long-standing knowledge that the connection with pleasure (especially sexual attraction) brings

23. Wolter, "John Duns Scotus on the Primacy and Personality of Christ," 140, 141.

24. See Michael Lynch, "Recovering Hopkins, Recovering Ourselves," 107–17. Hopkins felt free to call sexuality dangerous; professional literary criticism today (I recommend the December 1994 PMLA for an instance) has largely lost its ability to indwell the idea that unchastity might be morally destructive (except perhaps as a physical risk to others' health), disconnecting critics from a long, fruitful literary tradition.

the beautiful to notice.[25] Experientially, the desirable defines the good; it tells the animal "what good *means.*" The meter emphasizes the verb. Scotus asserts, in a passage Hopkins read, that "what is amicable for others has its roots in what is amicable for oneself."[26] We work, within the privacy of our "pitches," by analogy, and can only engage in charity by equating the other with ourselves. Only if the other's desires resemble ours can we know enough to do good to another. And here the distinction between restraining and extinguishing a desire becomes vitally important. To restrain a desire is to practice liberty; to extinguish desire is to extinguish both love and freedom, for there is no freedom where there is no desire.

Thus a glance, a restrained look, can "master more" than a gaze. The phrase "out of countenance" recalls the form of a face. The common meaning of "to put out of countenance" is to disconcert, to disturb the self-possession of a person. A gaze may discountenance the one who looks, the one who knows himself to be seen, or both. Hopkins leaves the application of the phrase ambiguous. What bothers us when we find ourselves being stared at? Having become an object of attention without personal engagement. One can also be, more subtly, put out of countenance—outside of approval, or at any rate worthiness of approval—by desiring such a degradation. It is a betrayal of charity to oneself, a failure of hope.

But Hopkins here is primarily addressing the one who gazes. What embarrasses us when we find ourselves staring at someone? Knowing that we have treated another person as a spectacle rather than as an object of personal respect; we feel shame at not having mastered our own impulses. To desire to possess a person for one's enjoyment, without such personal respect, militates against seeking the good of that person per se. To treat someone as such an object of pleasure disturbs the dignity of that other person—worthily called self-possession. Sometimes the object of such attention believes that such desire is love, and is consumed by an anxiety to preserve love by feeding the possessor's pleasure. Desiring to be the instrument of another's pleas-

25. Examples can be found in Edmund Burke's *Essay on the Sublime and the Beautiful,* already a classic in the nineteenth century.

26. *Ord.* 2, d. 6, q. 2, trans. Wolter, *John Duns Scotus on the Will and Morality,* 465.

ure, and no more, can crush freedom under the illusion that one must give the one who claims possession everything, even one's own integrity. The gaze of desire that masters either lover or beloved, rather than being itself mastered by the free will, engenders finally no friendship, no charity, not even the bare semblance of human justice.

So the first quatrain overflows into the second, where Hopkins exemplifies charity through an old legend about how it came about that Christian missionaries were sent to England. In the story, Pope Gregory saw some beautiful boys for sale at a slave market in imperial Rome. He asked about their race, and upon being told that they were Angles, he said that such beautiful creatures might better be called "angels"—the pun applies in Latin as well as in English—and soon thereafter dispatched missionaries to their tribe. Hopkins uses an example that might well be dangerous, for he himself sternly disapproved of his own susceptibility to temptation from the beauty of men. The description of the boys, full of liquid and sibilant consonants, wallows in rich vowel sounds. The loveliness of the boys is set against the dank flesh-crawling consonance of "swarméd Rome." Gregory "gleans" them like Edenic fruit fallen in the storm of war—a fortunate fall for heathen England. Hopkins suggests that God drew Gregory to charity for the Angles by alerting his eye through his affective will. His apprehension of beauty opened his heart to give others the good he knew: the knowledge of God. He first recognized the slave boys as attractive; then, having become aware of them, he recognized them freely as beings like himself; and finally, through his charity, he created a community.

The sestet addresses the problem posed in the octave. A Bible verse explains the connection between the sexual subtext of the octave and the apparently irrelevant opening of the sestet. Wisdom 14.12 in the Douay version reads:, "For the beginning of fornication is the devising of idols, and the invention of them is the corruption of life."[27] Gregory could presumably have bought a few of the slave boys and kept their

27. Moran, in "Manl(e)y Mortal Beauty," properly finds Hopkins dealing with sexual temptation in the poem, but seems unaware that he would have been quite conscious of it. Seduced by the current convention that "subversive" is always and everywhere a term of praise, on page 19 she misreads the biblical allusion; Hopkins has no reason to consider the God of Israel an idol, nor, especially, to use biblical language to do so—the language of the Prophets, who claimed to be speaking God's own condemnation of idols.

beauty in his eye. Resisting the temptation to self-deception and idolatry offered by their beauty, Gregory instead sent missionaries to their people. The law of God would free them, too, from the barren tyranny of their own idols, and free them to set the Highest Good in the highest place in their lives; thus could they love the "world's loveliest" with charity and justice, giving beauty its real due.

It is in human nature to worship; Hopkins's cardinal text from the *Spiritual Exercises* is "Man was created to praise." He preached on it: "This is the purpose of the world, the end of our being: when we have once said from our hearts / Glory be to God / we have answered the end of our being."[28] The reason for physical beauty is to lead us to justly appreciate God's creatures and their Creator, restraining love for self to bring the others forth in their fullness, as God did.

> Why did the Son of God go thus forth from the Father not only in the eternal and intrinsic procession of the Trinity but also by an extrinsic and less than eternal . . . one?—To give God glory and that by sacrifice.[29]

To notice beauty and rejoice in it—to instress it—is to wish it well. To instress beauty in itself is to glorify God. Sin arises when beauty is enjoyed not for itself but for some other purpose. In the poem, "Our law" is the moral law of the human race, which is also a natural law—an *inlaw*, as Hopkins called a thing's internal principle of development. To prefer less than full rational freedom in oneself, or one's beloved, is to damages one's own freedom and humanity. Idolatry is self-delusion; the stress falls heavily on "are" in "Love what are."

By the similarity of consonant sounds, Hopkins makes a subtle connection between "law" and "love's worthiest, were all known; / World's loveliest." And what is loveliest? Self, soul. Hopkins tried to explain the relationship between external beauty and self's beauty to Bridges: "[E]ven bodily beauty, even the beauty of blooming health, is from the soul, in a sense, as we Aristotelian Catholics say, that the soul is the form of the body."[30] Recall that the relationship of the soul to the body is so intimate that each is incomplete, not a full person, when

28. Hopkins, *Sermons and Devotional Writings*, 28.
29. Hopkins, *Sermons and Devotional Writings*, 110.
30. Hopkins, *Letters to Bridges*, 95 (25 Oct. 1879).

they are separated. That intimacy makes it so that "Self| flashes off frame and face." Alliteration underscores the relationship between the self, the action the self undertakes, and the vehicles for that action.

Why are human beings loveliest? They are not necessarily so physically, although Hopkins says cautiously that they would be "were all known." All is not known; much is hidden, but men are the fullest manifestation of the self-sacrificing creative power of God. God chose to dwell in one man bodily; the Image of God must be the loveliest creature. Beautiful bodies manifest souls which Christ would make lovely. Yet in humanity's fallen state such bodies present a danger to other souls. We must be cautioned not to listen to the affective will alone in seeing the beauty.

The advice comes with strong stress: "*Merely* meet it." We are not to avoid beauty, nor to kill desire; meeting beauty alerts us to know the good. We can even "own" it—in the sense of acknowledging it, he hastens to add. Hopkins allows the shade of possession to creep in before restraining it, as must the viewer of beauty: "own, / Home at heart, Heaven's sweet gift; then leave, let that alone." The liquids reappear, again with an "o" sound. The final line calls readers to the charity that Gregory practiced and that, Hopkins believes, Christ practices constantly in the Great Sacrifice.

And in the poem itself readers meet beauty, both in sound and in the associations the words have brought into our minds. The language is sometimes deliberately seductive in the sense that Jonathan Culler found so maddening in "The Golden Echo"; Hopkins is quite conscious that the reader has met "dangerous" sexual beauty in the poem. He has not only posed but phenomenologically presented the problem of dealing with perilous beauty. In turning the reader to Christ at the end, Hopkins is hoping that the experience of reading the poem will be an enactment rather than a mere acknowledgment of the poem's advice. Erudite and elaborate in its theological underpinnings, his poetic is nevertheless a poetic of experience, experience rooted in the pleasures of language which for him defined the specifically poetic art. And to reveal the inscapes of thought and sound so entangled together is his own gesture of charity to his readers. He has shown them beauty; his art should bring them to think about the beauty of God, rather than about Hopkins the artist, because his technique is only a lens through which to view the same message written larger in the language of sky and mountain and the human form.

Every attempt to get other people to understand real things is an act of sacrificial love for the human community. Hopkins's poetic project is participation in that sacrifice; it is the exercise of instress upon the inscapes of the world. To instress inscapes with disinterested love is to do justice. There are aspects of justice in the world that are much more urgent; our world is full of injustices far more damaging than the failure to notice beauty. Hopkins had greater damage to combat than lack of appreciation for the beauties of nature, keenly though he felt the lack. The human beings we cut down, did we but know it, are lovelier far than the most lovely poplars; therefore Hopkins wrote little, in scraps of time. But his muse was blinkered only because there was so heavy a load of sin upon the "bent world." If all were well, the apparently gratuitous act of praise would be the most fundamental human duty. In an unfallen world, it would be the sacrifice of Christ, wishing well to all creation.

Hopkins sees the poet in Christ, sees Christ as a poet—or rather, he sees being a poet as being Christ, an "AfterChrist," rejoicing in the "world's wildfire." Christ submerges himself in others' good. Thus a poet, looking upon loveliness, speaking of beauty as his heart most longs to do, becomes one with the Image of God, never losing the particularity and limitation that makes him a self. And in that emptying of self, that loving attention to all that is other, he, paradoxically, finds full humanity and perfect freedom, the flowering of all selfhood. Hopkins's grace and peculiarity was to see, as no one else had, the overing and aftering of the inscapes of language. He lovingly attends to the world as a word, and cries "Look! Listen!" When we do listen, when we do look, we see the beauty of the language, indeed. But "Still, if we care for fine verses how much more for a noble life!"[31] The poetry also opens our eyes to a self, to Hopkins the man, and for him and what he most loved, "fans fresh our wits with wonder," yields glory, gives praise.

31. Hopkins, *Letters to Bridges*, 61 (19 Jan. 1879).

CHAPTER 10

AFTERCOURSES
Literature, Love, and Hopkins

When Hopkins entered Oxford, he was a promising young poet with aesthetic concerns. He was also a serious young Anglican with religious concerns. There was a common thread in these preoccupations: the question of how one can be faithful to the truth. When he left Oxford, though his religious allegiances were different, his central concerns were the same. His fundamentally religious sense of obligation to the truth deepened as he matured, and was always at the center of his thought, uniting rather than dividing his thirst for mortal beauty and his thirst for God.

The conviction that he was bound in service to the truth suffused his life and his poetry. As both priest and poet, he felt called to proclaim God as Truth. In our day, fear of offending those who hold different cultural positions has led to condemnations of all evangelism as the arrogant attempt at imposing one's own will upon others; but Hopkins could hold the idea of a single unchanging truth without feeling threatened by differences in perspective, for he was convinced that he and his fellow human beings could claim to know truth only personally. He practiced long the discipline of learning to distinguish truth perceived in the world from the hungers of his own will. Whether he is trying to communicate about counterpoint meter or about justice in the universe, Hopkins does not domineer because he acknowledges the insistent uniqueness of his vision. He is odd, and he knows he is odd; the oddness, the personal flavor, is essential. Any true human vision is a limited one. Hopkins's confidence in the value of that which is "counter, original, spare, strange" sometimes seemed arrogant to his contemporaries; in fact, it is humble, because it does not seek to universalize his own perception. Hopkins is the subject, not the master, of the truths he sees; likewise others are subject to so much of the multifarious truth as they can perceive.

It is not easy to believe oneself bound to the service of truth if truth cannot be found. In Hopkins's intellectual world, philosophers embittered by moral corruption and enthralled by the degree to which the human mind could accurately discover the way the world works, had asserted that truth was objective. To hold the truth was a matter of pure intellectual assent to what the individual could perceive himself, rather than a matter of faith in what other human beings said. The systematic distrust of religious tradition was not founded upon any new evidence, but only upon a new style of thought that the Romantics recognized as a terrified, inhuman demand for certainty. As Blake put it,

> May God us keep
> From Single vision & Newton's sleep![1]

Wordsworth and Coleridge were among those who felt that the demand for such austere objectivity was untrue to human experience. They knew that people did not learn joy by ratiocination upon objective evidence, and moreover that the objectivity of any evidence and any reasoning can well be doubted. Looking within, they discovered the mind shaping its own world, and fearless of subjectivity, they embraced the reality of internal experience. Within it they located religion and morality. As might the most profound doubter, Coleridge insistently placed perception inside the human subject, exalting interpretation above objective description; yet he did not deny the world beyond the mind. Instead, he found reality in their interplay. But neither he nor Wordsworth sought reality entirely within individual experience, or there would have been no point to their writing poems. The Romantic endeavor of Wordsworth and Coleridge was social and leaned quite consciously upon a long moral tradition, though the Ro-

1. William Blake, letter to Thomas Butts, Nov. 22, 1802, in *The Letters of William Blake,* 2 vols., ed. Geoffrey Keynes (New York: Macmillan, 1956), 1:79.

mantics looked to the heart's practical knowledge rather than to authority for the confirmation of moral precepts. Thus Wordsworth confirmed his religious and moral education by appealing to homely incidents. The next intellectual generation, which included such diverse thinkers as Newman and John Stuart Mill, despite being surrounded by scientific and technological advances, found Wordsworth and Coleridge too convincing to dismiss.[2] Mill and Newman both doubted that human beings have access to any external world, and both felt a compelling power in romantic emotional intensity and interiority. If we may judge by the testimony of Mill's autobiography, for him poetry manifested a moral truth far more valuable than scientific facts.

English thought had uneasily sorted itself into two worlds: an external world of scientific fact and an interior world wherein resided emotion, morality, and poetry.[3] Faced with doubt regarding the objective, historical truth of the Scriptures, Christians began to fear for their religion's intellectual respectability, and often retreated into sentiment. Newman's Tractarians opposed the separation of truth from morality and religion. They took up the challenge in two ways: first, by an appeal to the intellectual authority of preceding generations, embodied in the study of the earliest Christian writings; and second, by a pattern of religious practice and devotion that emphasized an interior spirituality with a personal, romantic flavor. Hopkins aligned himself with the Tractarians and rejected the higher criticism as arrogantly mistrustful of the Christian forbears whose love and goodwill seemed too deep for question.

Already an artist, Hopkins cherished an intense interior life and a consciousness of the mysterious privacy of perception. He easily accepted the idea of art as a guide to moral truth and the true artist as

2. Ball, *Science of Aspects*, 5–10.

3. In the twentieth century, this epistemological embarrassment devolved into the reduction of all ethical discourse to a realm of hortatory "pseudostatements," making literature a pleasant and useful branch of technology rather than any sort of knowledge or communication of truth. See I. A. Richards, *Poetries and Sciences* (New York: Norton, 1970), esp. 57ff.

fundamentally religious, taking his keynote from Ruskin, whose religious rhetoric passed easily from aesthetics to commentary on the art of living. Ruskin's ideal artist unified aesthetics and sacrifice, heroically disciplining his desire for the lovely and the orderly in the interests of truth. Ruskin demanded "truth" in architecture and "truth" to the artist's own eye in painting. This ideal of the responsibility of the artist to the community rather than merely to himself Hopkins seized upon with fervor. Working in a Tractarian mode, he abnegated even the rich sensuality of his artistic perceptions in the hopes of arousing yet more noble sentiments.

Hopkins could make religious sense of Ruskin's doctrine of moral sacrifice in terms of the High Anglican teaching about the union of the individual Christian with Christ in his sufferings. He centered his interior life on the dogma that in Communion a believer entered body and soul into union with the sacrificed Christ. Hopkins considered that union not a submission to an irrational force but rather an acceptance of the incarnation of Divine Reason. Convinced of the importance of reason, especially in religious matters, Hopkins became uneasy with the vague anti-rational mysticism in Ruskin's divinized artistic imagination, which seemed dangerously sentimental and illogical. Hopkins sought certainty in the historical claims of authority upheld by the Tractarians. Respect for his forbears in religion led him to seek stronger authority than that church party could offer him for the dogma of the Real Presence, so central to his concept of Christian life as sacrifice. Rome attracted him with its strong, uniform tradition upholding that dogma, which the Anglican communion did not hold consistently. After an anguished decision to become Roman Catholic, he was received into that communion by the most famous convert in England, John Henry Newman.

Newman, who became a mentor to Hopkins, took up epistemology from a Romantic point of view. Romanticism colored his understanding of the degree to which the imagination, and the will, work upon the information gathered by the senses. Hopkins had feared and distrusted subjectivity; Newman taught him that the willful action of the mind, assent, is the only way we know even "scientific" facts, and that we first know most things by authority-that is, by trust in other people. No one has enough information, alone, to understand the world in even the most rudimentary way. We can and must believe things on the basis of authority rather than objective evidence. In fact, Newman argues, there is no absolute, objective certainty; there is only moral certainty. This moral and communal grounding for knowledge struck a powerful chord in Hopkins. Newman argues that truth is one, but not monolithic; many members of a community can perceive the same thing under a number of aspects, perhaps all true; only no truth can contradict another. Newman's philosophy of perception and language justified a view of the artist as something more than an advertising man for the known truths of religion. His theory about the multiplicity of true perceptions accorded well with Ruskin's esteem for the artist's particularity, and had the added advantage of keeping the artist from the prideful position of depending only upon himself. One could test one's perceptions against those of other people, since truth cannot contradict itself. At the Oratory, Hopkins began to use the key term of his artistic vocabulary, "inscape," which refers first of all to these unique perceptions: an artist "catches" truths no one else has seen and seeks to reveal them to others.

Building upon his acceptance of the multiplied reality of the Real Presence in the Eucharist, Newman had opened Hopkins's mind to multiple aspects of the ordinary things of this world, each perceived by faith. As he trained for the priesthood, his concept was expanded by sacramental theology. The *sacramentum* is a collection of things used as a conscious allegory, to some degree arbitrarily, for a symbolic purpose—like much early poetry of Hopkins. The really important thing, the *res,* in every sacrament, is access to God's grace, the acceptance or rejection of which is an event hidden in the privacy of the soul. But Hopkins's poetry engages the concept of the thing-which-is-also-a sign, the *res et sacramentum,* which exists in the world publicly—a marriage, priesthood, membership in an organization—and which also has a spiritual and social dimension present in all cases, with or without the consent or even the perception of the person receiving the sacrament. Hopkins takes up this dimension of the Church's symbols and applies it to the whole world. It is not that Hopkins sees God directly in the world, just as a sacramentally married couple is not literally transformed into Christ and the Church. The world is language about God without ceasing to be itself; every last element of the world, down to the very noises we make when we speak, is in some way news of God, and made to lead creatures to his love. Thus Hopkins approaches the ordinary things that he perceives as charged with God's meaning, ready to leap out at anyone willing to attend to them. Therefore he takes wild delight in detail and a complex interlayering of meaning in every aspect of his poems: inscape, even inscape of meter, is news of God, which he is eager to share. Poetic language functions for him like the physical things used for the symbols in a sacrament.

There is a danger of pure interpretive subjectivity in this growing understanding of the role of the will in the perception of beauty, and Newman offered little help in escaping it. Newman believed in logic and system, but as for the experiences of the senses, he believed that human beings encountered only phenomena that were not realities, and that every perception of which we became aware was always already interpreted. The regress into solipsism could be stopped only by an act of will: the decision to have faith in a good God who provides true access to the outside world. Then Hopkins discovered Duns Scotus and his concept of *formalitas,* which reverberated deeply with his concept of inscape. In Scotus what one encounters in a *formalitas* is a reality with a toehold outside the self, not a mental construct. Scotus posited that humans have intuitive knowledge preceding interpretation. Its content is minimal—only of the existence of incursions upon one's perceptions, and the state of one's own actions—but the information, while shaped by one's own peculiar experience, is real, and accessible to others. Rejoicing that his readers could encounter a reality just as he did, Hopkins wrote poems breathtaking in their boldness with language and their phenomenological immediacy. Scotus taught him to understand peculiar personal perception as essential to human fulfillment in salvation. Hopkins brought this vision into his thought about creation, redemption, and damnation, where it becomes a grounding for the moral and religious stress in his poetry, reawakening, on a deeper level, the Ruskinian sense of the moral importance of art.

Rarely has the philosophical sophistication of Gerard Manley Hopkins governed a reading of his poetry. His ideas about language, literature, God, and especially love present a challenge to the modern reader. Hopkins believes that literature can serve a rational, disinterested love—love of all sorts of things, from saints to syntax, from falcons to philosophies, from bluebells to blacksmiths. His poems are permeated by a subtle and complex understanding of the relationship between linguistic structures and the world of experience. At the center of it all is community: between God and his creation, between humans and the message of God in the world, and especially among humans trying to tell each other about it. Love is a fundamentally rational act, beginning with the desire for what is pleasant to one's own senses, proceeding to rational perception of the good experienced by like creatures, and coming to its crown in the faith that others also love the good. The faith that others are capable of loving what is good and true, and only that faith, is the foundation of trust among human beings. Scotus argues that without trust, there can be no language, no "sharing of concepts and affections of the mind, and the social life among human beings would be destroyed."[4] The poet's role is to train us in recognizing that other people do indeed see and love truth; for without that generosity of imagination we can scarcely hope for any good thing, certainly not for the good of one another.

But, of course, we do not all see the world alike. Hopkins's poetry should, at best, breed respect for the real goods that others perceive and we even find (as Bridges found Hopkins's poems) "repellent." It need not rob us of our proper revulsion to evil. Of course, judgment is necessary; to take all notions as truth would be to refuse to prefer reality to willful delusion—in other words, to make everything equally false. But Hopkins's oddity is an argument for attending to the unexpected and unwanted good. He offers us the opportunity to taste other realities in poetry, the beauty which he sees and which we can aban-

4. *Ord.* 3, suppl. dis. 38, trans. Wolter, *Duns Scotus on the Will and Morality,* 483.

don without harm if we "see nothing in it." His epistemology assigns to each human being a limited vision that can only be shared by means of the inadequate instruments of language and gesture. Nevertheless, Hopkins believes that we must love one another enough to share what we know, despite our deficiency, and trust one another enough to hear. For we all live, as Hopkins put it, in bat-light, but faith in one another's utterances can be

> Night's lantern
> Pointed with piercèd lights, and breaks of rays
> Discover'd everywhere.[5]

As we have seen, Hopkins lived in times when it had become fashionable to approach the written record of the past with a corrosive suspicion of the writers' motives. The reaction to that hermeneutic transformation gave birth, in time, to the Oxford Movement and precipitated Hopkins's personal religious crisis. Matthew Arnold sought to erect fictional barriers in religion and poetry against the moral decay that might result from the breakdown of a standard of religious truth. Newman merely mourned the numbers of those fallen away from God, who

> are very sceptical about the existence of principle and virtue; they think all men are equally swayed by worldly, selfish or sensual motives, though some hide their motives better than others, or have feelings and likings of a more refined character. . . . they have no higher principle within them to counteract the effect of what they see without. . . . and they use their knowledge to overreach, deceive, seduce, corrupt, or sway those with whom they have to do.[6]

Newman deplored this; but when I was a graduate student in literature in the 1980s and 90s, literary theorists were quite earnest in their attempts to convince me that the mistrust and deception he described with such alarm were in fact the normal function of language. The articles we were expected to read and emulate discounted the very idea of investigating whether the authors of the books we studied had any

5. Hopkins, *Poetical Works*, 47.

6. Newman, "Ignorance of Evil," in *Parochial and Plain Sermons* (Westminster, Md.: Christian Classics, 1968), 8:262–63.

wisdom to share. Graduate students were to mine texts for evidences of the social pathologies that produced them. Deaf to Hopkins when he talks about love, God, and beauty, Culler and Miller are not sad cases on the margins; they are respected authorities. As a teaching consultant, I saw their methods practiced in the classroom. Freshman composition teachers would lecture to their classes about how language subverts meaning and later, in conference with me, express bewilderment that their students seemed to find composition pointless.

Besides my love of Hopkins, which led me to read Scotus, two other things guarded me from the hermeneutic trap of refusing to see any love in language. One was a philosopher: I was explaining my dissertation to him, describing the epistemology behind Matthew Arnold's poetics in all the usual poststructuralist terms of domination and subversion. Usually people stumbled on the epistemology, but he dispatched all difficulty with that in a sentence or two. Then he looked me in the eye and asked: "But tell me this: do you love Arnold?" It was a fine and unnerving moment; no one had expected me to speak about love and literature in the same sentence for years, and the answer, though I did not know it then, was a turning point in my life.

For I was already beginning to taste by experience what the answer ought to be, had I thought of it. I was, at the time, beginning to hold English classes twice weekly under a tree in a circle made by a house and five toolsheds. There, thirty-six Mexican and Salvadoran immigrants lived, quite aware that their poverty, suffering, and helplessness—in a word, their oppression—was a direct result of their ignorance of the language of the powerful in our culture. I approached them with political liberation in mind—yet power interested them less than storytelling, politics less than attempts to share recipes and jokes and warnings, to tell what they knew and to get to know me. I thought then, and I think now, that these people knew what oppression is and knew what language is for. For a year and a half, as I read literary theory, the *clase de inglés* in East Palo Alto was living evidence that language need not be a tool for domination but might be an attempt to share knowledge about the world. Knowledge is sometimes power; what I discovered in that circle of shacks is that its origin is love.

This sort of talk is easily condemned as "metaphysical" or "mystification." It is indeed metaphysics—but only in the old sense of logic, ontology, and epistemology, not in the loose sense, which I have heard in the mouths even of respected scholars, of vague numinous sentiment or "things which cannot be proven."[7] Except in the sense that all existence is a wonder, there is nothing mysterious about believing that I am experiencing something outside myself, or accepting the consequences of the proposition that "being is and not-being is not." Nothing in it is contrary to the notion of proof, and it requires no special divine illumination. Here at the turn of the millennium, logic itself has its enemies in the U.S. academy, who think of it as a logocentric structure imposed by a past privileged class. The minimal assumptions of a good-faith epistemology provide language with its point of contact to the world outside the mind; I assert that these concepts do not belong to an exclusive class of religious initiates.

It is not arrogant to trust in the existence of some standard higher than one's personal feeling by which one might be proven wrong. Yes, the standards depend fundamentally on human witness. But to claim that truth cannot be known is far more dangerous, mystifying, and exclusive—and indeed, cruel. It savors of rot to draft the language of liberation to defend an idea that only an educated elite can believe; it is toxic to take that idea and live it. The very notion that deception is inherent to language offers nearly irresistible temptations for the cynical exploitation of verbal power. Much more flexible and accessible, and supportive of justice, is the position of Hopkins. Hopkins believed that a single point of view is insufficient—but that there is a way to judge truth and falsehood. We can look to logic and to our own experience and ask whether our various understandings contradict one another. If not, we can rejoice in new knowledge; for many realities can exist even in the same thing. We can know being, Scotus says; we can know truth, because truth means intelligibility. Hopkins, presuming the intelligibility of the things of the world, allows his readers to meet

7. It is not the first time I have heard such a usage, but I regret to report that at a conference on cosmology at Stanford University on February 12, 1999, I heard Nobelist in physics Steven Chu define "metaphysics" as "things that can't be proven."

him with their own experiences. The different perceptions of other minds are not merely different ways of expressing the same monolithic and exclusive truth; they are different truths, different *formalitates*, present in the one thing.

No one understands the world alone; we do not invent our own language. Nevertheless, as Hopkins is acutely aware, we live alone; we encounter the world from within the impenetrable privacy of our selves. Our own bodies; our own histories; our time, place, class; the training and instruments we have to hand; our cultural blindnesses and insights—all shape our abilities to recognize things. Trust in one's senses is necessary, but one cannot function exclusively upon the physical knowledge one has personally discovered. Even the most astute and capacious individual mind cannot exhaust the store of realities encountered in any trivial thing, from its cultural meanings to the interactions of its subatomic particles. To perceive many realities and reveal them to one another is fundamental to human community. And it is a loving service of truth, and of one another, to test our understandings against each other's perceptions and to protect each other against delusion and refusal to see.

Hopkins, too, could have chosen to accept the philosophical position that human beings live in a world of sheer discourse, in which nothing can be tested; he was wise enough to reject the fearful urge for definitive testing and the consequent despair. While he did not believe in Ruskin's magical access to truth through an infallible Imagination, Hopkins objected to despair of finding any truth—on moral grounds, as Scotus did. People do give evidence of knowing the difference between existence and nonexistence; to pretend that one does not, Scotus insists, is to argue in bad faith, from an impossible and inhuman standard of knowledge. Hopkins and Newman both accept as metaphysically justified the very variety of points of view that is often taken for evidence against metaphysics. Yet they accept limits to knowledge. Scotus admits only one kind of information as intuitive: knowledge of the existence or nonexistence of some event from outside the mind, before the mind has had occasion to analyze and interpret it. That minimal knowledge, however, coupled with the power of memory, suffices for judging truth in language.

We create communion with our world by speech and ordered thought, by sound and gesture, and by building physical structures. Of these media, the poet is concerned with speech, revealing the realities we encounter both in the particulate isolation of our own perceptions and in the commonalities we have discovered by talking to one another. For this purpose, a poet has only the tools forged in common, and must use them obliquely to uncover that which is individual. Among the things of this world, language is perhaps the most rich and various, being both instrument and subject, the image and outstressing of that most rich reality, embodied consciousness. So the poet attends to the body of language in sound and intonation, rhythm and pace; to its place in the world of thought—syntax, rhetoric, image, argument—and to its place in the living reality of our loves and aversions. Such loving intercourse with the world allows us to honor it; to treat every self in it as, in justice, equal to every other self; allows us to humble ourselves and by humility to serve justice, freedom, love. Hopkins saw it as union with the Great Sacrifice.

From the Romantic epistemology of John Henry Newman and the luminous philosophical theology of John Duns Scotus, Hopkins synthesized a powerful theory of words, the world, and the love that connects them. It is a poetics of revelation rather than competition, of inclusion rather than absence. Hopkins's poetics offers an opportunity for many voices to speak, and for the writer and the reader to negotiate in the light of a common reality that they can in fact encounter. Hopkins's Scotist idea of multiple realities that do not displace one another allows for discussions of literature characterized by both liberty of thought and a sense of grounding in the reality at hand. Literature, for him, serves a community that lovingly shares knowledge; literary scholars could profit by seeing themselves as such a community today, and form a community with writers who came before us, in despite of death.

So too the critic can seek not power over the past but real liberty in wishing the good of the works explicated. If a work is remembered, understood, explained, made to blossom forth in greater understanding, the critic has done a work that sets aside his or her own thought in order to serve the knowledge of another. To enter into community with a writer of the past and seek community with a reader of the future is a good like a poem itself. Yes, there are more pressing necessities in the political and economic and social realms; and in those realms we should do them, and set aside, perhaps, the less urgent task of loving the words of a poet. Nevertheless, all good things deserve praise, and it is no waste to reveal the inscapes in them.

Hopkins read Scotus, who taught him that inscape may be shared; therefore the poet found joy in having lived in a common world with that thinker so long dead:

> Yet ah! this air I gather and I release
> He lived on; these weeds and waters, these walls are what
> He haunted who of all men most sways my spirits to peace;
>
> Of realty the rarest-veinèd unraveller . . .[8]

Hopkins revealed to his readers an inscape of Scotus. Because we share a world, I can say *yes* and *is;* I can understand it. I hope that I have well inscaped the gift; such justice can only be done by love, which is not irrational but, according to Scotus, the very seat of rationality. We must, it is true, believe in goodness or beauty or logic or metaphysics of some kind to escape from the arid confinement of our personal obsessions—but we only need open the door a little way to let the new breath in; only as far as to acknowledge that we can have experience of being, and can know it. Then we can read each other with joy, our many voices in counterpoint opening new visions to one another; we can in love test each other's words against experience, and find beauty; and we can awaken to each other's eyes the grace in the mortal beauty of the speaking world.

8. Hopkins,"Duns Scotus's Oxford," in *Poetical Works,* 156.

BIBLIOGRAPHY

Adams, Marilyn McCord. "Ockham on Identity and Distinction." *Franciscan Studies* 36 (1976): 5–75.

Armstrong, Karen. *A History of God: The 4000-Year Quest of Judaism, Islam, and Christianity.* New York: Alfred A. Knopf, 1993.

Arnold, Matthew. "A Lay Sermon: On the Unveiling of a Mosaic in Whitechapel" and "An Address to the Wordsworth Society, May 2, 1883." In *Complete Prose Works,* 11 vols., ed. R. H. Super (Ann Arbor: University of Michigan Press, 1974), 10: 249–55 and 10:131–34.

———. "On Poetry (Preface to *The Hundred Greatest Men*)." In *Complete Prose Works,* 11 vols., ed. R. H. Super (Ann Arbor: University of Michigan Press, 1971–1978), 9: 61–63.

Augustine, Saint. *Concerning the City of God, against the Pagans.* Translated by Henry Bettenson. Harmondsworth, Middlesex, England: Penguin Books, 1984.

Averroes. *Averroes on Plato's "Republic."* Translated by Ralph Lerner. Ithaca, N.Y.: Cornell University Press, 1974.

———. *On the Harmony of Religions and Philosophy: A Translation, with introduction and notes, of Ibn-Rushd's* Kitab fasl al-maqal, *with its appendix (*Damina*) and an extract from* Kitab al-kashf 'an manahij al-adilla, by George Faldo Hourani. (United Nations Educational, Scientific and Cultural Organization (UNESCO) Collection of Great Works. Arabic Series.) ("E. J. W. Gibb Memorial" Series. New Series, 21) London: Luzac and Co., 1961.

Balíc, Charles. "The Life and Work of John Duns Scotus." In *John Duns Scotus, 1265–1965,* Studies in Philosophy and the History of Philosophy, vol. 3., ed. John Ryan and Bernardine Bonansea (Washington, D.C.: The Catholic University of America Press, 1965), 1–27.

Ball, Patricia. *The Science of Aspects: The Changing Role of Fact in the Work of Coleridge, Ruskin, and Hopkins.* London: Athlone Press, 1971.

Barfield, Owen. *What Coleridge Thought.* Middletown, Conn.: Wesleyan University Press, 1971.

Bazan, Bernardo Carlos. "*Intellectum Speculativum:* Averroes, Thomas Aquinas, and Siger of Brabant on the Intelligible Object." *Journal of the History of Philosophy* 19 (1981): 425–46.

Blake, William. *The Letters of William Blake.* 2 vols. Edited by Geoffrey Keynes. New York: Macmillan, 1956.

Bliss, Geoffrey. "In a Poet's Workshop." *The Month* 167 (Feb. 1936): 160–67.

Boyle, Robert, S.J. *Metaphor in Hopkins.* Chapel Hill: University of North Carolina Press, 1961.

Bridges, Robert, ed. *Poems of Gerard Manley Hopkins.* London: Humphrey Milford, 1918.

Brown, Daniel. *Hopkins's Idealism: Philosophy, Physics, Poetry.* Oxford, U.K.: Clarendon Press, 1997.

Buckley, Jerome Hamilton, and George Benjamin Woods, eds. *Poetry of the Victorian Period.* 3d ed. Glenview, Ill.: Scott Foresman, 1965.

Bump, Jerome. *Gerard Manley Hopkins.* Boston: Twayne, 1982.

———. "The Hopkins Centenary: The Current State of Criticism." In Eugene Hollahan, ed., *Gerard Manley Hopkins and Critical Discourse,* 7–40.

———. "Hopkins's Imagery and Mediaevalist Poetics." *Victorian Poetry* 15 (1977): 99–119.

Butterfield, Herbert. *The Origins of History.* New York: Basic Books, 1981.

Calvin, John. *Institutes of the Christian Religion.* Translated by Henry Beveridge. Grand Rapids, Mich.: Eerdmans, 1989.

Canon Law Society of America. *Code of Canon Law, Latin-English Edition.* Washington, D.C.: Canon Law Society of America, 1983.

Carroll, Martin C., S.J. "Gerard Manley Hopkins and the Society of Jesus." In *Immortal Diamond: Studies in Gerard Manley Hopkins,* chap. 1. New York: Sheed & Ward, 1949.

Catholic Church. *Catechism of the Catholic Church.* London: Geoffrey Chapman, 1994.

Cervo, Nathan. "'The ooze of oil / Crushed': Hopkins's Refurbishment of the 'Lady' of the Troubadour Poets." *Hopkins Quarterly* 16, no. 4 (Jan. 1990): 147–48.

Cochran, Leonard. "Instress and Its Place in the Poetics of Gerard Manley Hopkins." *Hopkins Quarterly* 6 (1979–1980): 143–82.

Coffey, Peter. *Ontology, or the Theory of Being.* 1912; Reprint, Gloucester, Mass.: Peter Smith, 1970.

Coleridge, Samuel Taylor. *Biographia Literaria.* 2 vols. Edited by James Engell and Walter Jackson Bate. Princeton, N.J.: Princeton University Press, 1983.

Collins, James. "Philosophical Themes in Hopkins." *Thought* 22 (1947): 67–106.

Cotter, James Finn. *Inscape: The Christology and Poetry of Gerard Manley Hopkins.* Pittsburgh: University of Pittsburgh Press, 1972.

Culler, Jonathan. "Lace, Lance, and Pair." *Profession 94.* New York: Modern Language Association of America, 1994.

Dahlstrom, Daniel O. "Signification and Logic: Scotus on Universals from a Logical Point of View." *Vivarium* 18 (1980): 81–111.

DeLaura, David. *Hebrew and Hellene in Victorian England: Newman, Arnold, and Pater.* Austin: University of Texas Press, 1969.

Deutsch, Babette. *Poetry Handbook: A Dictionary of Terms.* 2d ed. New York: Grosset & Dunlap, 1962.

Devlin, Christopher. "The Image and the Word, Parts 1 and 2." *The Month,* n.s., 3 (1950): 114–27, 191–202.

Downes, David Anthony. *The Great Sacrifice: Studies in Hopkins.* Lanham, Md.: University Press of America, 1983.

Dumont, Stephen. "Theology as a Science and Duns Scotus's Distinction between Intuitive and Abstractive Cognition." *Speculum* 64 (1989): 579–99.

Duns Scotus, John. *Doctoris Subtilis et Mariani Ioannis Duns Scoti, Ordinis Fratrum Minorum, Opera Omnia.* Ed. Studio et Cura Commissionis Scotisticae, præside P. Carolo Balic. Vatican City: Typis Polyglottis Vaticanis, 1950– .

———. *Duns Scotus on the Will and Morality.* Edited and translated (with facing Latin text), and with an introduction, by Allan Wolter, O.F.M. Washington, D.C.: The Catholic University of America Press, 1986.

———. *God and Creatures: The Quodlibetal Questions (Quæstiones Quodlibetales).* Translated and edited by Allan Wolter and Felix Alluntis. Princeton, N.J.: Princeton University Press; Reprint, with corrections, Washington, D.C.: The Catholic University of America Press, 1975.

———. "How God's Love Extends to All Things" (Ord. III suppl. d. 32). Translated in Allan Wolter, "John Duns Scotus on the Primacy and Personality of Christ," in *Franciscan Christology,* ed. Damian McElrath (St. Bonaventure, N.Y.: Franciscan Institute, 1980), 139–42.

———. *Jean Duns Scot sur la conaissance de Dieu et l'univocité de l'Étant.* Translated with an introduction by Olivier Boulnois. Paris: Presses Universitaires de France, 1988.

———. *Opera Omnia.* Edited by L. Wadding. Lugundi Sumptibus Laurentii Durand, 1639.

———. *Philosophical Writings.* Translated (with Latin text) and edited by Allan Wolter. Indianapolis, Ind.: Hackett, 1987.

———. "Prologue to the *Ordinatio* of Duns Scotus." Translated by Allan Wolter in "Duns Scotus and Revealed Knowledge," *Franciscan Studies,* n.s., 11 (1951): 231–72.

———. "Selections from the *Ordinatio,*" trans. James J. Walsh. In *Philosophy in the Middle Ages: The Christian, Islamic, and Jewish Traditions,* ed. Arthur Hyman and James J. Walsh (Indianapolis, Ind.: Hackett, 1973; Reprint, 1982), 560–604.

———. "Selections from the *Ordinatio.*" In *Selections from Medieval Philosophers,* 2 vols., ed. and trans. Richard McKeon (New York: Scribner's, 1930), 2: 313–50.

Elliott-Binns, L. E., D.D. *Religion in the Victorian Era.* 2d ed. London: Lutterworth Press, 1964.

Ellis, Virginia Ridley. *Gerard Manley Hopkins and the Language of Mystery.* Columbia: University of Missouri Press, 1991.

Ellsberg, Margaret. *Created to Praise.* New York: Oxford University Press, 1987.

Erb, Peter. "Perichoresis and the Poetry of Hopkins." *Hopkins Quarterly* 11, nos. 3–4 (Fall 1984–Winter 1985): 67–78.

Feeney, Joseph. "Four Newfound Hopkins Letters: An Annotated Edition, with a Fragment of Another Letter." *Hopkins Quarterly* 23, nos. 1–2 (Winter–Spring 1996): 3–40.

———. "Hopkins' 'Failure' in Theology: Some New Archival Data and a Reevaluation." *Hopkins Quarterly* 13, no. 3 (Oct. 1986–Jan. 1987): 99–107.

Frank, William A. Personal correspondence via email, 22 May 2000.

Frank, William A., and Allan Wolter. *Duns Scotus Metaphysician.* West Lafayette, Ind.: Purdue University Press, 1995.

Frye, Northrop. *The Great Code: The Bible and Literature.* New York: Harcourt Brace Jovanovich, 1982.

Fulweiler, Howard. *Letters from the Darkling Plain: Language and the Grounds of Knowledge in the Poetry of Arnold and Hopkins.* Columbia: University of Missouri Press, 1972.

Gardner, W. H. *Gerard Manley Hopkins: A Study of Poetic Idiosyncrasy in Relation to Poetic Tradition.* London: Oxford University Press, 1944.

Gardner, W. H., and N. H. MacKenzie, eds. *Poems,* by Gerard Manley Hopkins. 4th ed. New York: Oxford University Press, 1967.

Garfinkel, Paul, et al. "Body Awareness in Anorexia Nervosa: Disturbances in 'Body Image' and 'Satiety.'" *Psychosomatic Medicine* 40, no. 6 (1978): 487–98.

Gelber, Hester. "Logic and the Trinity." Ph.D. dissertation, University of Wisconsin, 1974.

Gilbert, Sandra, and Susan Gubar. *The Madwoman in the Attic: The Woman Writer and the Nineteenth-Century Literary Imagination.* New Haven, Conn.: Yale University Press, 1979.

Giles, Richard, ed. *Hopkins among the Poets.* Hamilton, Ont.: International Hopkins Association, 1985.

Girard, René. *Violence and the Sacred.* Baltimore: Johns Hopkins University Press, 1977.

Gracia, Jorge J. E. "The Transcendentals in the Middle Ages: An Introduction." *Topoi* 11 (1992): 113–20.

Grajewski, Maurice. *The Formal Distinction of Duns Scotus: A Study in Metaphysics.* Philosophical Series, Vol. 90. Washington, D.C.: The Catholic University of America Press, 1944.

Graziosi, Marco. "Hopkins' Aesthetic Theory." *Hopkins Quarterly* 16, no. 3 (Oct. 1989): 71–88.

Halliday, David, and Robert Resnick. *Physics,* 3d ed., Pt. 2. New York: John Wiley & Sons, 1978.

Helsinger, Elizabeth K. *Ruskin and the Art of the Beholder.* Cambridge, Mass.: Harvard University Press, 1982.

Heuser, Alan. *The Shaping Vision of Gerard Manley Hopkins.* London: Oxford University Press, 1958.

Hilton, Tim. *John Ruskin: The Early Years, 1819–1859.* New Haven, Conn.: Yale University Press, 1985.

Himmelfarb, Gertrude. *Marriage and Morals among the Victorians.* New York: Alfred A. Knopf, 1986.

Hoagwood, Terence Allan. "Hopkins's Philosophical Poetics." In Hollahan, ed., *Gerard Manley Hopkins and Critical Discourse,* 183–97.

Hollahan, Eugene, ed. *Gerard Manley Hopkins and Critical Discourse.* New York: AMS Press, 1993.

Hopkins, Gerard Manley. *The Correspondence of Gerard Manley Hopkins and Richard Watson Dixon.* Edited by Claude Colleer Abbott. London: Oxford University Press, 1955.

———. *The Early Poetic Manuscripts and Note-books of Gerard Manley Hopkins in Facsimile.* Edited by Norman H. MacKenzie. New York: Garland, 1989.

———. *Further Letters of Gerard Manley Hopkins, Including His Correspondence with Coventry Patmore.* 2d ed., rev. and enlarged. Edited by Claude Colleer Abbott. Oxford, U.K.: Oxford University Press, 1956.

———. *The Journals and Papers of Gerard Manley Hopkins.* Edited by Humphry House and Graham Storey. London: Oxford University Press, 1959.

———. *The Later Poetic Manuscripts of Gerard Manley Hopkins in Facsimile.* Edited by Norman MacKenzie. New York: Garland, 1991.

———. *The Letters of Gerard Manley Hopkins to Robert Bridges.* Edited by Claude Colleer Abbott. London: Oxford University Press, 1955.

———. *The Sermons and Devotional Writings of Gerard Manley Hopkins.* Edited by Christopher Devlin. London: Oxford, 1959.

Hyman, Arthur. "Averroes as Commentator on Aristotle's Theory of the Intellect." In Dominic J. O'Meara, ed., *Studies in Aristotle,* 170–73.

Hyman, Arthur, and James Walsh, eds. *Philosophy in the Middle Ages: The Christian, Islamic, and Jewish Traditions.* Indianapolis, Ind.: Hackett, 1973.

John of the Cross, Saint. *Ascent of Mount Carmel.* 3d rev. ed. Translated by E. Allison Peers. Garden City, N.Y.: Image Books, 1958.

Johnson, Margaret. *Gerard Manley Hopkins and Tractarian Poetry.* Brookfield, Vt.: Ashgate, 1997.

Johnson, Samuel. *Rasselas, Prince of Abyssinia: A Tale. In Poems and Selected Prose of Samuel Johnson,* ed. Bertrand Bronson (New York: Holt, Rinehart and Winston, 1952).

Johnson, Wendell Stacy. *Gerard Manley Hopkins: The Poet as Victorian.* Ithaca, N.Y.: Cornell University Press, 1968.

Kelly, J. N. D. *Early Christian Doctrines.* Rev. ed. San Francisco: Harper & Row, 1978.

Kirk, G. S., J. E. Raven, and M. Schofield. *The Presocratic Philosophers.* 2d ed. Cambridge, U.K.: Cambridge University Press, 1995.

Kitchen, Paddy. *Gerard Manley Hopkins.* Manchester, U.K.: Carcanet, 1989.

Kretzmann, Norman. "Evidence against Anti-Evidentialism." In *Our Knowledge of God,* ed. K. J. Clark (The Netherlands: Kluwer Academic Publishers, 1992).

———. "Reason in Mystery." In *The Philosophy in Christianity,* Royal Institute of Philosophy Lecture Series 25, Supplement to *Philosophy* 1989, ed. Godfrey Vesey (Cambridge, U.K.: Cambridge University Press, 1989), 15–40.

Lahey, G. F., S.J. *Gerard Manley Hopkins.* London: Oxford University Press, 1930; Reprint, New York: Haskell House, 1969.

Landow, George P. *The Aesthetic and Critical Theories of John Ruskin.* Princeton, N.J.: Princeton University Press, 1971.

Lewis, C. S. *The Four Loves.* New York: Collins Fontana Books, 1963.

———. *Miracles: A Preliminary Study.* New York: Macmillan, 1947.

———. *Studies in Words.* Cambridge, U.K.: Cambridge University Press, 1958.

Lichtmann, Maria. *The Contemplative Poetry of Gerard Manley Hopkins.* Princeton, N.J.: Princeton University Press, 1989.

Loomis, Jeffrey B. *Dayspring in Darkness: Sacrament in Hopkins.* Lewisburg, Pa.: Bucknell University Press, 1988.

Lowell, Robert. "Hopkins's Sanctity." In *Gerard Manley Hopkins, by the Kenyon Critics,* ed. John Crowe Ransom and Cleanth Brooks (Norfolk, Conn.: New Directions, 1945), 89–93.

Loyola, Ignatius, Saint. *Saint Ignatius: Personal Writings.* Translated by Joseph A. Munitz and Philip Endean. New York: Penguin Books, 1996.

———. *The Spiritual Exercises of St. Ignatius.* Translated by Anthony Mottola. Garden City, N.Y.: Doubleday Image Books, 1964.

Lynch, Michael. "Recovering Hopkins, Recovering Ourselves." *Hopkins Quarterly* 6, no. 3 (Fall 1979): 107–17.

MacClintock, Stuart. "Heresy and Epithet: An Approach to the Problem of Latin Averroism, Parts 1, 2, and 3." *Review of Metaphysics* 8 (Sept. 1954; Dec. 1954; March 1955): 526–45, 342–56, 176–99.

MacKenzie, Norman. "Introduction" to *Poems and Prose of Gerard Manley Hopkins.* Baltimore: Penguin Books, 1964.

———, ed. *The Later Poetic Manuscripts of Gerard Manley Hopkins in Facsimile.* New York: Garland, 1991.

———, ed. *The Poetical Works of Gerard Manley Hopkins.* Oxford, U.K.: Clarendon Press, 1990.

———. *A Reader's Guide to Gerard Manley Hopkins.* Ithaca, N.Y.: Cornell University Press, 1981.

Mariani, Paul L. *A Commentary on the Complete Poems of Gerard Manley Hopkins.* Ithaca, N.Y.: Cornell University Press, 1970.

Marrone, Steven P. *Truth and Scientific Knowledge in the Thought of Henry of Ghent.* Speculum Anniversary Monographs, Vol. 11. Cambridge, Mass.: Mediaeval Society of America, 1985.

Martin, Robert Bernard. *Gerard Manley Hopkins: A Very Private Life.* London: Harper Collins, 1991.

McChesney, Donald. *A Hopkins Commentary.* New York: New York University Press, 1968.

McKeon, Richard, ed. and trans. *Selections from Medieval Philosophers,* Vol. 2: *Roger Bacon to William of Ockham.* New York: Scribner's, 1930.

McNeeley, Trevor. "The Blissful Agony of Hopkins: Notes of a Neo-Reactionary." *Hopkins Quarterly* 12, nos. 3–4 (Oct. 1985–Jan. 1986): 97–114.

McNees, Eleanor J. *Eucharistic Poetry: The Search for Presence in the Writings of John Donne, Gerard Manley Hopkins, Dylan Thomas, and Geoffrey Hill.* Lewisburg, Pa.: Bucknell University Press, 1992.

Mental Health Abstracts Online, http//dialog.carl.org:3005/cgi-bin/cw_cgi?fullRecord+31422+1+11+5.

Miller, Joseph Hillis. *The Disappearance of God: Five Nineteenth-Century Writers.* Cambridge, Mass.: Harvard University Press, 1963.

———. *The Linguistic Moment: From Wordsworth to Stevens.* Princeton, N.J.: Princeton University Press, 1985.

Milward, Peter. *A Commentary on the Sonnets of G. M. Hopkins.* Chicago: Loyola University Press, 1969.

Moran, Maureen F. "Manl(e)y Mortal Beauty: Hopkins as Tractarian Aesthete." *Hopkins Quarterly* 22, nos. 1–2 (Winter–Spring 1995): 3–29.

Moore, Michael D. "Newman and the Motif of Intellectual Pain in Hopkins' Terrible Sonnets." *Mosaic* 12 (Spring 1979): 29–46.

Newman, John Henry. *Apologia pro Vita Sua.* Garden City, N.Y.: Doubleday Image, 1956.

———. *Discourses Addressed to Mixed Congregations.* Westminster, Md.: Christian Classics, 1966.

———. *An Essay in Aid of a Grammar of Assent.* Introduction by Nicholas Lash. Notre Dame, Ind.: University of Notre Dame Press, 1979.

———. "Ignorance of Evil." In *Parochial and Plain Sermons,* vol. 8. Westminster, Md.: Christian Classics, 1968.

———. *Loss and Gain: The Story of a Convert.* Edited by Alan G. Hill. New York: Oxford University Press, 1986.

———. *The Philosophical Notebook,* vol. 2. Edited by Edward Sillem. New York: Humanities Press, 1970.

Nixon, Jude. *Gerard Manley Hopkins and His Contemporaries: Liddon, Newman, Darwin, and Pater.* New York: Garland, 1993.

Noone, Timothy B. "Individuation in Scotus." *American Catholic Philosophical Quarterly* 69 (1995): 527–42.

Norman, Edward. *The English Catholic Church in the Nineteenth Century.* Oxford, U.K.: Clarendon Press, 1989.

O'Meara, Dominic J., ed. *Studies in Aristotle.* Studies in Philosophy and the History of Philosophy, Vol. 9. Washington, D.C.: The Catholic University of America Press, 1981.

Ong, Walter, S.J. *Hopkins, the Self, and God.* Toronto: University of Toronto, 1986.

Ott, Ludwig. *Fundamentals of Catholic Dogma.* Rockford, Ill.: Tan, 1974.

Pater, Walter. *The Renaissance: Studies in Art and Poetry.* Edited by Donald Hill. Berkeley and Los Angeles: University of California Press, 1980.

Perler, Dominik. "Signification in Scotus." *Medieval Philosophy and Theology* 3 (1993): 97–120.

Peters, W. A. M. *Gerard Manley Hopkins: A Critical Essay towards the Understanding of His Poetry.* Oxford, U.K.: Oxford University Press, 1948; Reprint, Basil Blackwell and Johnson, 1970.

Phillips, Catherine, ed. *Gerard Manley Hopkins.* Oxford Authors Series. New York: Oxford University Press, 1986.

Pick, John. *Gerard Manley Hopkins, Priest and Poet.* London: Oxford University Press, 1966.

———. *A Hopkins Reader.* Garden City, N.Y.: Doubleday Image Books, 1966.

Plotkin, Cary H. "To Give Being Back: Hopkins's Theodic Language." In Hollahan, ed., *Gerard Manley Hopkins and Critical Discourse,* 217–32.

Pohle, Joseph. *The Sacraments: A Dogmatic Treatise.* 4th rev. ed. Edited by Arthur Preuss. St. Louis, Mo.: B. Herder Book Co., 1923.

Polanyi, Michael. *Personal Knowledge: Towards a Post-Critical Philosophy.* Chicago: University of Chicago Press, 1958.

Potts, Michael. "Hopkins and Metaphor." *American Catholic Philosophical Quarterly* 68, no. 4 (1995): 501–13.

Quasten, Johannes. *Patrology.* 4 vols. 1950; Reprint, Westminster, Md.: Christian Classics, 1986.

Raiger, Michael. "'Poised, But on the Quiver': The Paradox of Free Will and Grace in Hopkins's 'Spring' and '(Carrion Comfort).'" *Religion and the Arts* 3, no. 1 (Spring 1999): 64–95.

Renan, Ernest. "M. Feuerbach et la nouvelle école Hégélienne." In *Oeuvres completes de Ernest Renan,* 10 vols., ed. Henriette Psichiari (Paris: Calmann-Lévy, 1947), 7:286–95.

Richards, I. A. *Poetries and Sciences.* New York: Norton, 1970.

Ricouer, Paul. "The Metaphoric Process as Cognition, Imagination, and Feeling." In *Philosophical Perspectives on Metaphor,* ed. Mark Johnson (Minneapolis: University of Minnesota Press, 1981).

Ritz, Jean-Georges. *Robert Bridges and Gerard Manley Hopkins: A Literary Friendship, 1863–1889.* London: Oxford University Press, 1960.

Robinson, John. *In Extremity: A Study of Gerard Manley Hopkins.* Cambridge, U.K.: Cambridge University Press, 1978.

Ruggles, Eleanor. *Gerard Manley Hopkins: A Life.* New York: W. W. Norton, 1944.

Ruskin, John. *The Works of John Ruskin.* 39 vols. Edited by E. T. Cook and Alexander Wedderburn. New York: Longmans Green, 1903–1912.

Ryan, John K., and Bernardine M. Bonansea, eds. *John Duns Scotus, 1265–1965.* Studies in Philosophy and the History of Philosophy, Vol. 3. Washington, D.C.: The Catholic University of America Press, 1965.

Sadie, Stanley, ed. *The New Grove Dictionary of Music and Musicians.* Washington, D.C.: Macmillan, 1980.

Salman, Dominique, O.P. "Note sur la premiere influence de Averroes." *Revue Neoscolastique de Philosophie* 40 (1937): 203–12.

Salmon, Rachel. "'Wording it How': The Possibilities of Utterance in *The Wreck of the Deutschland.*" *Hopkins Quarterly* 10, no. 3 (Fall 1983): 87–108.

Schleiermacher, Friedrich. *On Religion: Speeches to Its Cultured Despisers.* Translated by John Oman. New York: Harper Torchbooks, 1958.

Schneider, Elizabeth. *The Dragon in the Gate: Studies in the Poetry of G. M. Hopkins.* Berkeley and Los Angeles: University of California Press, 1968.

Scotus. See "Duns Scotus, John."

Sheriff, John K. *The Fate of Meaning: Charles Pierce, Structuralism, and Literature.* Princeton, N.J.: Princeton University Press, 1989.

Sprinker, Michael. *A Counterpoint of Dissonance: The Aesthetics and Poetry of Gerard Manley Hopkins.* Baltimore: Johns Hopkins University Press, 1980.

Sulloway, Alison. *Gerard Manley Hopkins and the Victorian Temper.* New York: Columbia University Press, 1972.

Swift, Jonathan. *Gulliver's Travels,* vol. 8 of *The Prose Works of Jonathan Swift, D.D.,* ed. G. Ravenscroft Dennis (London: George Bell & Sons, 1909; Reprint, AMS Reprint, 1971).

Tempier, Stephen, Bishop of Paris. "Condemnation of 277 Propositions." Translated in Hyman and Walsh, *Philosophy in the Middle Ages,* 542–50.

Templeman, William B. "Ruskin's Ploughshare and Hopkins's 'The Windhover.'" *English Studies* 43 (1962): 103–6.

Tennyson, G. B. "Removing the Veil: Newman as Literary Artist." *Renascence* 42 (Fall 1990–Winter 1991): 29–44.

———. "Sacramental Imagination." In *Nature and the Victorian Imagination.* Berkeley and Los Angeles: University of California Press, 1977.

———. *Victorian Devotional Poetry: The Tractarian Mode.* Cambridge, Mass.: Harvard University Press, 1981.

Tertullian. *Against Praxeas.* Translated in *The Ante-Nicene Fathers,* ed. A. Roberts and J. Donaldson (1884–1886; Reprint, Grand Rapids: Eerdmans, 1989), 597–627.

Thomas, Alfred, S.J. *Hopkins the Jesuit: The Years of Training.* London: Oxford University Press, 1969.

Thomas Aquinas, Saint. *Summa contra Gentiles.* Translated by Vernon Bourke. New York: Image Books, 1956.

———. *Summa Theologica.* First complete American edition. Translated by the Fathers of the English Dominican Province. New York: Benziger Brothers, 1947.

Trilling, Lionel, and Harold Bloom. *Victorian Prose and Poetry,* vol. 5 of *The Oxford Anthology of English Literature.* New York: Oxford University Press, 1973.

von Balthasar, Hans Urs. *The Glory of the Lord: A Theological Aesthetics,* vol. 4 of *Studies in Theological Style: Lay Styles.* Translated by Andrew Louth et al. Edited by John Riches. Edinburgh: T. & T. Clark, 1986.

Walhout, Donald. "Scotism in the Poetry of Hopkins." In *Saving Beauty: Further Studies in Hopkins,* ed. Michael Allsopp (New York: Garland, 1994), 113–32.

———. *Send My Roots Rain.* Athens: Ohio University Press, 1981.

Waller, John O. "Matthew Arnold and Thomas Arnold: Soteriology." *Anglican Theological Review* 44 (Jan. 1962): 57–70.

Walter, James. "Perspectives of Symbol and Allegory in 'The Windhover.'" *Hopkins Quarterly* 12, nos. 3–4 (Oct. 1985–Jan. 1986): 115–17.

Ward, Bernadette Waterman. "Ernest Renan's Averroism in the Religious Thought of Matthew Arnold." *Nineteenth Century Prose* 22 (Spring 1995): 34–53.

———. "Poet and Priest in the Terrible Sonnets: Gerard Manley Hopkins." Senior honors thesis, Harvard University, 1981.

Warren, Austin. "Gerard Manley Hopkins, 1844–1889," and "Instress of Inscape." In *Gerard Manley Hopkins by the Kenyon Critics,* ed. John Crowe Ransom and Cleanth Brooks (Norfolk, Conn.: New Directions, 1945), 1 14 and 72–88.

Watson, S. Y. "A Problem for Realism: Our Multiple Concepts of Individual Things and the Solution of Duns Scotus." In Ryan and Bonansea, eds., *John Duns Scotus.*

White, Norman. *Hopkins: A Literary Biography.* Oxford, U.K.: Clarendon Press, 1992.

Wolter, Allan. *Duns Scotus on the Will and Morality.* Washington, D.C.: The Catholic University of America Press, 1986.

———. "The Formal Distinction of Duns Scotus." In Ryan and Bonansea, eds., *John Duns Scotus,* 45–60.

———. "John Duns Scotus on the Primacy and Personality of Christ." In *Franciscan Christology,* ed. Damian McElrath (St. Bonaventure, N.Y.: Franciscan Institute, 1980), 139–82.

———. *The Philosophical Theology of John Duns Scotus.* Edited by Marilyn McCord Adams. Ithaca, N.Y.: Cornell University Press, 1990.

———. *The Transcendentals and Their Function in the Metaphysics of Duns Scotus.* Washington, D.C.: The Catholic University of America Press, 1946.

Wordsworth, William. *Wordsworth: Selected Poetry.* Edited by Mark Van Doren. New York: Modern Library, 1950.

Wuellner, Bernard, S.J. *Dictionary of Scholastic Philosophy.* Milwaukee: Bruce, 1956.

Zaniello, Tom. "A 'Beautiful but Broken Arc.'" In *Critical Essays on Gerard Manley Hopkins,* ed. Alison G. Sulloway (Boston: G. K. Hall, 1990), 155–68.

———. *Hopkins in the Age of Darwin.* Iowa City: University of Iowa Press, 1988.

Zemka, Sue. "The Arnolds and the Bible in the Age of the Great Reform Bill." Unpublished paper, West Coast Association for British Studies, March 1986.

———. "Victorian Testaments: The Uses and Abuses of the Bible in Early Nineteenth-Century British Literature." Ph.D. dissertation, Stanford University, 1989.

INDEX

www.ingramcontent.com/pod-product-compliance
Lightning Source LLC
LaVergne TN
LVHW041114090826
844660LV00060B/305